FRONT COVER: The seated seamtress doll is an all original Schilling papier-mâché with a cloth body stamped "American Pet." The 18in (45.7cm) French fashion doll has a Gesland body. *Photograph by Carolyn Cook.*

BACK COVER: The 14in (35.6cm) bisque doll has a solid dome neck, blue sleep eyes, closed mouth and a composition ball jointed body. It is marked only with a "6." *Photograph by Carolyn Cook.*

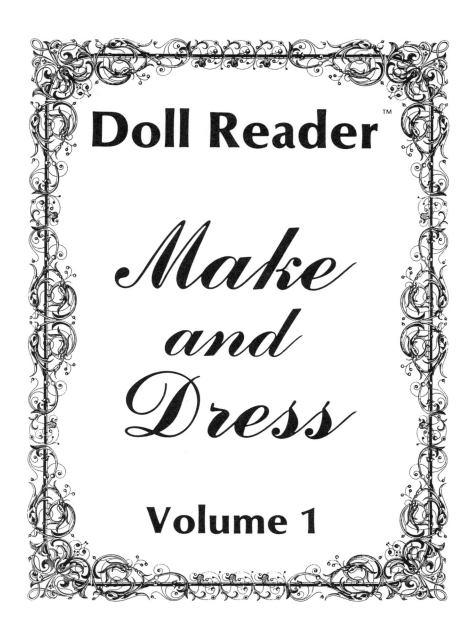

Doll Reader™

Make and Dress

Volume 1

edited by Virginia Ann Heyerdahl

Article Reprints 1975 - 1981

Published by  HOBBY HOUSE PRESS, INC.

Cumberland, Maryland 21502

ISBN: 0-87588-193-9

Table of Contents

Doll Making

Doll Costuming & Patterns

Miniature Projects For Dolls

Doll Repair

Introduction

Since its inception in December 1972, the **Doll Reader** has been proud to bring to its readers a variety of the finest articles on doll collecting, making and dressing. Due to the many requests received, Hobby House Press, Inc. has compiled a series of doll making and dressing articles which we believe will be of immense value.

This book is divided into four parts. The first section on dollmaking includes patterns and instructions for making cloth dolls and for carving your very own wooden dolls. There are detailed instructions for making a Queen Anne doll, pincushion dolls, rag dolls in regional dress, cloth dolls of the 1890s and even felt dolls.

The second section is devoted to doll costumes and patterns. Among the helpful articles to be found here are fascinating peddler doll costumes, outfits for French fashion lady dolls, doll shoes and bonnets, Summer costume patterns for dolls, bridal and morning dress designs, fashion pages from old issues of *The Delineator* magazine describing just how dolls of the time should be attired, and a host of other patterns and designs for doll clothing.

Miniature enthusiasts will delight in the third section containing mini-sewing, quilting and needlepoint projects.

The last section of this book features ways of repairing dolls compiled from articles written by experts who offer sensible and practical methods to use.

It is my sincere hope that doll makers and doll dressers of today will derive as much enjoyment and help from this volume as our letters from subscribers have indicated. More articles on doll making and doll dressing will appear in future issues of the **Doll Reader**. I suggest that you subscribe to our publication and add to your enjoyment of making and dressing dolls.

Virginia Ann Heyerdahl
Editor - March 1983
Gary R. Ruddell
Publisher - March 1983

Doll Making

From *The Mary Francis Sewing Book* by Jane Eayre Fryer.

Dolls N' Things -- *Emily*, a mini-historical Doll

by **Sandy Williams**

Emily is a mini-historical doll, circa 1750. She stands 6½in (15.2cm) tall and is made of unbleached muslin. The original sack dress was made of a beige silk fabric and brocaded with silver flowers and leaves. The dress has wide elbow panniers with slits for access to pockets. Her stomacher is decorated with ribbon bow éshelles. A double row of lace from her chemise shows from the sleeves and a single row of lace at the neckline. A woman of 1750 usually wore her hair cut short in front and drawn back in curls. The curls were held in place with pomatum and flour and were powdered for full dress.

This mini doll may be used for a variety of uses such as display, pincushion, Christmas tree ornament, and other uses.

Materials needed: Unbleached muslin, thin cardboard (from cereal box); silver, light gray, red, blue acrylic paints; brush-on rouge; very thin point black magic marker or india ink and pen; hair spray; Q-tip; polyester stuffing; glue and perhaps light gray embroidery thread.

Press muslin, lay fabric over drawings and trace doll with a sharp pencil onto fabric. Paint hair light gray, eyes blue, lips red, flowers and leaves silver, fan with perhaps gold and blue. Go over pencil lines with magic marker and spray with hairspray to set colors. Cut out doll on dotted line. Pin the right sides of front and back doll together -- sew doll together with very fine stitches, leaving bottom of dress open. Clip all curves and notch corners. Turn doll right side out.

sewing line ⟶

cutting line ⟶

Stuff head lightly --poke Q-tip into neck area, stuff lightly around Q-tip. It is helpful to place a dab of glue up inside the points of the sleeves and then put stuffing into these areas -- this will hold the stuffing in these small areas. Stuff rest of doll lightly -- but enough so that material is not wrinkled in any area.

For the base of the doll: Trace onto muslin with magic marker. Cut out on dotted line, clip seam allowance to sewing line. Out of thin cardboard, cut out a base on the sewing line. Place cardboard base piece onto wrong side of muslin base, glue muslin seam allowance up on to the top of cardboard base. Let dry. Blind stitch base to hem of dress (make sure toes of shoes face to front of doll!), stuffing bits of filling into doll so that doll will stand straight and unwrinkled.

You may want to sew light gray embroidery thread on for hair. Use three strands. To make the curls, moisten a long strand of the embroidery thread with hairset and wind the thread around a round toothpick. Let dry. Remove thread from toothpick and snip into tiny curls -- glue to back of head.

Lightly rouge cheeks and spray with hair spray to protect doll.

1890s Cloth Doll

by **Sandy Williams**

Margaret Rose is an 9¼in (23.6cm) cloth doll. She is "painted" with liquid embroidery or fabric acrylic paints onto unbleached muslin and stuffed with polyester fiberfill. A perky black satin bow is tacked at the back of her head.

Margaret is ready for a promenade on the boardwalk in her dress of striped light and navy blue surah. Her white jersey and sleeves are embroidered in navy blue thread. Navy blue stockings and black and white beach shoes complete her outfit. She has blonde hair and blue eyes.

Comfort was not the keynote for beach wear in the 1890s -- modesty was. Bathers were clothed from neck to toe. From babyhood, women were taught to protect their skin from the harmful effects (freckles and a tan) of the sun. Hats and parasols were a must. Even lemon juice was splashed on their skin after a brief encounter in the sun in order to keep their prized pink and white complexions. How different than today when bikinis and a deep tan are the rage.

Materials Needed: unbleached muslin; polyester fiberfill; ½yd (.46m) of 1in (2.5cm) wide black satin ribbon; liquid embroidery or fabric acrylic paints in light blue, navy blue, black, yellow, brown, red, pink; fine point waterproof black magic marker; iron-on transfer pencil; tracing paper.

Place tracing paper over doll. Trace doll with transfer pencil (keep point sharp). Place traced doll face down on muslin; leave at least a 2in (5.1cm) margin around doll. Press with hot iron until doll is entirely transferred onto the muslin. Do *not* cut doll out yet. "Paint" the doll: alternate navy blue and light blue stripes on the dress, navy blue stockings, tan and brown starfish, blonde hair with brown lines, pink cheeks and lips, highlight lines in lips red, eyes blue, eyebrows brown. Use the black magic marker to outline the doll, all fine lines on her face and dress and her shoes. Carefully follow the manufacturer's instructions on how to use the liquid embroidery or fabric acrylic paints.

Cut doll out on cutting line. With right sides of front and back of doll together, sew around doll from dot to dot; use small stitches. Clip curves and notch corners. Turn doll right side out. Firmly stuff with polyester fiberfill. Blind-stitch opening closed. Make a large 1½in (3.8cm) bow of the black satin ribbon; trim ends. Tack to back of head at the x so that the top third of bow is seen over the front of the head.

If "painting" the doll is just not your style, the doll is very attractive if just drawn with the black magic marker and the black bow added.

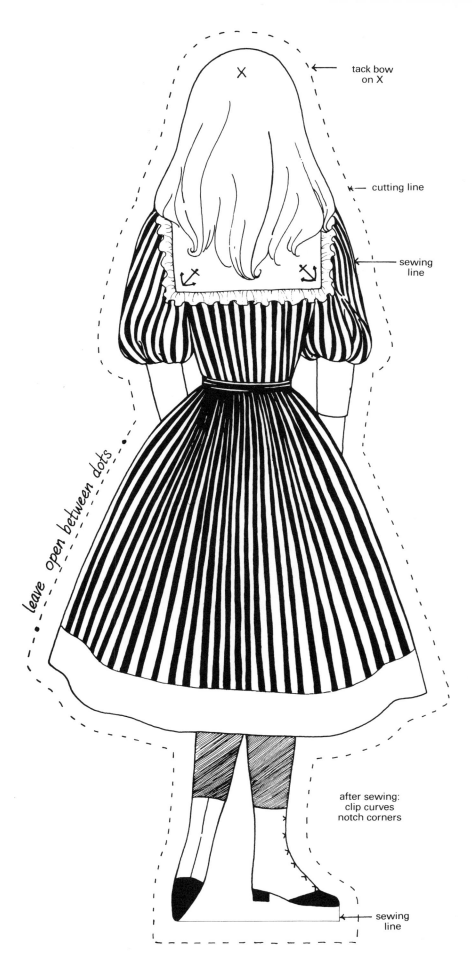

tack bow on X

cutting line

sewing line

leave open between dots

after sewing: clip curves notch corners

sewing line

EUGENIA......a lady of quality
by Susan Sirkis

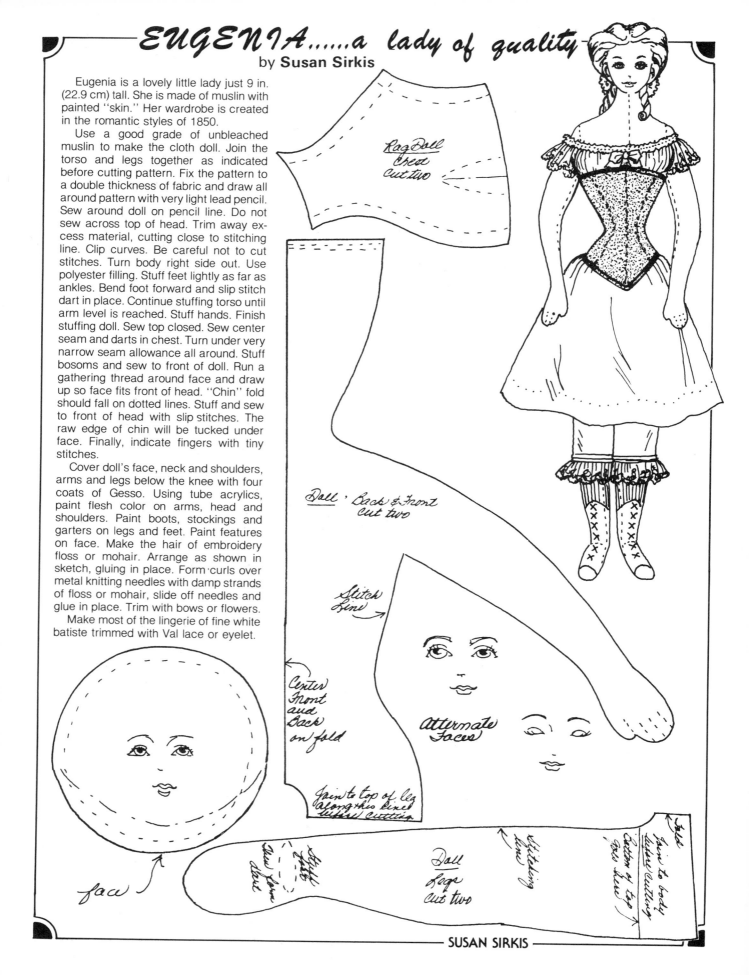

Eugenia is a lovely little lady just 9 in. (22.9 cm) tall. She is made of muslin with painted "skin." Her wardrobe is created in the romantic styles of 1850.

Use a good grade of unbleached muslin to make the cloth doll. Join the torso and legs together as indicated before cutting pattern. Fix the pattern to a double thickness of fabric and draw all around pattern with very light lead pencil. Sew around doll on pencil line. Do not sew across top of head. Trim away excess material, cutting close to stitching line. Clip curves. Be careful not to cut stitches. Turn body right side out. Use polyester filling. Stuff feet lightly as far as ankles. Bend foot forward and slip stitch dart in place. Continue stuffing torso until arm level is reached. Stuff hands. Finish stuffing doll. Sew top closed. Sew center seam and darts in chest. Turn under very narrow seam allowance all around. Stuff bosoms and sew to front of doll. Run a gathering thread around face and draw up so face fits front of head. "Chin" fold should fall on dotted lines. Stuff and sew to front of head with slip stitches. The raw edge of chin will be tucked under face. Finally, indicate fingers with tiny stitches.

Cover doll's face, neck and shoulders, arms and legs below the knee with four coats of Gesso. Using tube acrylics, paint flesh color on arms, head and shoulders. Paint boots, stockings and garters on legs and feet. Paint features on face. Make the hair of embroidery floss or mohair. Arrange as shown in sketch, gluing in place. Form curls over metal knitting needles with damp strands of floss or mohair, slide off needles and glue in place. Trim with bows or flowers.

Make most of the lingerie of fine white batiste trimmed with Val lace or eyelet.

Rag Doll Chest Cut two

Doll Back & Front cut two

Stitch Line

Center Front and Back on fold

Alternate Faces

Join to top of leg along this line before cutting

face

Stitch Dart (turn over dart)

Doll Legs cut two

Stitching line

Join to body before cutting. Bottom of top seam line

Fold

SUSAN SIRKIS

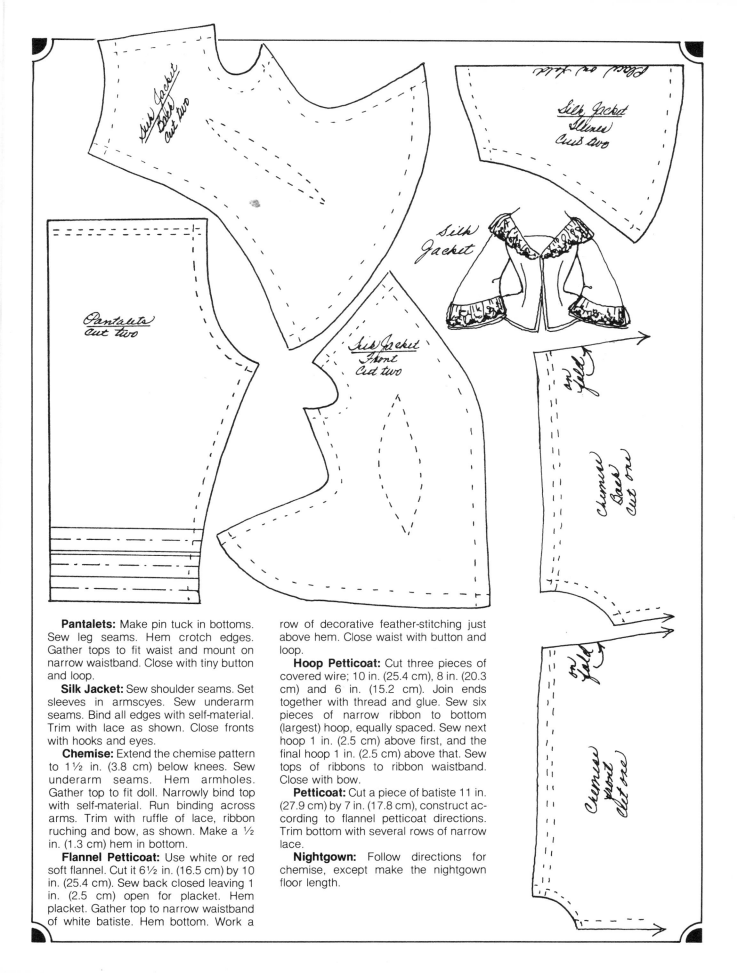

Pantalets: Make pin tuck in bottoms. Sew leg seams. Hem crotch edges. Gather tops to fit waist and mount on narrow waistband. Close with tiny button and loop.

Silk Jacket: Sew shoulder seams. Set sleeves in armscyes. Sew underarm seams. Bind all edges with self-material. Trim with lace as shown. Close fronts with hooks and eyes.

Chemise: Extend the chemise pattern to 1½ in. (3.8 cm) below knees. Sew underarm seams. Hem armholes. Gather top to fit doll. Narrowly bind top with self-material. Run binding across arms. Trim with ruffle of lace, ribbon ruching and bow, as shown. Make a ½ in. (1.3 cm) hem in bottom.

Flannel Petticoat: Use white or red soft flannel. Cut it 6½ in. (16.5 cm) by 10 in. (25.4 cm). Sew back closed leaving 1 in. (2.5 cm) open for placket. Hem placket. Gather top to narrow waistband of white batiste. Hem bottom. Work a row of decorative feather-stitching just above hem. Close waist with button and loop.

Hoop Petticoat: Cut three pieces of covered wire; 10 in. (25.4 cm), 8 in. (20.3 cm) and 6 in. (15.2 cm). Join ends together with thread and glue. Sew six pieces of narrow ribbon to bottom (largest) hoop, equally spaced. Sew next hoop 1 in. (2.5 cm) above first, and the final hoop 1 in. (2.5 cm) above that. Sew tops of ribbons to ribbon waistband. Close with bow.

Petticoat: Cut a piece of batiste 11 in. (27.9 cm) by 7 in. (17.8 cm), construct according to flannel petticoat directions. Trim bottom with several rows of narrow lace.

Nightgown: Follow directions for chemise, except make the nightgown floor length.

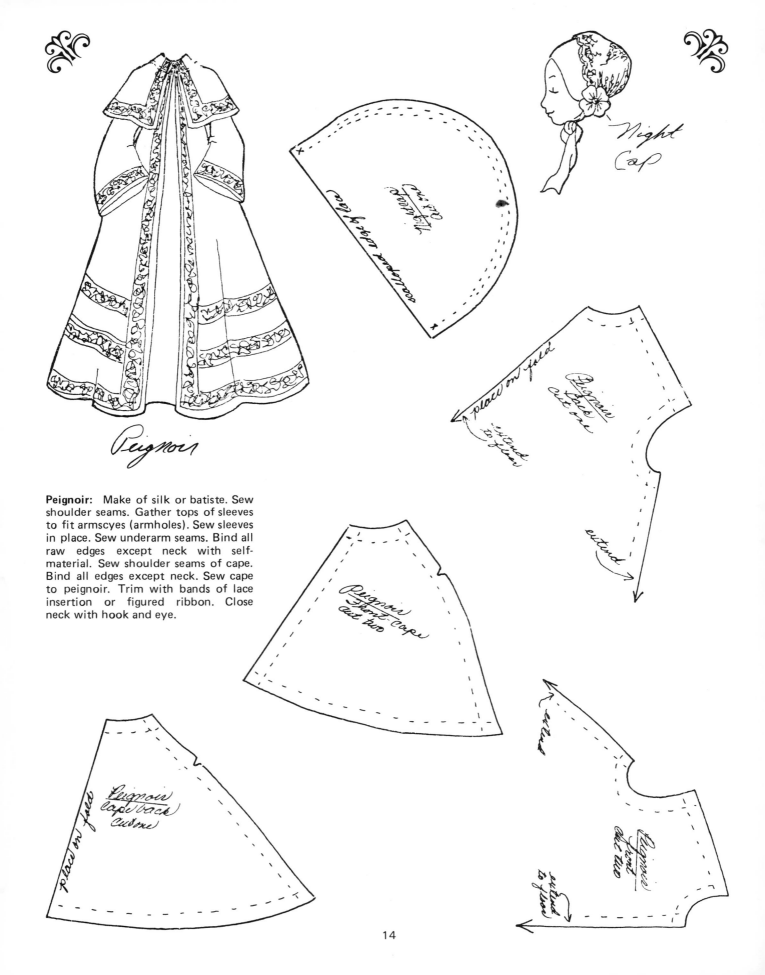

Peignoir

Night Cap

Peignoir: Make of silk or batiste. Sew shoulder seams. Gather tops of sleeves to fit armscyes (armholes). Sew sleeves in place. Sew underarm seams. Bind all raw edges except neck with self-material. Sew shoulder seams of cape. Bind all edges except neck. Sew cape to peignoir. Trim with bands of lace insertion or figured ribbon. Close neck with hook and eye.

Corset: Make the corset of colored cotton or silk. Sew darts. Cut narrow covered wire and whip to solid lines for bones. Bind top, bottom and back edges with self-material. Lace up back with strands of embroidery floss.

Dinner Dress

Dinner Dress Sleeve Cut two

Dinner Dress Bodice Front Cut two

Dinner Dress Bodice Back Cut two

Peignoir Sleeve Cut two

Dinner Dress: Make the dinner dress of pale blue silk - a checked or striped design would be appropriate. It should be worn over the batiste blouse. Cut the skirt 17in x 6½in. (43.2cm x 16.5cm). Sew center back seam leaving 1in. (2.5cm) open at top for placket. Make a ½in. (1.3cm) hem in bottom. Gather top to fit waist and sew to narrow waist band. Close with button and loop. Sew the shoulder and under arm seams of bodice. Sew center back seam and make inverted box pleats in back. Sew sleeve seams and set sleeves in armscyes. Bind narrowly all raw edges with self-material. Trim with ruching of narrow silk ribbon and bows as shown. Close back with concealed hooks and eyes.

Bloomer costume: Make the jacket of colored cotton. Make the blouse, skirt and bloomer of white batiste. The wide brimmed straw hat may be worn with the Bloomer costume. Sew bloomer crotch seams. Sew leg seams. Make narrow casing and draw up to fit doll. Cut the skirt 13 in. x 4 in. (33cm x 10.2cm). Sew center back seam leaving 1 in. (2.5cm) open at top for placket. Make a ½ in. (1.3cm) hem in bottom. Hem placket. Gather top to fit doll's waist and mount on narrow waist band, close with tiny button and button hole. Sew back side pieces to center back of jacket. Make darts in front. Sew shoulder and under arm seams. Narrowly bind neck and waist edges. Close front with concealed hooks and eyes sewn to dots. Sew sleeve seams. Bind bottom of sleeves and set sleeves into armscyes. Trim jacket as shown with bands of ribbon, lace or embroidery. Sew shoulder and underarm seams of blouse. Hem back facings. Gather neck to fit doll and bind narrowly with self-material. Trim with narrow lace frill. Sew sleeve seams. Gather tops of sleeves slightly so sleeves will fit. Sew sleeves to armscyes. Gather bottoms of sleeves, bind and trim to match neck. Hem bottom. Close back with tiny buttons and button holes.

Evening Dress: Make the evening dress of white net and lace over pale peach silk. Cut bodice front and backs of silk. Make darts in front and sew underarm and shoulder seams. Hem back facings and narrowly bind bottom and top edges with self-material. Cut sleeves of silk. Trim each with a row of slightly gathered ¼ in. (.65cm) lace. Sew sleeve seams, gather tops and set sleeves into armscyes. Gather bottom to fit, bind and trim with lace ruffle. Make bertha of net: gather on double dotted lines. Sew front and shoulder seams. Edge bottom with ¼ in. (.65cm) lace ruffle. Cover seams and top of lace ruffle with narrow lace insertion or decorative stitching. Turn under narrow hem at top and sew to neckline of dress. Turn under raw edge at back and blind stitch to bodice. Make two skirts (described with the dinner dress) one of silk and one of net. Trim the net skirt with three rows of 1½ in. (3.8cm) wide lace, slightly gathered. The skirts should be gathered together and mounted on a single waist band. Close bodice and skirt with concealed hooks and eyes.

Evening Headdress: Cut a piece of white covered wire long enough to make shape shown. Twist into shape. Cover one side lightly but completely with white glue and place on a piece of white net which has been laid upon wax paper. When glue has dried remove from wax paper and trim net away from outside of headdress as closely as possible, leaving only the inside of the petal shapes covered. Glue ¼ in. (.65cm) lace to wire and trim with pastel ribbon bows and streamers.

Muff: Cut the muff in wool or velvet to match burnouse. Work embroidery in chain stitch with single strand embroidery floss. Pad with thin layer of cotton and line with silk. Sew ends together. Bind each end with narrow strips of white velvet. Do lazy-daisy stitches with one strand of black embroidery floss to simulate ermine.

Burnouse: Make the burnouse of very fine light weight wool or velveteen. Edge completely with white or silk ribbon. It may be black, white or a soft color. Fold down center back. Tack two sides together at x's. Make five tassels of matching embroidery floss. Sew tassels to o's.

Hat: Cut the hat pieces of heavy paper - such as index card. Sew together. Dampen very narrow straw. Using invisible polyester thread, sew the straw together around and around until the form is covered. Begin at the outside and sew only the first round to the form. Knot thread. Continue sewing with over cast stitches. Let dry. Snip stitches around brim, releasing hat from form. Trim with ribbon. Flowers may be added if you wish.

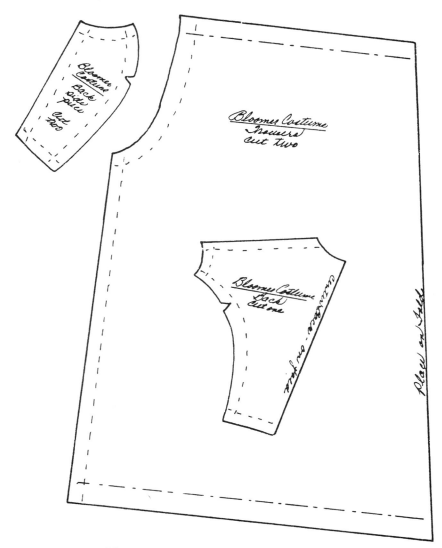

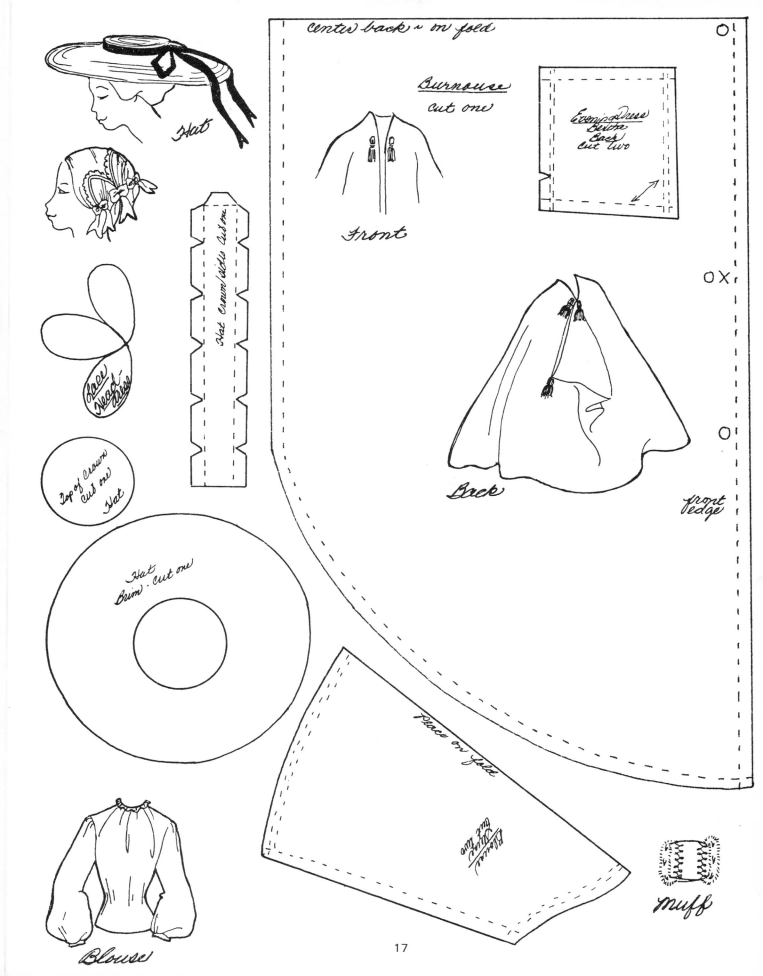

Hat

Lace Head Dress

Top of Crown
Cut one
Hat

Hat Crown/side Custom

Hat
Brim . cut one

Center back ~ on fold

Burnouse
cut one

Front

Back

Evening Dress
Bertha
Back
cut two

front
edge

Place on fold

Blouse
cut two

Blouse

muff

17

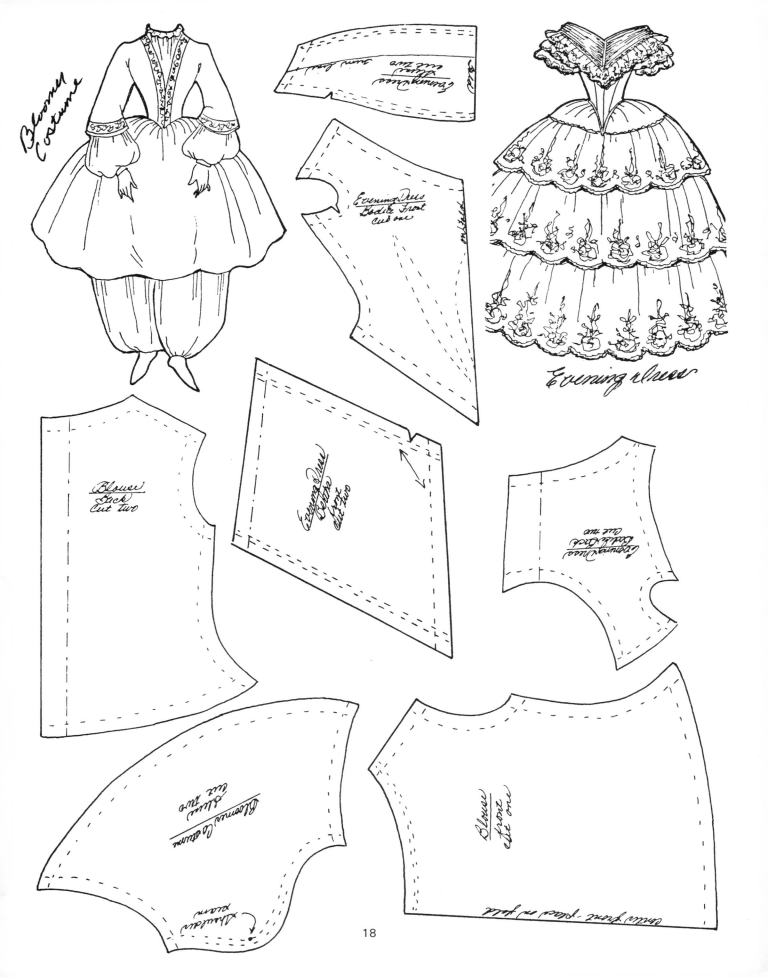

Bloomer Costume

Evening Dress

Evening Dress Skirt cut two

Evening Dress Bodice Front cut one

Evening Dress Skirt front cut two

Evening Dress Bodice Back cut two

Blouse Back Cut two

Blouse front cut one

Bloomer Costume cut two

Shalara seam

Skirt front - Place on fold

18

all purpose doll body

by **Susan Sirkis**

There is no point in trying to make a beautiful doll dress on a lumpy doll body. Sometimes in the case of antique dolls which are being restored to a supposed original state not much can be done. Modern dolls, however, are a different story. Artists' dolls, and reproduction dolls, in a variety of mediums may be fitted out with this all purpose adaptation of the classic milliners' model body. It has the chief attributes of a dressmakers dream: a slender waist and tapering limbs. It also has the distinct advantage of being quickly and easily made. The height of the dolls can be adjusted by shortening or lengthening the legs. The directions are the same for all sizes. The body may be made in heavy unbleached muslin but I prefer felt. Make sure the bottom of the body legs are wide enough for the kit legs.

DIRECTIONS
1. Make darts.
2. Sew front and back seams.
3. Sew leg seams.
4. Turn body inside out.
5. Run a thin stream of Elmer's glue all around top of kit legs. Insert into bottom of body legs. Make sure the toes point forward! Wrap heavy thread around leg to hold cloth in place.
6. Stuff legs to crotch.
7. Tie ribbon around legs, holding them together while stuffing is completed. This will prevent them from spreading.
8. Complete stuffing. Make an envelope fold in top to close.
9. Cut a piece of fabric wide enough to go around tops of arms and long enough to reach from the top of one arm to the top of the other when they are arranged on each side of the body with the wrists at hip level. Sew long edges together. Insert and secure arms using the same method as was used for the legs.
10. Sew the top of the arm tube across the top of the body.
11. Place the head on the shoulders and sew in place. Use cotton tape through sew-holes if necessary. The inside of the shoulder plate may be spread with Elmer's glue if necessary. The joint of arms and legs may be cornered with strips of lace if desired.

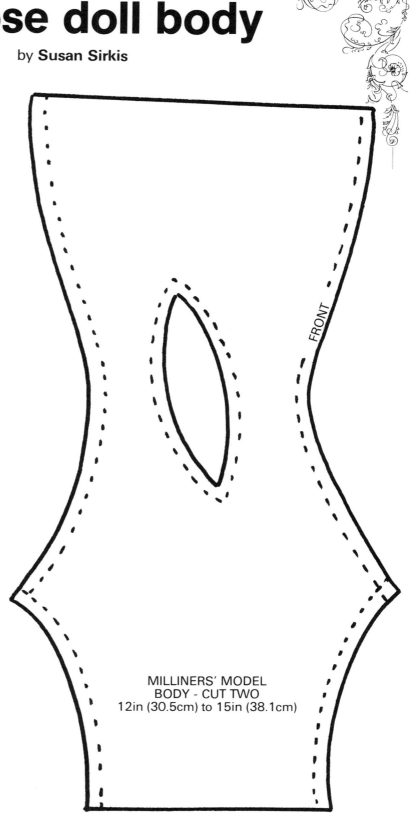

FRONT

MILLINERS' MODEL
BODY - CUT TWO
12in (30.5cm) to 15in (38.1cm)

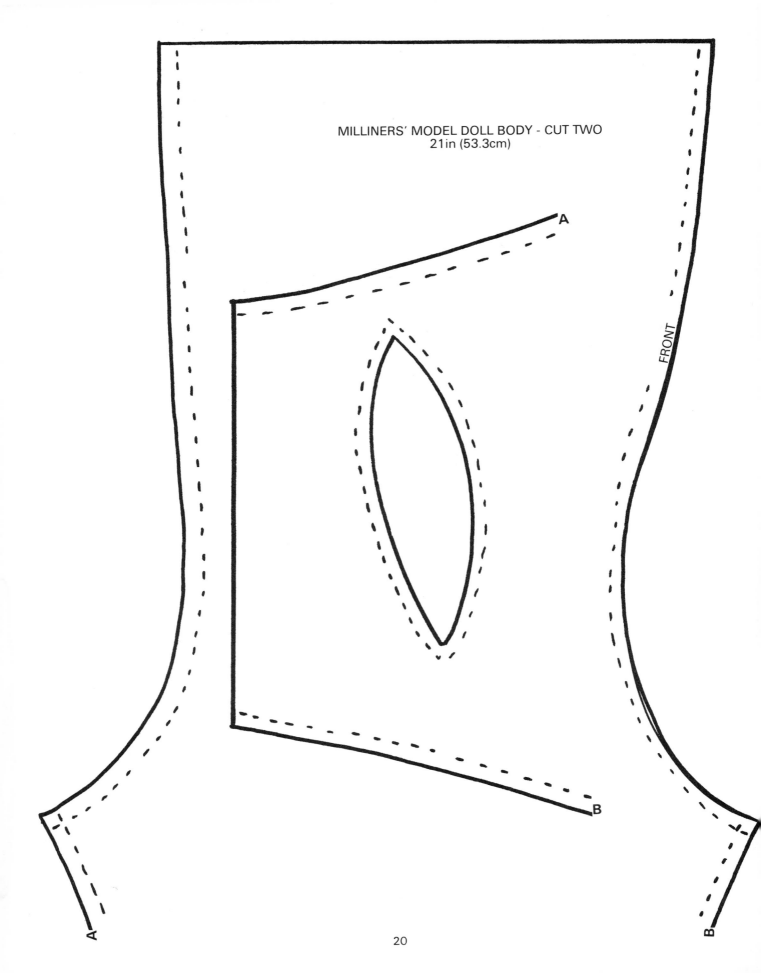

MILLINERS' MODEL DOLL BODY - CUT TWO
21in (53.3cm)

A

FRONT

B

A

B

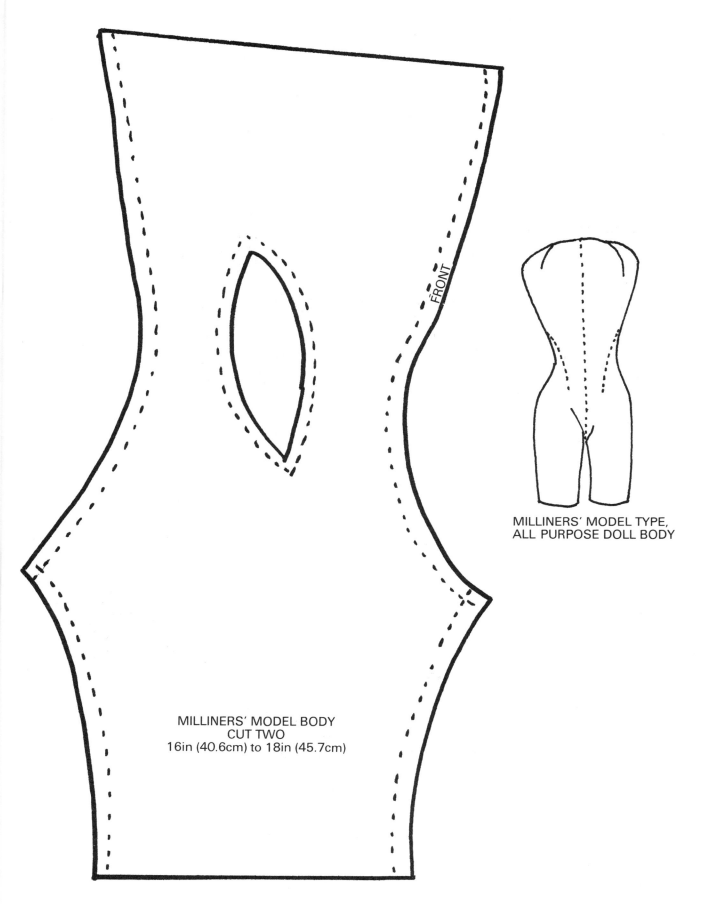

FRONT

MILLINERS' MODEL BODY
CUT TWO
16in (40.6cm) to 18in (45.7cm)

MILLINERS' MODEL TYPE,
ALL PURPOSE DOLL BODY

21

A Rag Doll In Regional Dress
Salzburg, Austria

by **Susan Sirkis**

Many years ago when I was living in Austria with my parents, my mother was gifted with a beautiful old scarf. Of a deep blue figured silk, it has a colorful woven floral border and deep hand knotted silk fringe, also in blue. The scarf, soft as a cobweb, was the type worn with several of the regional costumes in Austria. My mother's scarf dated from the 1890s. Its beauty engendered in me an interest in regional costume which endures today. One of

the chief ways I have enjoyed my interest has been to periodically costume dolls in regional dress. Many doll collectors casually dismiss any doll in regional costume as cheap souvenir merchandise. However, many of the most sought after dolls in collections today may have originally emerged from the toy factory in exquisite smaller version of the full size regional or peasant dress. Indeed, many so-called French Fashion dolls (far from cheap toys!) were appareled in regional clothing.

One of my favorites of the regional costumes I have made over the years was for a 16in (40.6cm) tall doll named *Magda* and represented "Land Salzburg," or the state of Salzburg in Austria where "Stadt Salzburg," or the city of Salzburg is located. *Magda's* costume was based on a dirndl of 1900, with long skirt and leg-o-mutton sleeves popular in the fashionable world of that time.

MAGDA HERSELF: Make the doll of unbleached muslin. Trace pattern pieces onto tisue paper (never use patterns printed on newspaper -- ink may smudge and ruin your fabric). Pin the body pattern to the muslin. Cut pieces out. Carefully trace the face with all of its outlines. The outlines will match the front of the doll's body. Pin the tracing to a piece of cardboard. Pin the muslin face over the drawing. Carefully trace the features and wisps of hair onto the muslin using light pencil lines. You may want to practice first on a scrap of muslin. You may also complete the face on a piece of muslin and then whip it onto the front of the doll, after it is stuffed, as a sort of mask. Embroider the features with a single strand of embroidery floss using satin and outline stitches as shown in diagram.

When the embroidery is complete begin to make the body by gathering the torso back along double dotted lines. Draw up to match front. Make dart in front neck to tilt head forward a little. Place right sides of back and front together and sew along stitching line. Leave top open for stuffing, carefully clip all curves. Sew arms and legs together in a similar manner. Turn all pieces. Stuff firmly and smoothly with polyester fiberfill. Turn under a narrow seam allowance at top of head and stitch closed. Close tops of arms and legs with envelope folds: hold the back of the leg (inside of arm) toward you and push the top edge down towards the front; fold each side in towards the center, thus making a point at center front (top of arm). Whip arms and legs to doll as shown in sketches.

Make the hair of brown yarn. Sew it along line of center part with matching thread, using backstitch. Arrange a knot of twisted yarn at back. Sew in place with thread.
PANTALETS: Make the pantalets of white batiste. Turn under seam allowance at bottom of legs. Trim with lace. Sew front crotch seam. Sew back crotch seam below dot. Hem back opening above dot. Gather to fit waist. Fold waistband down middle. Sew ends together. Turn. Press under seam allowance. Insert top of pantalets. Topstitch along bottom of waistband. Close with button and buttonhole. Close leg seams.

UNDER PETTICOAT: Make of white batiste. Cut a piece 9in (22.9cm) wide by 24in (61cm) long. Sew back seam leaving 2in (5.1cm) open at top for placket. Hem placket. Gather top to fit waist and mount on waistband (described for pantalets). Hem bottom and trim with lace. Close with button and buttonhole.
PETTICOAT: Make the under petticoat of blue and white checked or flowered gingham. Cut it 10in (25.4cm) wide by 27in (68.6cm) long. Sew back seam. Make a narrow casing in top and thread with cotton tape. Gather and tie around waist. Bind bottom with blue bias binding.
STOCKINGS: Use an old T-shirt, baby socks or finger bandages. Cut to fit just above knees. If T-shirt or socks are used sew center back seam. Trim tops with stretch lace.
SHOES: Make the shoes of felt. Sew center back seam. Sew soles to the uppers with an overcast stitch. Use six strands of embroidery floss to sew shoe to doll's foot as shown in diagram.
DIRNDL: *Magda's* dirndl is her Sunday best so it should be made of black silk. Line the bodice with self-material; place two layers of silk together, right sides facing; sew top edges together including armholes; turn and press. Cut skirt 10in (25.4cm) by 28in (71.1cm). Gather top to fit bottom of bodice. Sew to bodice. Sew center front seam leaving 2in (5.1cm) open at top for placket. Face bottom of skirt under 2in (5.1cm) with red silk. Sew sleeve seams. Hem bottom of sleeves. Turn under seam allowances at top and gather to fit arm. Sew to armscye (armhole) on bodice, positioning armscye between notches on sleeve.

STOMACHER: Cut the stomacher of red silk. Line with self-material, cover with white lace.
SCARF: Cut a piece of pale blue silk 6in (15.2cm) square. Fringe sides by pulling threads to a depth of ¼in (.65cm).
APRON: Cut the apron 10in (25.4cm) long by 8in (20.3cm) deep. Make a ½in (1.3cm) hem along one 10in (25.4cm) side. Narrowly hem two 8in (20.3cm) sides. Gather top and draw up to 2¼in (5.8cm). Mount on waistband ½in (1.3cm) wide and long enough to wrap around waist and tie in front.
HAT: Make the hat of black felt over an index card base. Cut two brims. Cut the cardboard brim by the same pattern, but without the seam allowances. Sew the felt pieces together around outside of circle. Turn. Press. Insert cardboard into brim. Sew center back seam of crown. Sew top of crown to crown. Sew crown to brim. Insert cardboard crown pieces into crown and carefully glue in place. Trim crown with gold middy braid tied in a knot at the back. Fringe ends of braid. Sew 1in (2.5cm) silk ribbon to underside of brim on either side at crown seam. Tie in a bow at back under chignon allowing ends to float down back.

To get *Madga* dressed, place her shoes, socks, pantalets, under petticoat and petticoat on her. Arrange the scarf over her shoulders. Pin the stomacher in place over her chest and over scarf. Place dirndl on doll and lace front closed with embroidery floss. Tie at waist. Place apron on doll. Suspend a small gold medalion around her neck on narrow black velvet ribbon. *Magda's* dress, apron, and scarf may be made of cottons for everyday wear.

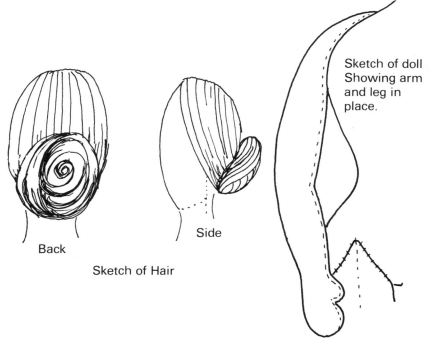

Back

Side

Sketch of Hair

Sketch of doll Showing arm and leg in place.

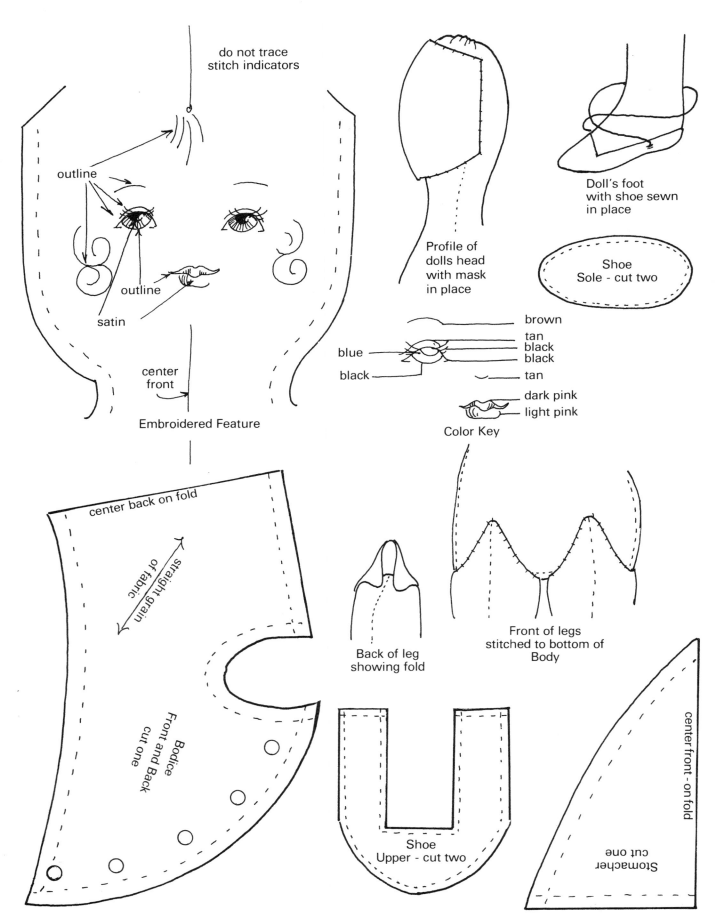

do not trace
stitch indicators

outline

outline

satin

center
front

Embroidered Feature

Profile of
dolls head
with mask
in place

Doll's foot
with shoe sewn
in place

Shoe
Sole - cut two

brown
tan
black
black
tan

blue

black

dark pink
light pink

Color Key

center back on fold

straight grain
of fabric

Bodice
Front and Back
cut one

Back of leg
showing fold

Front of legs
stitched to bottom of
Body

Shoe
Upper - cut two

center front - on fold

Stomacher
cut one

24

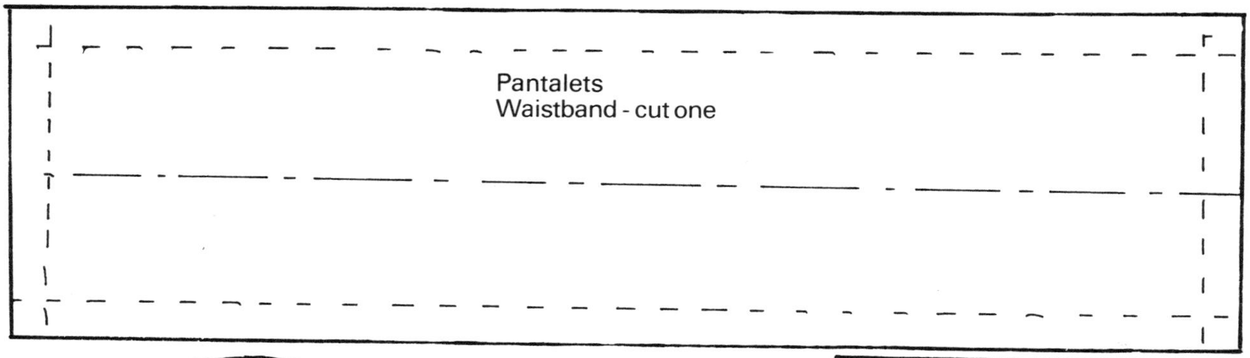

Pantalets
Waistband - cut one

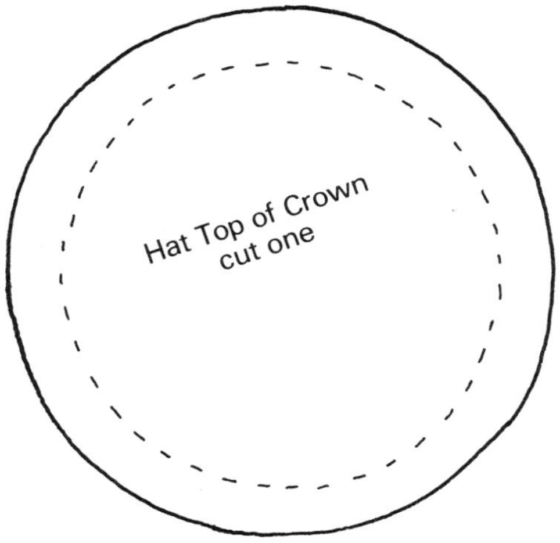

Hat Top of Crown
cut one

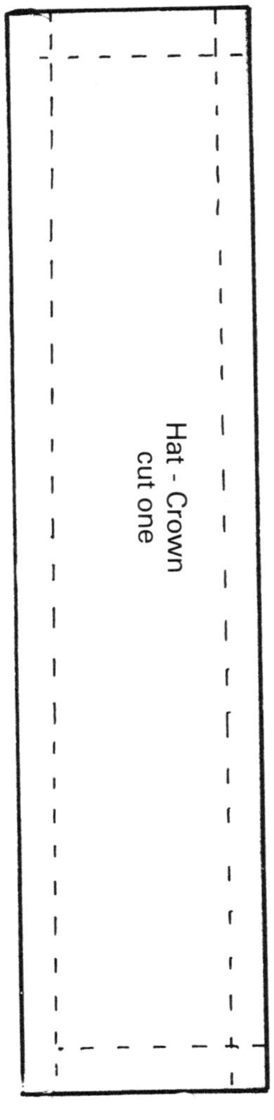

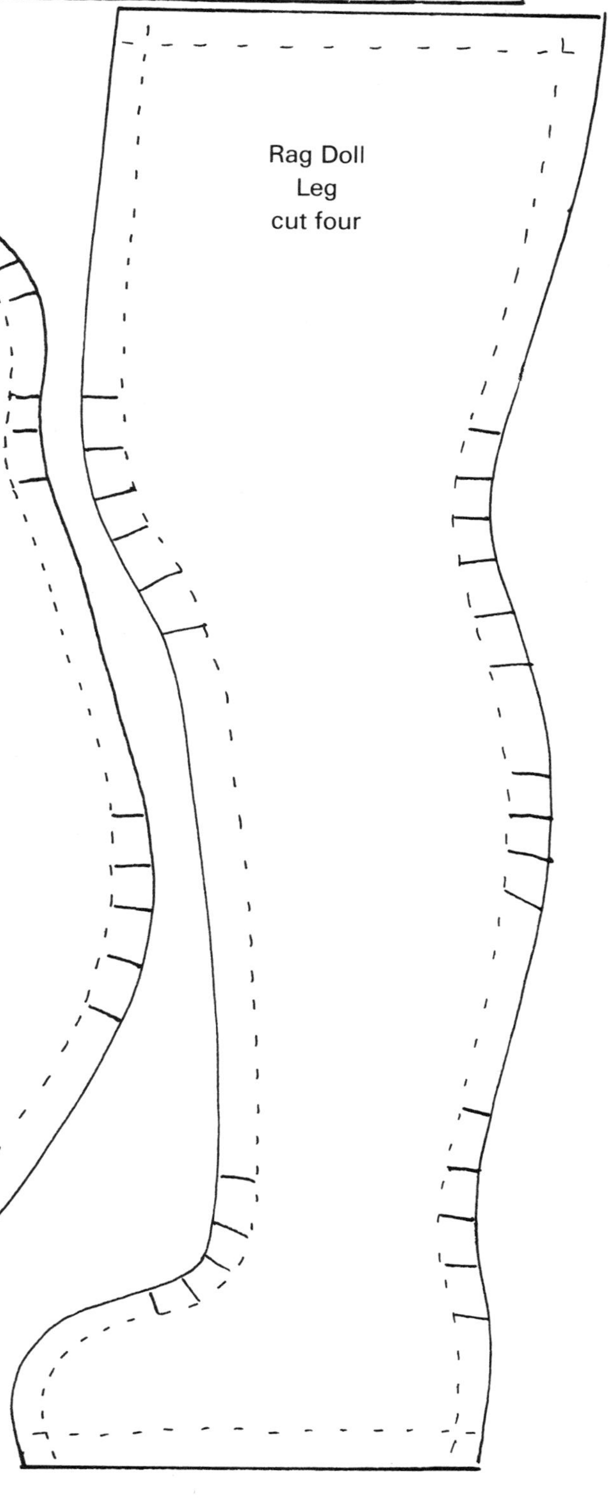

Rag Doll
Leg
cut four

Hat - Crown
cut one

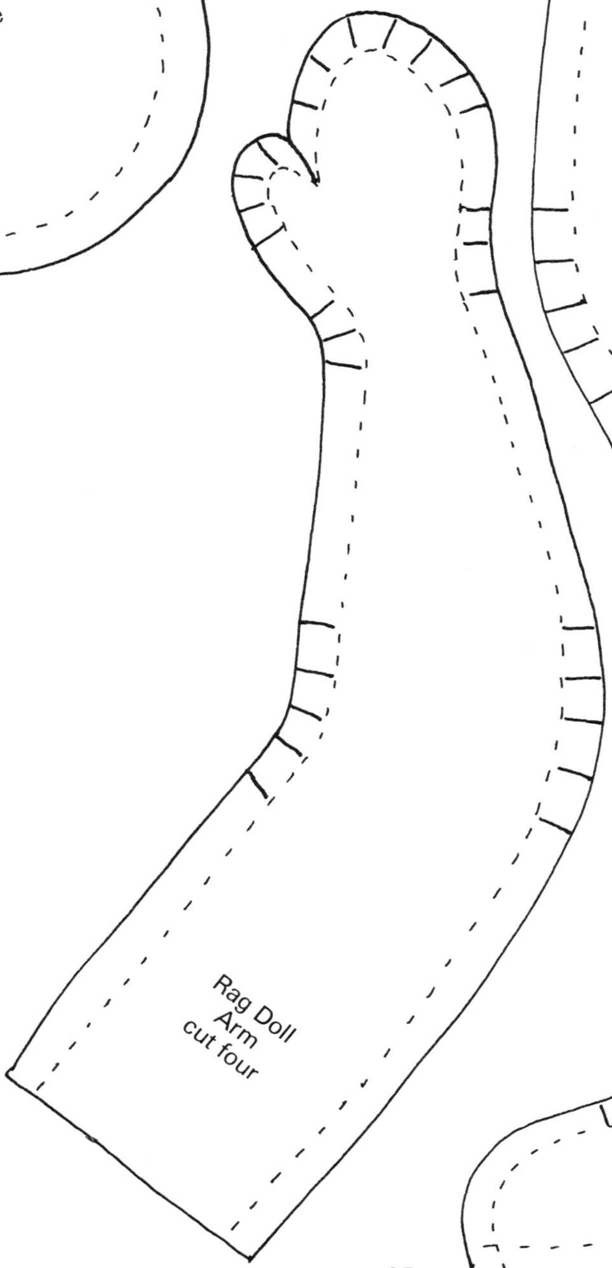

Rag Doll
Arm
cut four

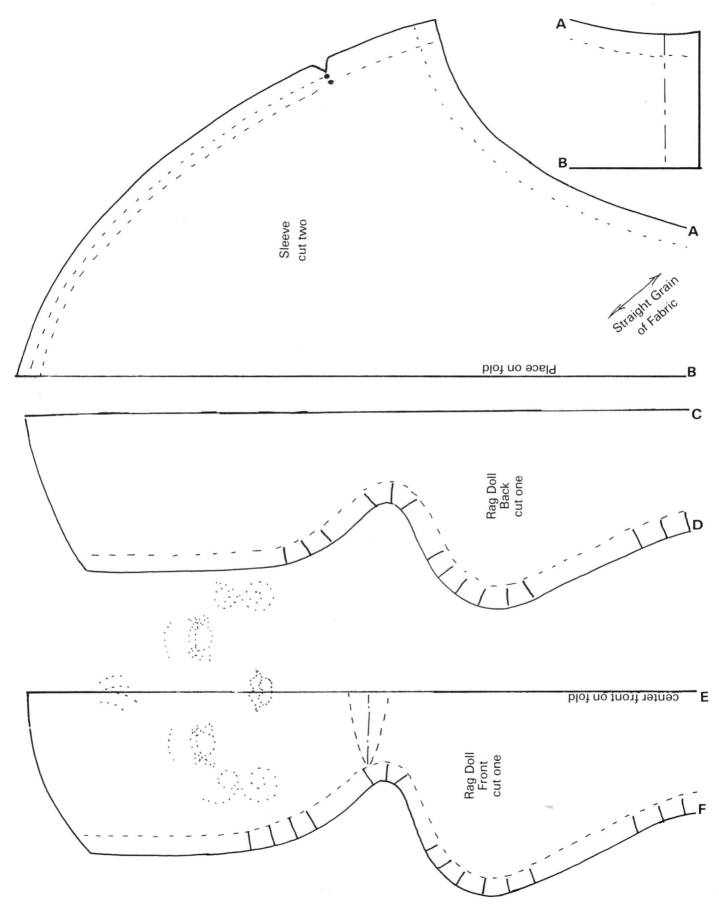

Sleeve
cut two

A

B

A

Straight Grain
of Fabric

Place on fold

B

C

Rag Doll
Back
cut one

D

center front on fold

E

Rag Doll
Front
cut one

F

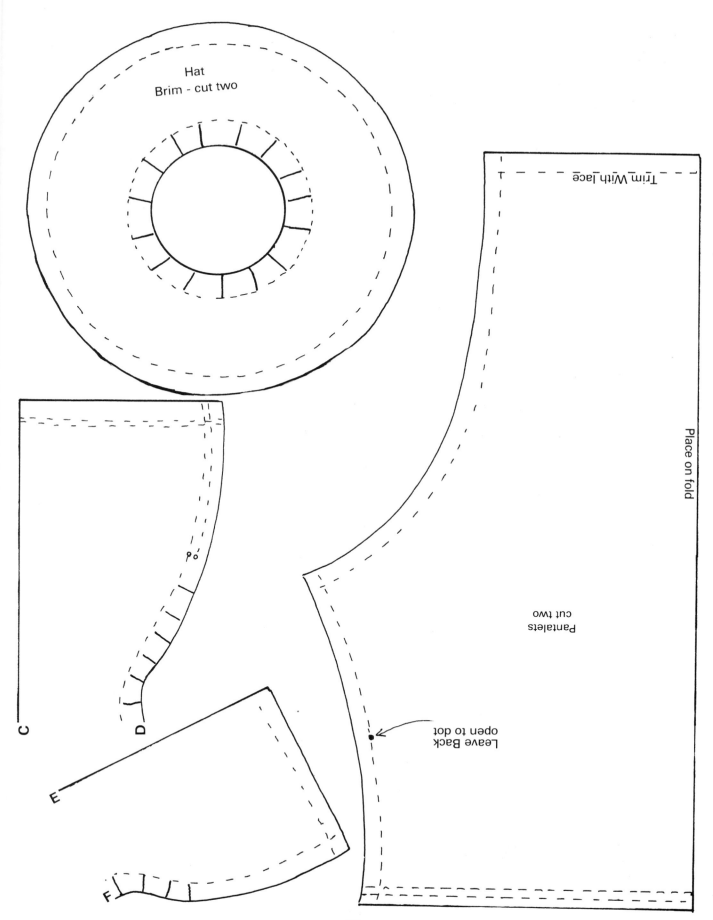

Hat
Brim - cut two

Trim With Lace

Place on fold

Pantalets
cut two

Leave Back
open to dot

C

D

E

F

27

THE COMPANION

by Susan Sirkis

Here is presented *Hans*, also costumed in the regional costume of Salzburg, as a companion to *Magda*. The directions for making the body are just the same as for *Magda*, but I will repeat them here for your convenience. *Hans* will be about 17in (43.2cm) tall.

HANS: Make the doll of unbleached muslin. Trace pattern pieces onto tissue paper (never use patterns printed on newspaper -- ink may smudge and ruin your fabric). Pin the body pattern to the muslin. Cut pieces out. Carefully trace the face with all of its outlines. The outlines will match the front of the doll's body. Pin the tracing to a piece of cardboard. Pin the muslin face over the drawing. Carefully trace the features and wisps of hair onto the muslin using light pencil lines. You may want to practice first on a scrap of muslin. You may also complete the face on a piece of muslin and then whip it onto the front of the doll, after it is stuffed, as a sort of mask. Embroider the features with a single strand of embroidery floss using satin and outline stitches as shown in diagram.

When the embroidery is complete begin to make the body by gathering the torso back along double dotted lines. Draw up to match front. Make dart in front neck to tilt head forward a little. Place right sides of back and front together and sew along stitching line. Leave top open for stuffing, carefully clip all curves. Sew arms and legs together in a similar manner. Turn all pieces. Stuff firmly and smoothly with polyester fiberfill. Turn under a narrow seam allowance at top of head and stitch closed. Close tops of arms and legs with envelope folds: hold the back of the leg (inside of arm) toward you and push the top edge down towards the front; fold each side in towards the center, thus making a point at center front (top of arm). Whip arms and legs to doll as shown in sketches.

Make the hair of brown yarn. Using long stitches, sew the hair to the head as shown in diagram.

DRAWERS: Make the drawers of white batiste. Sew back crotch seam. Sew front crotch seam. Make a narrow casing in top. Sew leg seams. Hem bottoms. Run a narrow tape through top and draw up to fit waist.

STOCKINGS: Use an old T-shirt, baby socks or finger bandages dyed dark blue. Cut to fit just above knees. If T-shirt or socks are used make a seam up center back. Hem tops.

SHOES: Make the shoes of felt. Sew seams on uppers. Attach soles. Cut buckles of cardboard painted gold. Sew to shoes.

SHIRT: Make the shirt of white batiste. Sew shoulder seams. Sew underarm seams to dots. Hem front edges and bottoms. Sew collars together around outer edges. Turn and press under seam allowance on bottom. Insert raw edges of shirt. Blindstitch collar in place. Work buttonholes up front. Sew buttons in place. Sew sleeve seams above dots. Slightly gather tops and set into armscyes. Hem openings below dots. Mount narrow cuffs on each sleeve. Close with small buttons.

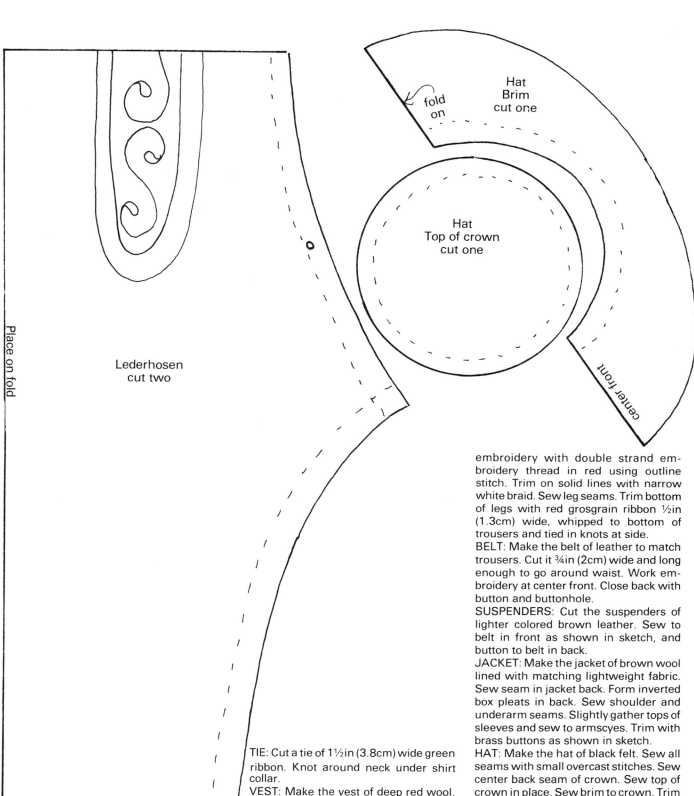

Place on fold

Lederhosen
cut two

Hat
Brim
cut one

fold on

Hat
Top of crown
cut one

center front

TIE: Cut a tie of 1½in (3.8cm) wide green ribbon. Knot around neck under shirt collar.

VEST: Make the vest of deep red wool. Sew shoulder and underarm seams. Sew narrow yellow braid to solid lines. Narrowly bind all raw edges. Work buttonholes in front. Close with small brass buttons.

LEDERHOSEN:Make the lederhosen of brown leather. Sew crotch seams, leaving front open above dots. Work the embroidery with double strand embroidery thread in red using outline stitch. Trim on solid lines with narrow white braid. Sew leg seams. Trim bottom of legs with red grosgrain ribbon ½in (1.3cm) wide, whipped to bottom of trousers and tied in knots at side.

BELT: Make the belt of leather to match trousers. Cut it ¾in (2cm) wide and long enough to go around waist. Work embroidery at center front. Close back with button and buttonhole.

SUSPENDERS: Cut the suspenders of lighter colored brown leather. Sew to belt in front as shown in sketch, and button to belt in back.

JACKET: Make the jacket of brown wool lined with matching lightweight fabric. Sew seam in jacket back. Form inverted box pleats in back. Sew shoulder and underarm seams. Slightly gather tops of sleeves and sew to armscyes. Trim with brass buttons as shown in sketch.

HAT: Make the hat of black felt. Sew all seams with small overcast stitches. Sew center back seam of crown. Sew top of crown in place. Sew brim to crown. Trim with a narrow gold braid band and feathers as shown.

Dress *Hans* in his drawers, shirt, tie and vest; then his trousers, suspenders and jacket.

Now, take *Hans* and introduce him to *Magda* -- I have a notion they will be a perfect couple!

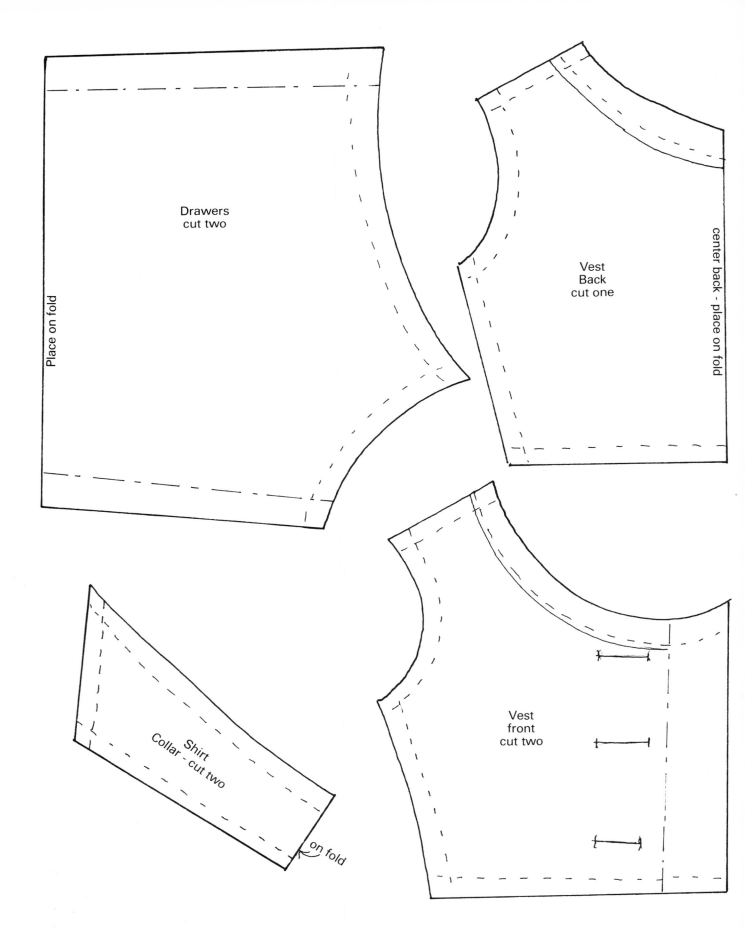

Drawers
cut two

Place on fold

Vest
Back
cut one

center back - place on fold

Shirt
Collar - cut two

on fold

Vest
front
cut two

30

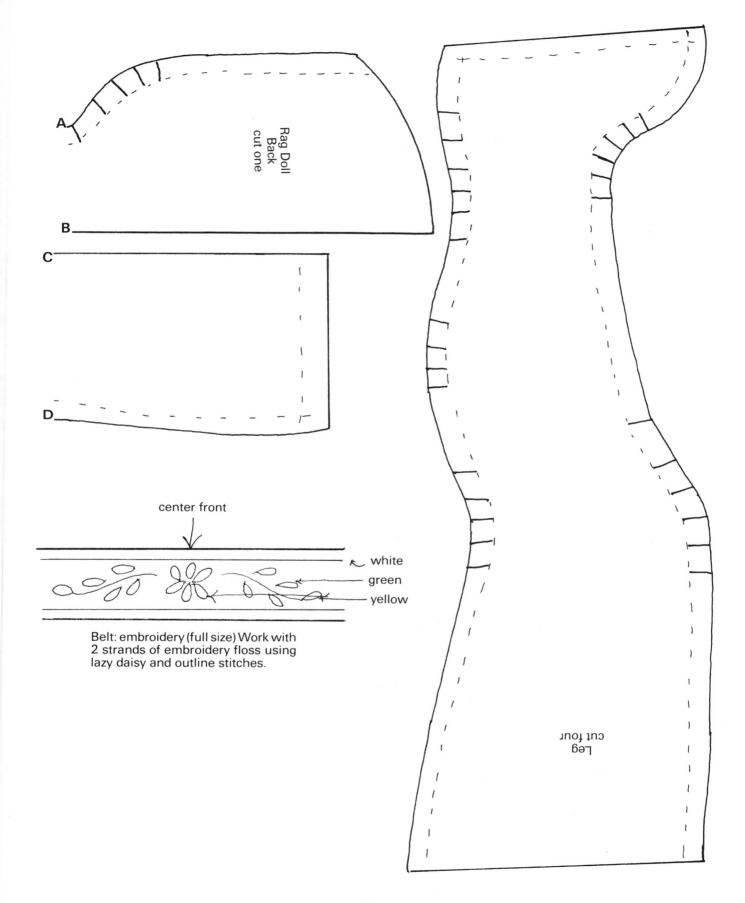

A

Rag Doll
Back
cut one

B

C

D

center front

↙ white
← green
← yellow

Belt: embroidery (full size) Work with
2 strands of embroidery floss using
lazy daisy and outline stitches.

Leg
cut four

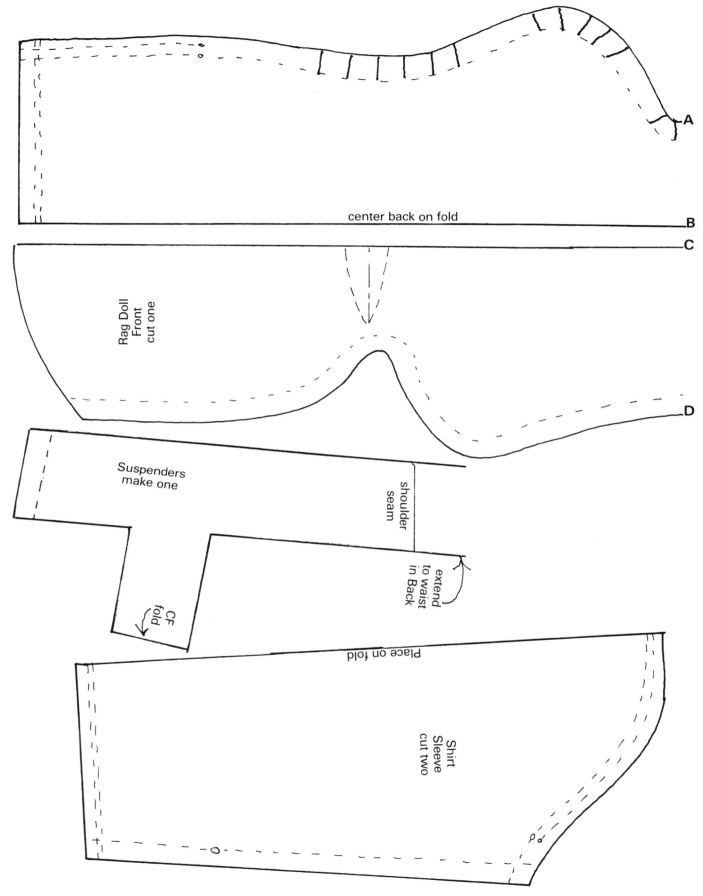

A

center back on fold

B

C

Rag Doll
Front
cut one

D

Suspenders
make one

shoulder
seam

extend
to waist
in Back

CF
fold

Place on fold

Shirt
Sleeve
cut two

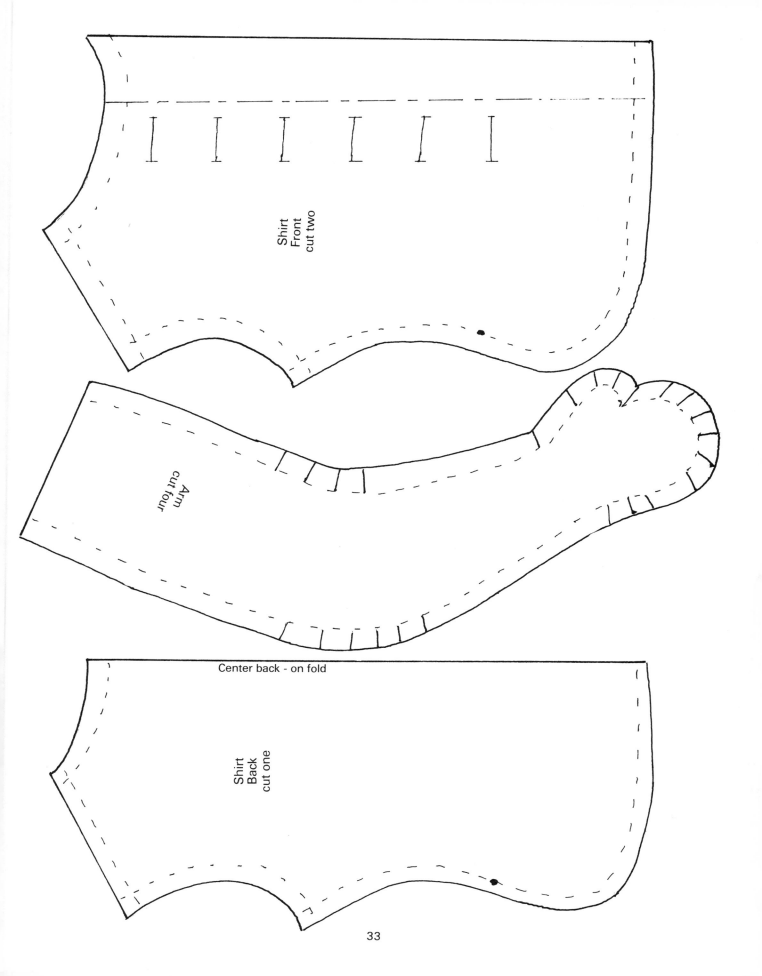

Shirt
Front
cut two

Arm
cut four

Center back - on fold

Shirt
Back
cut one

33

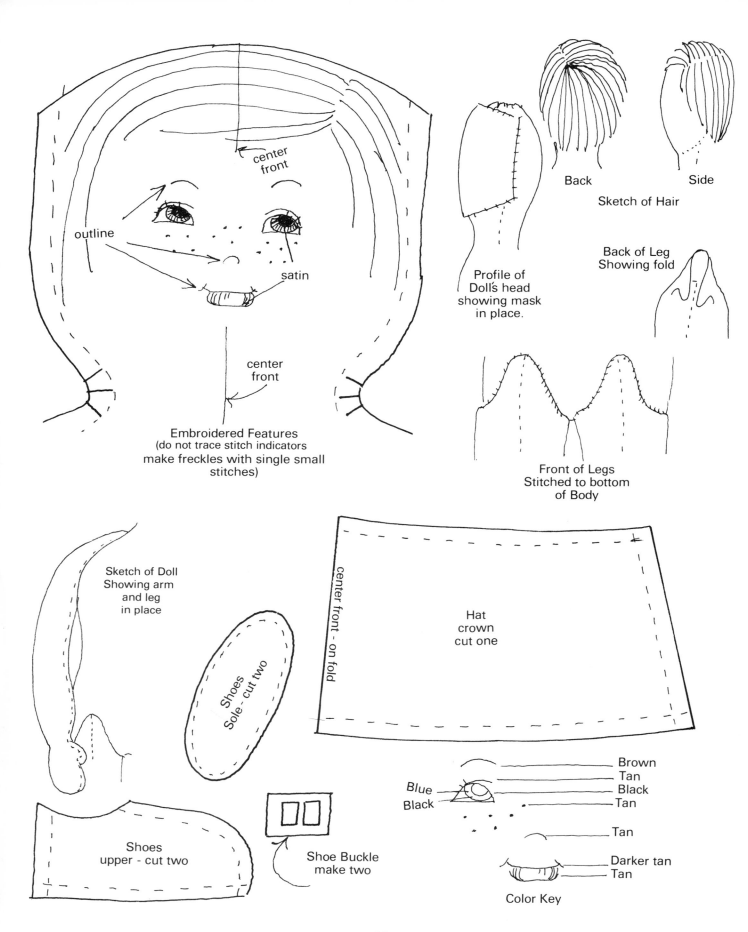

center front

outline

satin

center front

Embroidered Features
(do not trace stitch indicators
make freckles with single small
stitches)

Back

Side

Sketch of Hair

Profile of
Doll's head
showing mask
in place.

Back of Leg
Showing fold

Front of Legs
Stitched to bottom
of Body

Sketch of Doll
Showing arm
and leg
in place

Shoes
Sole - cut two

center front - on fold

Hat
crown
cut one

Shoes
upper - cut two

Shoe Buckle
make two

Brown

Tan

Blue   Black

Black   Tan

Tan

Darker tan

Tan

Color Key

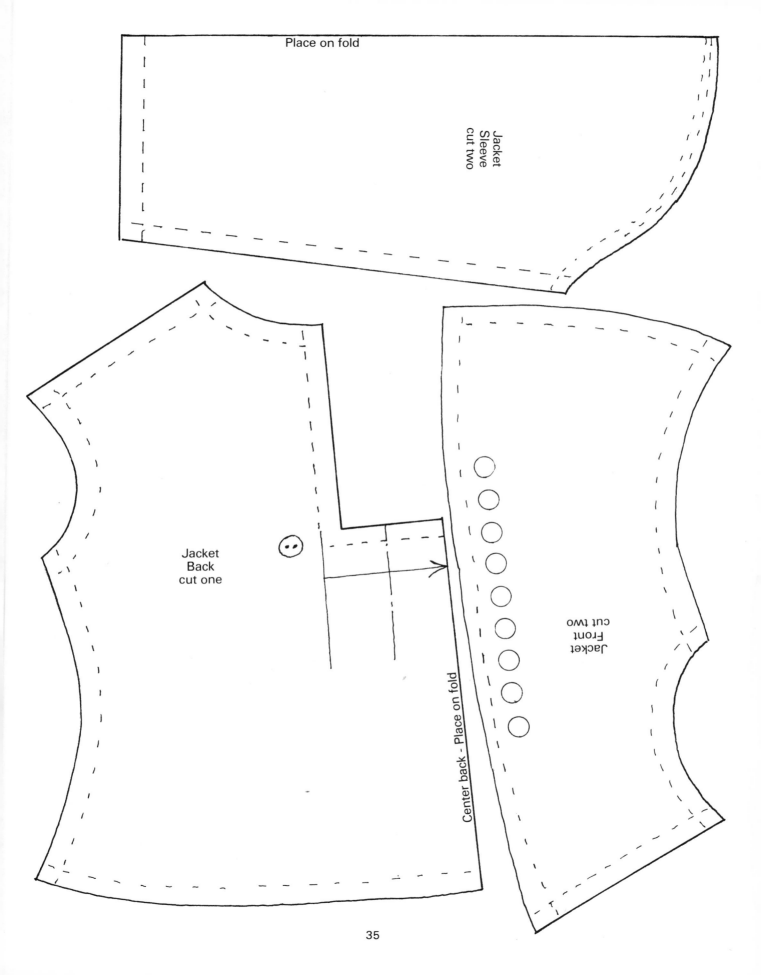

Place on fold

Jacket
Sleeve
cut two

Jacket
Back
cut one

Center back - Place on fold

Jacket
Front
cut two

35

Illustration 1. "Clara," (left), has hair painted with little curls around her face. She is turned slightly to show the bun at the back of her head. Tiny slippers with straps are painted on her feet. A chemise of batiste (from *The Doll Book)* is worn over lace-trimmed pantalets. "Viola," (right), has plain, painted hair and shoes. She holds an antique wooden doll which is less than 2in. (5.1cm) tall. Her lace-trimmed pantalets are of batiste. The white batiste dress in the trunk and the blue checked one directly above are made from the pattern included here as is the white sunbonnet above "Viola."

This little favorite of mine is so inexpensive and simple to make that you can do as the Princess Victoria did with her little wooden dolls and dress scores of them in the styles of the early-to-mid 19th century fashions.

"Viola," (right, *Illustration 1*) who resembles an old wooden doll, is one of a series of designs which I call "Old Timeys." Three different designs appear in my book, *Dolls, Puppedolls & Teddy Bears* (Van Nostrand Rienhold, 1977). They are simple, cloth dolls which capture something of the essence of antique dolls. Their character comes from the design; the way the cloth is cut in order to achieve just the right angle of their arms, legs and body. Construction involves two main pieces; a front and a back. They do have small darts at the neck and sometimes the addition of a small bun of hair at the head to give them depth. Some of my "Old Timeys" have legs cut separate from the body while others are in one piece from head to toe as is "Viola" shown here.

Her facial features are suitable for either embroidery (with a single strand of floss), felt-tip pen, paint or colored pencil. In order to give her the stiff and shiney look of a painted wooden doll, I

"Viola" An "Old Timey" Doll

by **Estelle Ansley Worrell**

paint her head, shoulders and feet with three or four coats of thick, white liquid glue such as "Elmer's" or "Sobo." During the glue-painting process, I place a tiny felt triangle on her nose within the embroidered or painted lines. When this triangle is covered with glue and hardened it looks almost exactly like the old carved or inserted wood noses on the original wooden dolls.

A comb can be added at the top of her head. About half of Victoria's dolls have combs, while half have plain heads.

Sewing across the hips where the legs join the body will enable her to sit

Illustration 2. "Clara," (left), wears a white batiste empire dress with blue sash and rosette. A batiste mobcap frames her curls. She holds a fan. "Viola," (right), wears a yellow checked cotton dress and white pique sunbonnet. Both dresses are from *The Doll Book*. The Victorian chair from *The Dollhouse Book* has petit point upholstery. A miniature "lithographed" cloth cat rests on the seat.

down if you like, but she will lose some of her characteristic stiffness as a result.

"Viola" looks especially like a wooden doll when you construct her of a beige, tan or yellowish fabric—the color of the light woods used for the little homemade or imported wooden dolls.

Named in honor of my mother, Clara Viola (Henson) Ansley, "Viola" has the hair style and shoes of the old dolls which were painted by simply dipping the heads and feet directly into the paint can.

Many of the period clothes in my earlier book, *The Doll Book*, will just fit "Viola," especially those intended for my 8-9" (20.3-22.9cm) child doll (see *Illustrations 2* and *4*). The dollhouses and doll furniture of period styles from my book, *The Dollhouse Book*, are perfectly scaled for her also. She is particularly at home with my Federal and early-Victorian style furniture (see *Illustration 2*).

"Clara," (left, *Illustration 1*), also named for my mother, has little curls painted around her face and dainty slippers painted on her feet.

Illustration 3. Here "Viola" wears satin ribbons which cross the bodice of her blue checked gingham dress, and then tie on the shoulders. A nosegay of tiny ribbon rosettes decorates the sash. The reticule purse is crocheted.

Illustration 4. "Clara" is dressed in blue wool which was used for the stole; white fur cloth was used for the muff. The felt bonnet is trimmed with satin ribbons and flowers. Patterns are from *The Doll Book*.

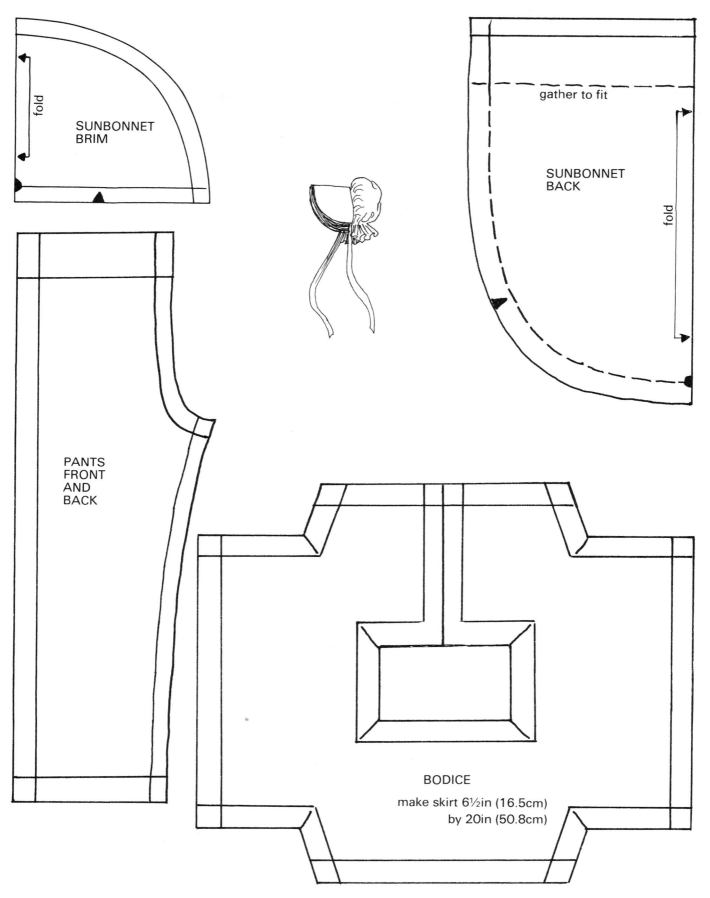

SUNBONNET
BRIM

fold

gather to fit

SUNBONNET
BACK

fold

PANTS
FRONT
AND
BACK

BODICE

make skirt 6½in (16.5cm)
by 20in (50.8cm)

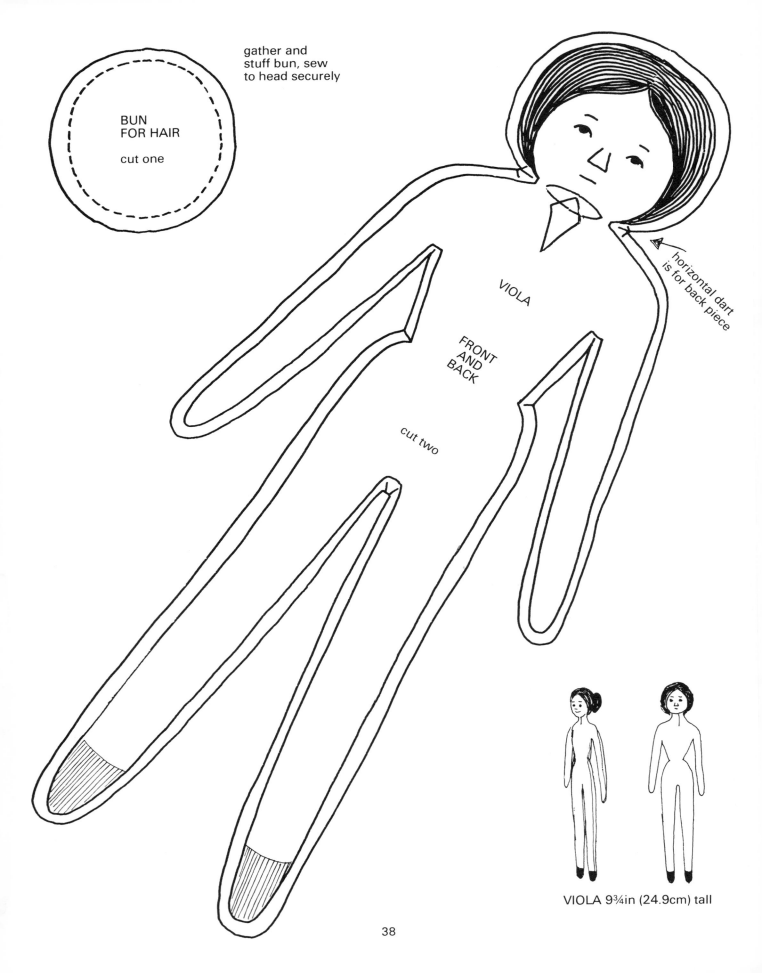

BUN
FOR HAIR

cut one

gather and
stuff bun, sew
to head securely

VIOLA

FRONT
AND
BACK

cut two

horizontal dart
is for back piece

VIOLA 9¾in (24.9cm) tall

38

Penny & Albert

"Old Timey" Children Dolls

by ESTELLE ANSLEY WORRELL

Photographs by STERLING WORRELL

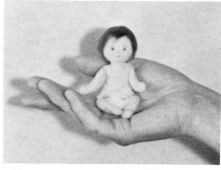

Illustration 1. A curved-leg "Penny" sits in the palm of my hand clad only in her white felt contoured diaper. She is very pleasing to cuddle in ones hand!

On page 36 I gave you "Viola" from my "Old Timey" series of miniature cloth dolls. This series was originally seen in my book, *Dolls, Puppedolls and Teddy Bears* (Van Nostrand Reinhold 1977). Something of the essence of antique dolls is captured through the design of their proportions and features yet they are so simple and inexpensive to construct that you can have as many as your heart desires. As promised, here are my patterns for "Viola's Children" -- a baby named "Penny" and a child named "Albert" (or "Vicky"). The baby can have either curved or straight limbs, the child can have straight or curved arms with his straight legs.

Only two pieces are required for each little doll and they can be cut from small scraps from your larger dolls. Only a handful of stuffing is needed for their dainty bodies. They can be made to represent any skin color but, if you want them to look

ABOVE: Illustration 3. Mama "Clara" takes her family for a stroll. A little boy "Albert" sports a blue cotton satin suit over a frilly lace blouse. His blouse is the jacket pattern turned around so that it opens in back. A lace frill was added to the front. His red and white striped stockings have slippers painted on the feet. Straw-colored felt was used for the sailor hat with blue grosgrain ribbon band and streamers. The outfit can be seen on the wall in Illustration 2 above the dark-skinned baby. "Albert" holds a teddy bear, one of my "Tiny Teddies," in his hand. Sleeping in the carriage is an infant "Penny" with her eyes embroidered closed. She is dressed in a tan wrapper and cap trimmed with blue embroidery worn over a white batiste dress and satin sash. The wrapper and cap appear at the lower right in Illustration 2.

Illustration 2. (Left to right) A dark-skinned baby I call "Leroy" is made of brown cotton cloth with black embroidery floss hair worked in French knots. A curved limb "Penny" of beige cotton/polyester broadcloth has auburn fur cloth hair glued to her head. A blond straight-legged baby has yellow floss hair while an older child, called "Albert" when a boy and "Vicky" when a girl, has long yellow fur cloth hair. Their clothing, displayed above them, is described in the following illustration discussions.

like old-fashioned wooden dolls, use a tan or yellowish fabric to resemble the light woods used for the little homemade or imported wooden dolls.

The facial features are suitable for embroidery with a single strand of floss or for painting. Hair can be floss, fur cloth, yarn, human hair or painted hair. To further capture the look and feel of an old wooden doll, the head and shoulders can be painted or dipped in white liquid glue to make it hard. The feet and hands or the whole doll can be hardened with glue if you like. (Just be sure to test your paint on a scrap first to make sure it does not run.) This baby is the same size as my baby in *The Doll Book* (Van Nostrand Reinhold 1966). Their clothes can be interchanged.

NO SEAM ALLOWANCES ARE GIVEN on patterns. For such a small doll it works best if you *draw* around the pattern with a pencil to indicate the stitching line. When cutting, allow about 1/8 in. (.31cm) to the outside of the pencil line as you cut with a good pair of sharp scissors. For real accuracy on very small pieces I often draw around the pattern, pin securely, and then sew directly on the pencil lines BEFORE cutting. Sew with a small stitch on your sewing machine or with a backstitch by hand. Be sure to clip the seam allowance at the neck, underarms, and arm and leg curves before turning with a small dowel or kelly forceps.

Stuffing should be done with a small dowel or swab stick to push the polyester filling into the head and limbs. Leave space at the hips and shoulders so that the arms and legs will move easily after stitching. Just pin a safety pin at the indicated line as you stuff the doll to hold the filling back until you are ready to sew across it.

These little dolls make nice gifts and prizes for doll club gatherings. Children enjoy them too. They not only are charming for babies for your small dolls but can serve as accessory "dolls" for your larger dolls to hold.

Chairs are from *The Dollhouse Book* (Van Nostrand 1964), the carriage and all miniatures are from the author's collection.

Illustration 4. "Vicky" models a party dress of lace made with the jacket pattern turned so that it opens in back. A lace jabot enhances the front bodice, an embroidered pink and green flower embellishes the skirt. This little dress can be made any length from very short to floor length according to the period style you prefer. Her stockings are a striped knit fabric with the shoes painted on. The dress is at the top left in Illustration 2. On the Chippendale chair sits an infant reflecting the pose of the real baby in the antique photograph on the wall above. Her dress of blue lawn is trimmed with ecru lace and satin ribbon. It is made like the white batiste dress at the upper right in Illustration 2. The hem is trimmed with a pulled-thread open work band as well as lace. A blue and ecru cap matches the dress. Sitting on the floor, a curved-leg baby plays with miniature alphabet blocks. She models an embroidered bib, diaper and crocheted booties. The bid and diaper are seen in Illustration 2 at lower center.

Illustration 5. Baby "Penny" sits in a wing chair dressed in a long christening dress which is seen at the top center of Illustration 2. Three rows of open work around the skirt were formed by pulling threads from the soft white lawn. An antique silk ribbon rosette decorates the waist. My original "Viola" doll stands between her children. In the rosewood Victorian chair a blond straight-legged baby wears the sleeveless dress with the salmon pink satin ribbon sash and pink embroidery. It can be seen on the wall just left of the center in Illustration 2. Her little lace brimmed bonnet can be seen at top center. An "Old Timey Penny," who most resembles her mother, stands beside the chair. Her hair and face are painted and her head and shoulders are hardened with several coats of glue to make her resemble an old penny wooden doll of the nineteenth century. Her sweater, bonnet and booties were crocheted of fine baby yarn using the jacket-sacque and cap patterns for guides. A matching blanket was woven on a small potholder loom with a crocheted scalloped edging added. (Blankets can be knitted, crocheted, or cut from cotton flannel 4 in. [10.2cm] to 5 in. [12.7cm] square.) She holds a 2 in. (5.1cm) tall teddy bear from my "Tiny Teddies" series of miniature bears.

"Old Timey Babies"

by Estelle Ansley Worrell

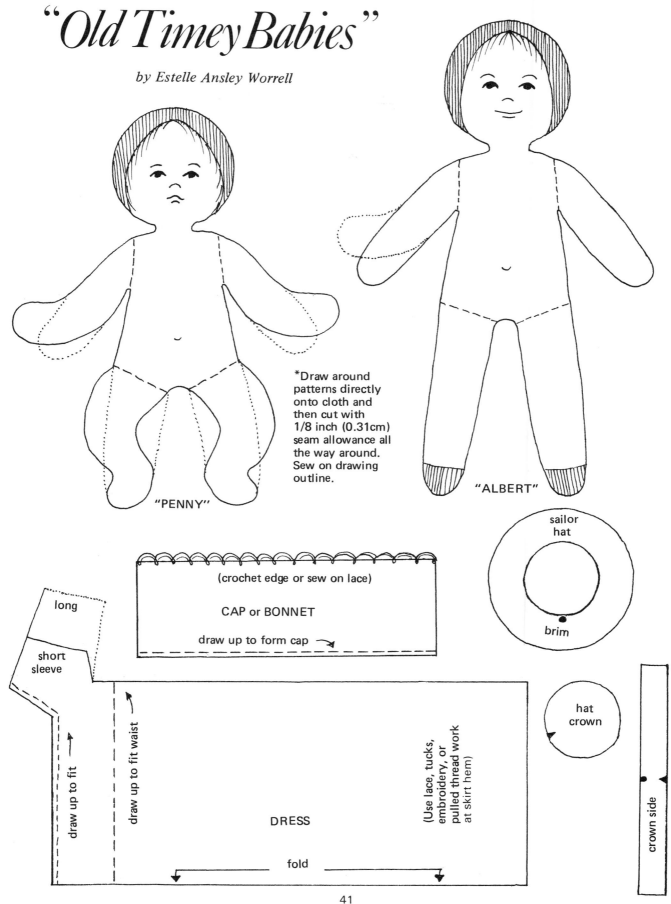

*Draw around patterns directly onto cloth and then cut with 1/8 inch (0.31cm) seam allowance all the way around. Sew on drawing outline.

"PENNY"

"ALBERT"

sailor hat

brim

(crochet edge or sew on lace)

CAP or BONNET

draw up to form cap →

hat crown

long

short sleeve

draw up to fit →

draw up to fit waist

(Use lace, tucks, embroidery, or pulled thread work at skirt hem)

DRESS

fold

crown side

No seam allowances are given. Draw around pattern for stitching line then allow about 1/8 inch (0.31cm) seam when cutting.

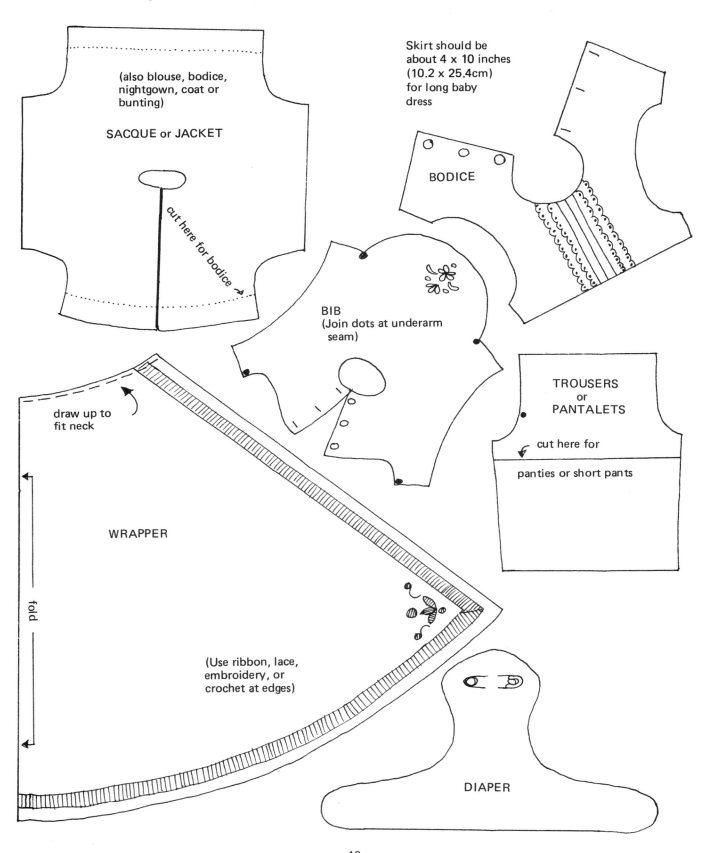

(also blouse, bodice, nightgown, coat or bunting)

SACQUE or JACKET

cut here for bodice

Skirt should be about 4 x 10 inches (10.2 x 25.4cm) for long baby dress

BODICE

BIB
(Join dots at underarm seam)

TROUSERS
or
PANTALETS

cut here for

panties or short pants

draw up to fit neck

WRAPPER

fold

(Use ribbon, lace, embroidery, or crochet at edges)

DIAPER

DOLLS N' THINGS

by Sandy Williams

This 3in (7.6cm) Queen Anne doll is made of a round-headed wood clothespin with wooden matches for the arms and legs. I made the dress up in royal blue cotton with a white batiste underskirt but you may make her in silks and taffeta if you prefer. Use the drawings as a guide in making her up. File all rough wood edges with an emery board and let each piece dry after gluing it on the doll. Use 1/4in (.65cm) white lace throughout. First saw the tips of the clothespin off, leaving a slight leg notch. Bend a pipe cleaner in half and glue in leg notch. Cut two matches for the legs -- each 1¾in (4.5cm) long, twist the pipe cleaner around the tops of the legs and glue, cut off excess pipe cleaner. With watercolors paint the face, arms and legs a flesh color. Paint eyes black, lips and shoes red and cheeks pink. Glue embroidery floss on for hair only where it would peek out from under her mobcap. Hem underskirt, gather waistline and glue to front of doll's waist. The overskirt; sew darts (forms the side panniers), hem front and bottom edges, gather waist to fit doll, glue to doll's waist, placing darts at doll's sides. Glue a small ball of tissue to *inside* of darts to make the sides protrude for wide panniers. Turn up waist hems of bodice and glue to doll, turn in sides so bodice fits doll snugly and glue. Cut two matches for the arms -- each 1¼" long. Turn up hem in sleeve and glue. Glue sleeve to arm to fit tight, gather a small length of lace and glue to bottom edge of sleeve. Glue shoulder tab of sleeve to shoulder of doll. Fold a length of lace in half and glue to the raw edges of bodice making a V down front of bodice. Cut stomacher out of index card, cut a piece of blue cotton a little bigger than card stomacher, turn excess material to back of stomacher and glue in place. Make two tiny bows of 1/4in (.65cm) blue ribbon -- one bow a little larger than the other and glue to front of stomacher. Glue stomacher to front of bodice. Sew lace to edge of mobcap -- gathering as you sew, glue to head of doll.

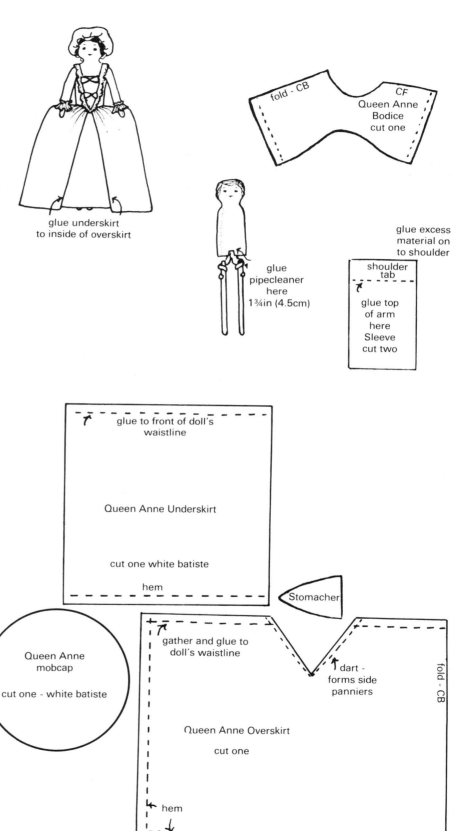

glue underskirt to inside of overskirt

glue pipecleaner here 1¾in (4.5cm)

fold - CB

CF

Queen Anne Bodice cut one

glue excess material on to shoulder

shoulder tab

glue top of arm here Sleeve cut two

glue to front of doll's waistline

Queen Anne Underskirt

cut one white batiste

hem

Stomacher

Queen Anne mobcap

cut one - white batiste

gather and glue to doll's waistline

dart - forms side panniers

fold - CB

Queen Anne Overskirt

cut one

hem

12in.(30.5cm) Felt Doll

by Sandy Williams

Illustration 1. *Front view. Photograph by Paul Emmett Hamilton.*

Illustration 2. Back view. *Photograph by Paul Emmett Hamilton.*

Felt is one of the easiest fabrics from which to make a doll. It is easily molded with your fingers and by the amount of stuffing used. You can "plump-up" cheeks by inserting a sewing needle into fabric and pulling gently.

This chubby toddler doll can sit up or stand due to its button-jointed legs. You have a choice of making the arms with either a mitt hand or a hand with separated fingers—both are easily sewn if you carefully follow the directions.

There are a few "tricks" to working with felt: Carefully match all pattern pieces (easing one piece upon the other if necessary); sew seams in smooth continuous lines (you will have to lift up the machine presser foot often to achieve smooth lines around curves and fingers but the result will be more than worth the little extra effort); carefully turn the felt pieces inside-out taking care not to pull the felt out of shape; set your sewing machine at 12 stitches per inch; use small pieces of fiberfill when stuffing,

"tamping" down the fiberfill firmly with the "poker" (see *Materials needed*). Most seam allowances are ⅛in. (3.2mm) unless noted. Blindstitch all openings closed, tucking in seam allowances; stuff extra bits of fiberfill into opening as you sew. If you are artistic and wish to paint your doll's face (use acrylic paints), first snip off felt fuzz where you wish to paint. Next, paint several white "base" coats on features; let dry between coats. If you make a mistake, first let paint dry then carefully "pick" paint off with a small pair of scissors.

Materials needed: 3 Squares of 9 by 12in. (22.9 by 30.5cm) flesh-colored felt; flesh-colored thread; buttonhole twist thread; two four-hole ½in (12.7mm) buttons; polyester fiberfill; dry, powdered cake rouge with brush; embroidery thread in dark and medium brown, white, pale and medium pink; dark brown felt; hair spray; dark brown "fun" fur; and a "poker." To make a poker to stuff bits of fiberfill into doll, cut an 8in. (20.3cm) piece of ⅛in. (3.2mm) round dowel rod, sand one end to a blunt point (great for pushing in bits of stuffing for fingers) and sand the other end flat.

Cut out all patterns pieces except for the arms. Mark darts. Sew all darts in pattern pieces.

Head: Pin side head to center section starting at each neck and work your way to top of head. Ease center section to side section; sew together. Repeat with other side section except leave open between dots in which to turn head right-side-out. Finger press all head seams. Stuff head firmly through this opening. Blindstitch opening closed.

Body: Sew CB seam, leaving open between dots. Sew CF seam. With right sides of front and back bodies together, pin and sew on shoulder, sides and crotch seams in one continuous seam. Snip corners of crotch seam off, turn right-side-out through back opening and finger press all seams. Stuff firmly and blindstitch opening closed.

Attach head to body: Run a basting guideline ¼in. (6.2mm) in on neck of head and body pieces. Pin and baste head to body using ¼in. (6.2mm) seams (align chin dart with body CF seam and side head darts with body shoulder seams). You can change the whole character of your doll by placing the head in different positions (such as doll looking to side). Using blindstitches, sew neck seam closed, going around neck twice.

Legs: Sew CF seam of leg together. With right sides of foot and leg seams together, pin and sew ankle seam. Sew CB seam of leg and foot together from dot of leg to heel of foot. Clip curve bottom of foot, matching CF and CB seams. For the other leg, reverse the foot sole. Turn legs right-side-out and finger press seams. With a double-threaded needle sew button to wrong side of *inner* (same side as big toe) leg with an X stitch; go over X stitch two more times. Repeat with other leg. Stuff foot and leg firmly keeping foot sole as flat as you can. Blindstitch leg opening closed. With a large needle threaded with a double strand of buttonhole twist, insert needle through X stitch on one leg, then insert needle through side hip of doll and out other side hip, insert needle through X stitch of other leg and reinsert needle back through doll's hip (see *Illustration 3*). Pull cord tight and tie cord ends into a knot; snip ends off.

Arms: Decide which type of hand you want for your arms—either separated fingers or a mitt hand. If you decide mitt hands use the following directions—you may either hand-stitch in the finger lines or leave the mitt hand plain.

Cut the arm pattern out on the cutting line. Pin pattern to a double thickness of felt. Machine-stitch as close as you can to the pattern, leaving open between the dots. To keep the sewing line flowing smoothly, you have to frequently lift the presser foot of your machine to get around the curved parts of the pattern. Cut arm out leaving a ⅛in. (3.2mm) seam allowance; slash between fingers; remove pattern and repeat for other arm. Turn arm right-side-out, being careful not to pull felt out of shape. The fingers are pulled out by using straight pins. Using the pointed end of "poker," twirl a long thin wisp of fiberfill around tip. Insert poker into a finger, grasp finger and pull out poker. Repeat with each finger; stuff hand. Using a single strand of flesh thread, insert needle into base of fingers (between middle and ring fingers). Pull needle up through top of fingers, pulling thread tight. Take tiny stitches up and down through fingers, pulling thread after each stitch. If you are sewing mitt hands, mold fingers toward palm of hand as you sew the finger lines. Stuff rest of arm firmly, molding it to a nice round shape. Blindstitch opening closed. Firmly sew arms to shoulder of doll.

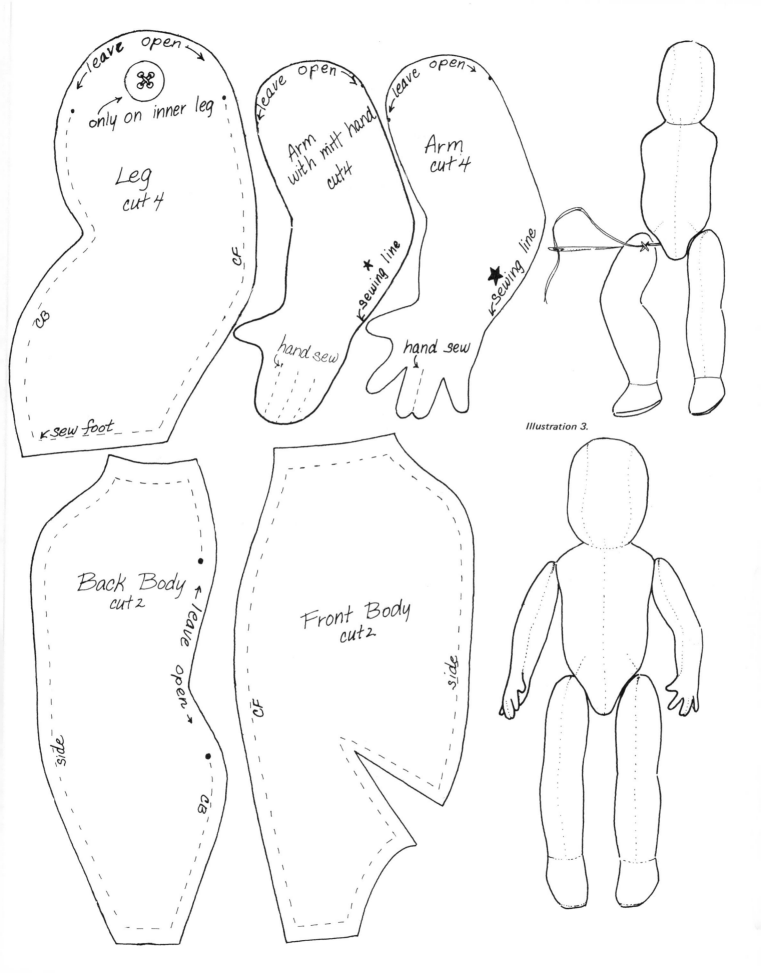

← leave open →

only on inner leg

Leg
cut 4

cB

cF

κ sew foot

← leave open →

Arm
with mitt hand
cut 4

★ sewing line

hand sew

← leave open →

Arm
cut 4

★ sewing line

hand sew

Illustration 3.

Back Body
cut 2

side

← leave open →

cB

Front Body
cut 2

cF

side

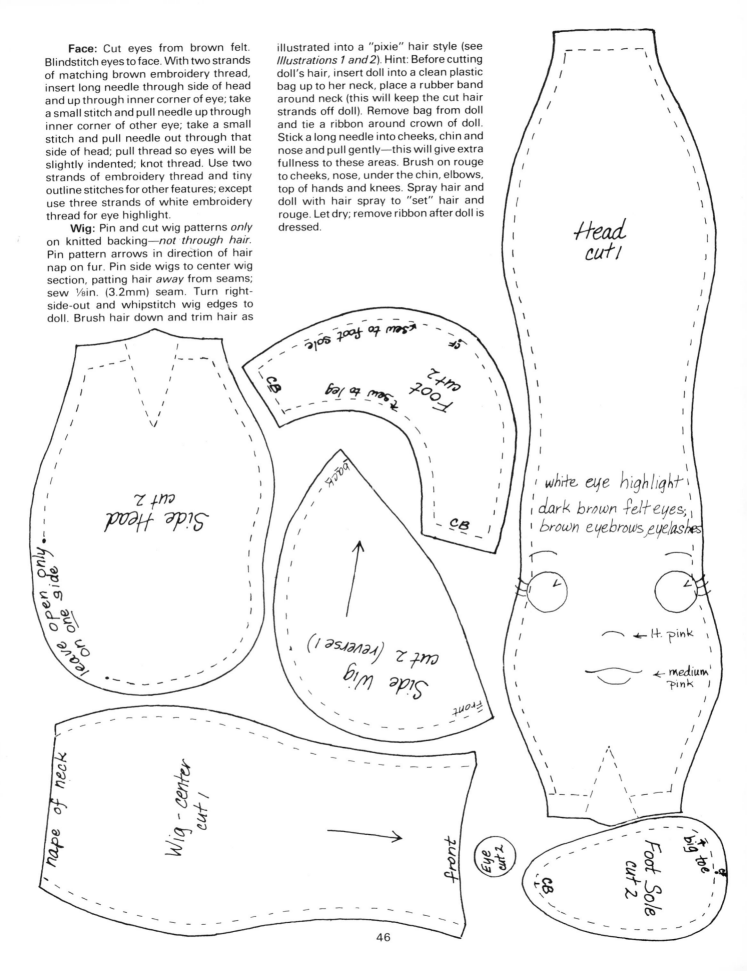

Face: Cut eyes from brown felt. Blindstitch eyes to face. With two strands of matching brown embroidery thread, insert long needle through side of head and up through inner corner of eye; take a small stitch and pull needle up through inner corner of other eye; take a small stitch and pull needle out through that side of head; pull thread so eyes will be slightly indented; knot thread. Use two strands of embroidery thread and tiny outline stitches for other features; except use three strands of white embroidery thread for eye highlight.

Wig: Pin and cut wig patterns *only* on knitted backing—*not through hair.* Pin pattern arrows in direction of hair nap on fur. Pin side wigs to center wig section, patting hair *away* from seams; sew ⅛in. (3.2mm) seam. Turn right-side-out and whipstitch wig edges to doll. Brush hair down and trim hair as illustrated into a "pixie" hair style (see *Illustrations 1 and 2*). Hint: Before cutting doll's hair, insert doll into a clean plastic bag up to her neck, place a rubber band around neck (this will keep the cut hair strands off doll). Remove bag from doll and tie a ribbon around crown of doll. Stick a long needle into cheeks, chin and nose and pull gently—this will give extra fullness to these areas. Brush on rouge to cheeks, nose, under the chin, elbows, top of hands and knees. Spray hair and doll with hair spray to "set" hair and rouge. Let dry; remove ribbon after doll is dressed.

Head
cut 1

white eye highlight
dark brown felt eyes;
brown eyebrows/eyelashes

lt. pink

medium pink

Side Head
cut 2

leave open only on one side

Foot
cut 2

sew to foot sole

CB

CB

sew to leg

Side Wig
cut 2 (reverse 1)

back

front

Eye
cut 2

nape of neck

Wig – center
cut 1

front

big toe

Foot Sole
cut 2

CB

Making Bread Dolls

by **Elizabeth Andrews Fisher**
Photographs and Sketches by **Elizabeth Andrews Fisher**

If your church needs dolls to sell at fairs or to raise funds, or just because you love dolls and want more, here are ways of making them:

First: Find a store that sells newspapers, and since newspapers around here are delivered in bundles tied with wire, ask the storeman to save the wire for you. It is just the right size and kind to use for making wire frame bodies.

BREAD DOLLS. Get a loaf of stale bread from the "second hand" counter, the biggest you can find. WHITE BREAD. Cut off all the crust, spread out on a tray to dry. Turn the bread over night and morning so it will dry evenly. When the bread is BONE DRY, and snaps like wood when broken, put the slices in a strong paper bag, and smash the slices with a rolling pin or even an empty bottle, until the slices are just meal. (Be careful when cutting off the crust not to leave your fingerprints in the bread because they will turn into hard lumps.)

Measure the bread crumbs. One cup of crumbs for one quarter cup of salt. Mix dry in a bowl. Then, add water slowly and with care, stirring all the while. When the mixture gets to the handleable clay stage, and sort of leaves the edges of the bowl, it is ready to use.

Cut a piece of wire 18in (45.7cm) long and bend into a hairpin shape. Push the open ends into holes in a large button, and pull the button right up to the loop in the wire.

Then squeeze a large walnut size lump of the bread around the wire against the button and go to work on the head.

Have you seen the beans that are white and have a black patch on one side? They make fierce looking eyes. Or you may use beads, buttons, rolling eyes from a craft counter (they come in all sizes). Push the eyes into the head while the bread is soft. Even glass headed pins will not be pushed into the dry head.

Hang the head up to dry while you make the hands and feet. Strip the paper from plastic bag ties, and use that wire to form hands and feet. When you have the frame made, cover with the bread.

Wrap the wire with ¾in (2cm) strips of old sheet. Be sure to fasten the ends securely so the strips will not unwind. When doing the winding, attach the hands and feet at the proper places to the body. Make your doll short waisted. You do not want the crotch dragging on the floor.

Dress the doll to suit yourself, keeping in mind that accessories MAKE the doll.

Measure from the bottom of the head to the bottom of the feet for the length of arm. This gets wound with the strips of old sheet when you do the body.

Eyebrows and lips may be colored with proper color in Sharpie pens. Cheeks may be perked up with a dab of dry cake rouge.

Fabulous hair styles may be obtained by using mohair, a little patience, your creative ability, glue and a needle and thread.

If any filling out is needed, stuff the clothes.

Make doll house dolls the same way, but smaller. They will pose for you and even bake or sit quietly and read.

This mixture will keep for a year in a well sealed (air tight) jar in the refrigertor. **Mark it well-Doll Stuff.**

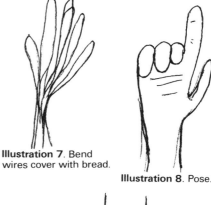

Illustration 7. Bend wires cover with bread.

Illustration 8. Pose.

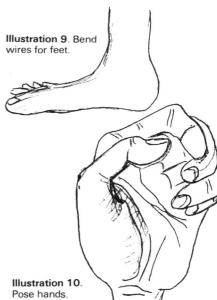

Illustration 9. Bend wires for feet.

Illustration 10. Pose hands.

Illustration 11. This is Mr. Plushbottom, a comic strip character, created by Lucy White, from bread and wire and felt. He has a cigar, pince-nez glasses, a watch chain over his fat tummy, a black and gold cane, spats, and shiny black shoes. His eyes are glass headed pins.

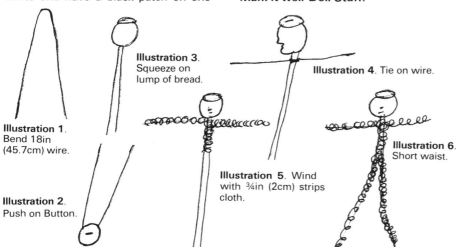

Illustration 1. Bend 18in (45.7cm) wire.

Illustration 2. Push on Button.

Illustration 3. Squeeze on lump of bread.

Illustration 4. Tie on wire.

Illustration 5. Wind with ¾in (2cm) strips cloth.

Illustration 6. Short waist.

Make Your Own Doll Collection

by ARTIE SEELEY

Illustration 1. LEFT TO RIGHT: Laughing Jumeau, Steiner, A. T., Marque. All reproductions by Artie Seeley.

Illustration 2. This old head is wire-eyed and is the one reproduced in the article.

You want a doll collection? Why not make one? (Illustration 1).

I have chosen an old favorite doll with a very simple head with which to begin. When purchased about 15 years ago, this doll (Illustration 2) was approximately $50.00. When offered $450.00 for the same doll, I felt I could not afford to keep it. Since I was making china arms and legs for people who collected dolls, I thought, why not make a mold of the head and I could make my own doll.

With my husband Bill's help I came up with a fairly good mold and we have been making Googlies ever since. Because each detail of this doll is simple, I believe it would be best for anyone who wants to make or paint a doll, to begin with this model or one similar. Here is a doll without fancy eyebrows or lashes, therefore, simple to make.

Begin work on a head fresh out of the mold. I always work on damp clay, which is best when leather hard. When holding the head, lay it gently on your hand; do not use any pressure, as the slightest pressure may cause a crack, particularly in the large opening in the top of the head. So - - - be careful!

First, remove seam lines with an Exacto tool. Then, feeling this surface with finger tips, check for smoothness. Using a very soft damp Mediterranean silk sponge, lightly rub the area of the mold line; then check the surface again with your finger tips; sometimes it helps to close your eyes. If there are any rough areas or lines on the face, use this same technique of gently sponging and slight finger tip pressure to smooth the surface. Do not wash or rub the face or the clay will lose nose and lip detail.

Make a mark around the eye with a sharp tool (pencil or Kemper needle). Mark just inside the actual opening line and criss cross the circle you want to remove. Using the Exacto blade, cut more deeply around the outer circle; slowly and gently deepen the cut and the four sections will fall out (Illustration 3). Smooth a bit with the blade. Using a wet round sable brush (size 6), go carefully around and around until you have the rest of the material washed away and the eye is a near perfect circle.

If your clay is cast thin, a little wiping on the inside of the opening will bevel the edge enough to match the curve of the eyeball. If your clay is thick, turn the head face down in your hand and, working through the top of the head, very carefully carve a bevel around the inside of the eye opening, using the curve of the Kemper tool (Illustration 4).

Now dip a size 8 or 10 round camel hair or watercolor brush into water. Press it down into a damp towel to remove the excess moisture and then roll it around the beveled edge inside the eye. Turn the head over, put the brush into the eye opening and circle around to make sure you have a smooth surface. Work gently as you do not wish to enlarge the shape you now have.

Carefully try an eye in the opening for size and fit (Illustration 5).

This would be a good time to sign the head using a very sharp pencil. Also, the date might be in order. If you have smoothed all surfaces, the neck opening and the head, even though it is still wet, pop it in your kiln or set it aside until you have more to go with it. Fire porcelain to Cone 6. The next step is sanding the surface with 220 garnet finishing

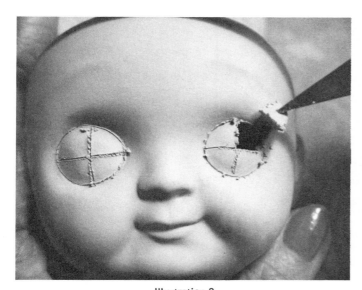

Illustration 3.

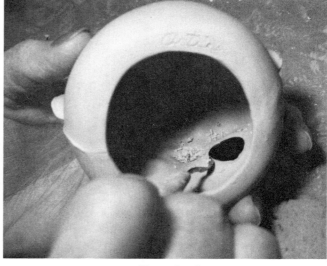

Illustration 4.

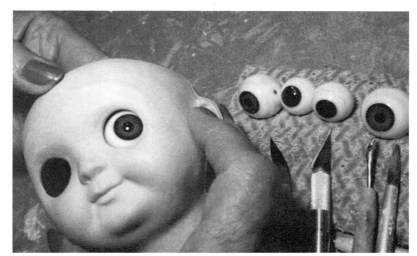

Illustration 5.

paper until the porcelain is satin smooth to the touch.

Mix a small amount of black china paint, another of rich brown and some lip color. I use Fern's red lip color, probably pompadour. You will need a mixing or tinting oil and some turpentine to clean your black and brown brushes. My red brushes **NEVER** touch any other color and are **NEVER** cleaned in turpentine; they are rolled in the tinting oil. Turpentine makes the red very dark and this is undesirable. You will need a 5/0 (00000) brush for fine work and two larger brushes for brows and lips. Actually, I use nearly 20 different brushes, and my hand seems to know just what I need for the job at hand. So all turpentine brushes lay by my right hand, lip and red brushes lay by my left; almost the same sizes by each side as I like both a fine and heavy for lips and the same for brows and lashes.

On this head, work first around the eyes. Pull some black china paint from the main bulk. Pick it up on your brush. This will tint around the eyes with a gray black shadow. Using a

Illustration 6.

small flat 1/8 in. (.31cm) sable brush (Illustration 6) wipe the opening and gently pull the color out so it is just the shadow of the color. There were no eyelashes on the original. Now fill a small round brush with black paint and wipe carefully around the inside edge of the eye. If you look at almost any old doll, you will see this is done to the area where the eyelashes generally grow. That is all there is to the eye.

Now for the eyebrows. The head has a nice raised area that shows exactly where the paint should go. However, play it safe and make a small dot with a pencil at the start (Illustration 6), middle and end of the brow. For an inexpert hand it is easier to follow the dots. Having a fine line painted, proceed to widen until it looks like the illustration of the original. The eyebrows should be thin at start and finish and wider in the middle. Use brown for the brows.

When painting the lips, put your fingertip into the edge of your red paint and pull away until you have an area covered thinly with paint. Do not try thinning with oil at this point, as it does not work. Using a small brush (Marx Princess) or a retouching brush, draw the upper lip. Using the paint you have drawn out, the lips should be rather light in color. If you want it darker, pick up closer to the bulk color. The upper lip is usually an elongated **M** and the lower lip is usually a **U** (Illustration 6). Fill in both areas with color, then wipe your retouching brush off so that it is almost dry of color and go over the areas, smoothing color and line (Illustration 7).

A tiny touch of red in the nostrils with your 5/0 (00000) brush and with the dry but slightly stained retouch brush, touch lightly at the sides of the nose. This makes an almost unseen shadow.

Now you are ready to paint the cheeks. Touch the tip of your little finger in the tinting oil and massage each cheek area. Wipe it dry with

Illustration 7.

Illustration 8.

another finger and the surface is now ready for color. I do hope that among the things you have saved over the years you will find a small piece of chiffon. You can probably use a piece of silk, but I like the texture of chiffon. Get a small piece of cotton and form it into a ball about the size of your fingernail. Now wrap the chiffon around it and you have a small pounce. Pounce it lightly into the drawn-out red color and try not to have any deep spots of color on the little ball. Now pounce lightly on the center of the cheek and work your way out (Illustration 7), up toward the eye and ear on to the lower cheek. There should be no break in your color. If there seems to be an edge that is sharp, use the ball of the finger to blend the outer edge. Repeat on the other cheek. There will not be much color left in the pounce but enough to tint the ears and a hint of color on the chin. You may even wish to tint the tip of the nose and a bit above — not much — just a hint. Smooth out with your fingertip.

If you have not smeared the cheeks and wiped off the eyebrows, you are ready for a china fire, Cone 019. In Illustration 5 you saw a round eye being tried for size and fit. This eye is at least 2 mm larger than needed in the finished head; if this fits properly, I know a smaller size will fit after

firing. If you have difficulty holding this round eye, try touching the balls of your middle and index fingers to your tongue; this moisture will hold the glass eye nice and firm. You will probably be able to try the eye in both eye holes without it slipping. This method of finger wetting also works for flat-back eyes.

The head is now out of the kiln and you have measured and determined the right eye size. I have a very easy way to set the eyes; perhaps you have your own way. I always hunt for the simple way of doing things, so give this a try.

You will need some modeling clay or florist clay. Even children's Playdough might work. Take the eye between your fingers as noted above and place inside the head with the eye looking to the left or right. When you have it in the proper position, press tightly in its socket and, with your other hand, press a small ball of clay on to the outside of the eye (Illustration 8) and a small area of the cheek. Now remove your left hand and see if the eye holds firmly. Repeat with the other eye making sure that the pupils are even directly across from each other. Now lay the head gently on its face on a towel. If you have several heads needing eyes, prepare them the same way. I have often done a dozen or more at one time. I think you will be surprised how easy it is. It takes about a tablespoon of water in your plaster to set a pair of eyes. I do not measure the plaster, just use enough to make a heavy gravy or a thick paste, just so it will drop off a spoon. Water first, then add the plaster. Start with a tablespoon of water for each pair. I have found that the little plastic coffee spoons from McDonald's are ideal for mixing plaster and placing it up into small

heads. Now drop a blob of plaster into the head on the outside of each eyeball; then use enough to bridge across the center connecting both eyes. Add to the blob on the outside, so you have a larger surface; this gives greater surface tension and the eye cannot be easily poked out. In a matter of minutes the plaster will set and you can remove the modeling clay and see if the eyes look right. If not, at this point a slight pressure will force the eyes out and you just begin over again using fresh plaster. If you wait, as I sometimes do, and do not look for a couple of days, a quick soak in warm water will enable you to remove the eyes easily.

Once you try this method, I am sure you will agree that it beats the old wax method and definitely is better than trying to gouge eyes out after some well-meaning person has poured in half a cup of plaster.

On to the finish. Use a small section of a styrofoam ball to make a dome. Glue it on and you are ready for a wig. I like the styrofoam dome because I can attach the wig with a pin and there is never a need to glue it on. Who knows — we may want to be a blond tomorrow! All done - - - isn't she a cutie? (Illustration 9).

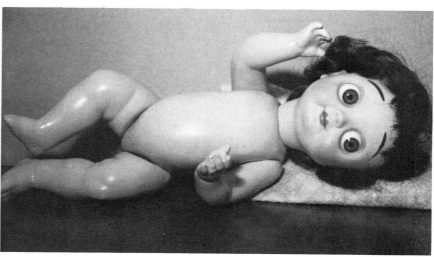

Illustration 9.

CARVING DOLLS
by **Clara H. Fawcett**

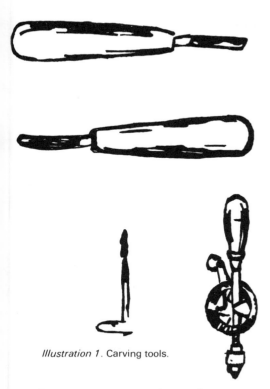

Illustration 1. Carving tools.

Ed. Note: These pattern instructions were taken from *On Making, Mending and Dressing Dolls* by Clara H. Fawcett. This doll makes up to be 10in (25.4cm) high. The patterns are full size so all you need to do is to transfer them via carbon paper to your wood-stock.

Claire Fawcett, daughter of the writer, tells the story of how to carve a doll. She has made hundreds, from tiny figures 1in (2.5cm) high to jointed "play" dolls of 20in (50.8cm) or more. For tools she relies mostly upon an ordinary pen knife or X-acto blade, but in carving the hair, finds carving tools (See *Illustration 1*) a help. The drill and awl shown in the sketch are used for drilling holes where the limbs are joined to the body. Wood is purchased from a lumber yard, often salvaged from a scrap heap at no cost. Preferences are white pine, cypress, gumwood, white wood, all easy to carve; but for a small hand with separate fingers one would have to use a hard wood like cherry; otherwise the fingers would chip off on the slightest provacation.

The work seems easy to Claire. "It's like peeling potatoes," she says. However, it is not easy for the beginner; it does require practice. In carving, many small things have to be taken into consideration. For instance, one does not start to carve a little doll on just the right

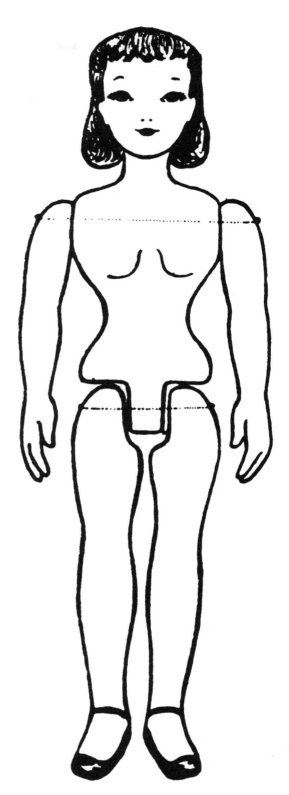

Illustration 2. Pieces shown in place.

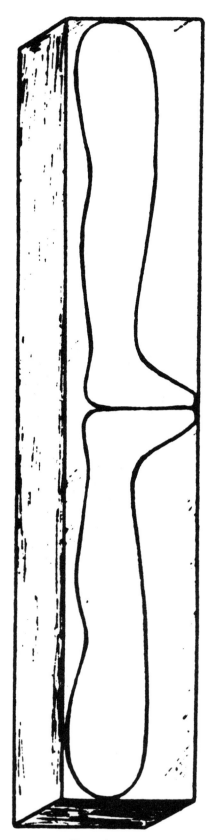

sized wood to contain the little figure. One must leave a "handle" to hold on to while carving. Choice of wood is important. Be careful that the wood you choose has no knots or cracks and is fine-grained. Sometimes the cracks are not apparent until one looks at the end and sees them spiraling out from the center.

Claire warns that every attempt at carving goes through what she calls "a discouraging stage." Even today, after years of practice, she always comes to a point in her carving where she thinks, "Heavens, this thing will never look like anything!" But it always turns out satisfactorily.

First make a rough sketch of what you want to carve. "You will find your figure changing as you go along," warns Claire, "but the sketch will help in the matter of proportions. Start with the head."

When the carving is finished, smooth with fine sandpaper or emery cloth. A stiff emery paper file is just the thing to take care of edges, such as the ruff of a clown. Start with something simple. Elaborate carving is not necessary for a doll. A face with good proportions and simple lines can be made as lovely as you wish with paint properly applied. If the doll is tiny, use pen and India ink for lashes and eyebrows. Leave a highlight in the pupil of each eye and on the mouth. If you will study the sketches, you will find that the lips do not meet on one side. This gives a better effect than it otherwise would. Study your own face in the mirror for proportions.

In carving arms and legs for *Dorothy*, a piece of wood the length of the two legs placed foot to foot, and another piece the length of the two arms placed end to end, was used. (See *Illustrations 3* and *4*.) This facilitates carving. Saw off the ends of the stick of wood on which the hands and arms are sketched before starting to carve. And it will help in carving the legs if you will first eliminate the rather large piece of unnecessary wood between point 1 and 2.

Dotted lines in Illustration 2 between the shoulders and hips show where the drill has been used to make a passage way for wires to hold the movable limbs in place.

Illustration 3. Legs.

Illustration 4. Arms.

Dorothy's corn-colored hair is shaded, and there is a small red bow painted on either side of the head. Mary Jane slippers are also painted on.

If you will make a small waist for your "growing girl" doll, she will look more attractive when dressed. In making a pattern for this doll, place paper over the torso and sketch an outline, making sure that you allow for seams. Sleeves are straight pieces of cloth, rounded a bit at the top. The plain skirt is slightly gored.

Illustration 5. Dorothy completed.

53

Wooden Dolls Fisher Style

by Elizabeth Andrews Fisher

Do you like wood? Do you like wooden dolls? Do you want to make one? The wood may be bass wood, sugar pine, shop quality redwood, anything except balsa. Balsa is for the nothing people.

Wood needed:

One piece 3in (7.6cm) by 1in (2.5cm) by 1in (2.5cm)

Two pieces ½in (1.3cm) by ½in (1.3cm) by 1½in (3.8cm) for arms

Two pieces ¾in (2cm) by ½in (1.3cm) by ½in (1.3cm) for hands

Two pieces ⅞in (2.2cm) by ½in (1.3cm) by ½in (1.3cm) for feet

Two pieces 1½in (3.8cm) by ⅝in (1.6cm) by ⅝in (1.6cm) for legs

One or two wooden Q-tips or similar cotton covered swab stick

Small drill in a pin vise

Some Titebond glue

Sharp jackknife, X-acto knife or other similar knife

If you do not have and can not find a pin vise, you may use the small drill bit in your fingers.

One thing to remember absolutely is this: CUT do not pry.

Ladies who have NEVER whittled anything in their whole lives have made excellent dolls. So you can give it a try too.

Let us start with the 3in (7.6cm) by 1in (2.5cm) by 1in (2.5cm) piece that will be the head and shoulders. Measure off 1½in (3.8cm) and draw a line across the stick. Measure ½in (1.3cm) beyond your first mark and draw a line, you will have 1in (2.5cm) left. With your trusty knife round off the 1½in (3.8cm) section into an egg shape. If you want to make features, now is the time to do it, if not just round it off nice and easy. Then thin down the ½in (1.3cm) section for the neck. Now you have the 1in (2.5cm) section left. That has to be gouged out so that it will form shoulders and fit over a cloth stuffed body.

The two little pieces for the hands will be carved next. As you KNOW, you need a right hand and a left hand so...please keep that in mind. Cut a "v" into one side of the wood about a third of

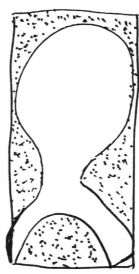

Illustration 1. Head.

the way down. Do the same to the other piece on the opposite side. See *Illustrations 2, 3 and 4.*

A quarter of the way in to the palm, cut straight down for the thumb. Shape the back of the hand, and the wrist. See *Illustration 5.*

Now with your pin vise or with just the small bit in your fingers bore a hole in the center of the wrist -- about ⅛in (.31cm) deep. If you want your doll to be especially nice and somewhat flirty, cut the wrist off at an angle. Now bore a hole into the small end of one of the arm sticks, right in the center, about ⅛in (.31cm) deep. Your drill should be number 42 that just fits a swab stick. Put some glue on the end of a swab stick, and push it into the hole in the hand. Cut off the swab stick so it will be about ¼in (.65cm) long, and put glue on it, and push it into the hole of the armstick. Then shape the arm properly with your trusty knife. The top of the arm should have a ridge so cloth may be put around and attached to the body later. See *Illustration 7.*

Shape the shoe as shown or go off on your own. "Pin" the shoe to the leg stick as you pinned the hand to the arm stick and shape the leg. Be sure you leave a ridge at the top to hold the cloth for attaching to the body.

If you want to shape the hair, use epoxy putty and have a ball arranging the hair. Paint it later. Or, if you want a softer effect, use mohair. With glue, needle and thread, you can make elegant hairdos with the mohair.

Milliners' models were made on this same idea, except the body was made of kid, and the arms and hands hung straight down.

If you did not cut the features, rely on your painting to give the desired effect. Dry cake rouge can be used for the cheeks as the kind with "creme" in it smudges.

For painting the features, you may use Testor's, or Pactra paints in the small bottles, and a brush with three hairs in it. If you do not want to use dry cake rouge, dip a piece of cloth in your red paint, just a slight touch of paint, then wet the spot where the paint is with Carbona, and rub on the cheeks.

The shoes and stockings may be painted AFTER sanding. If you want to have the knife cuts show, let them, just do not sand.

The body may be cut to your size, and stuffed with sawdust. If you use the cotton-like substance, put a small piece of lead in the body to give the right weight. Dolls that are too light lose something in the picking up.

One time when I cut the shoes too small for a specific doll I covered the shoes with leather and it made them the right size. Jersey may be glued around the legs for stockings. Clothes make the man, ahem...they also make the doll, but most of all accessories make the doll for sure.

In case you are not good with paints, waterproof pens work very well.

Illustration 2. Hand.

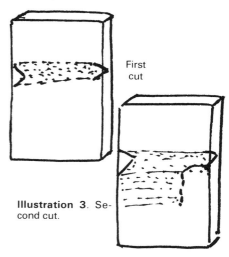

First cut

Illustration 3. Second cut.

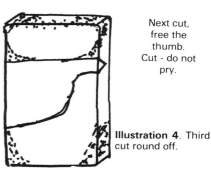

Next cut, free the thumb. Cut - do not pry.

Illustration 4. Third cut round off.

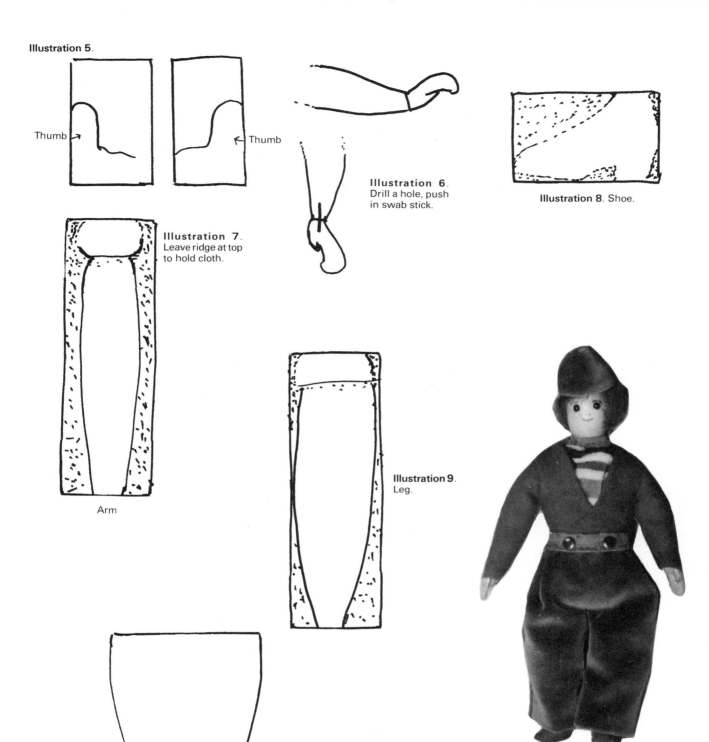

Illustration 5.

Thumb →

← Thumb

Illustration 6.
Drill a hole, push
in swab stick.

Illustration 8. Shoe.

Illustration 7.
Leave ridge at top
to hold cloth.

Arm

Illustration 9.
Leg.

Illustration 10. Body
Pattern. Modify to suit
your doll.

Illustration 11. Wooden Dutch boy created
by Pauline Zembko. He has nicely shaped
wooden shoes, and set-in black beads for
eyes.

To Make A Pincushion Doll Powder Box

A Mother's Day Gift Idea

by Jane Thompson

Illustration 1.

Illustration 2.

"Pincushion dolls" became more interesting, more popular and, alas, more expensive after the publication of Frieda Marion's *China Half Figures Called Pincushion Dolls*. Her more recent and more comprehensive book produced with Norma Werner, *The Collector's Encyclopedia of Half Dolls*, makes it still easier to classify, identify and evaluate these lovely miniatures. However, even before all that welcome information was compiled, I suspect most doll collectors had a few examples on their shelves simply because they were charmed by the graceful little beauties.

With Mother's Day approaching, why not put one of your unattached pincushion figures to use in a thoughtful gift? Of course, you could attach it to a stuffed cloth base for pins, but how about putting it on a box for a change? Then the container could be used to hold powder, candy, sewing needs, small jewelry or whatever you like.

The pincushion doll will serve as a knob on the lid, so it should be one that could be washed easily if soiled by handling. It would be practical to use one with molded hair and bodice so that no wig or clothing could become mussed. Also, selecting one with the arms close to the body would eliminate the possibility of breaking one of these delicate limbs. The china lady in illustration #1 is 2¾in. (7.1cm) tall and is incised "5823 Germany" at the back of the waist. She has light brown hair, blue eyes and a royal blue bodice. Her original cream colored skirts are bias-cut satin and net gathered at the waist and trimmed with a yellow satin sash and white velvet flowers. Attached to the box base she is 5in. (12.7cm) tall.

The pattern printed here makes a round box as in illustration #2 and fits the powder puffs available in the dime stores today. You will need cardboard as thick as the kind used on the back of pads of paper, scissors,

Elmer's Glue-All, very fine sandpaper or an emery board, muslin, needle and thread, sawdust and fancy trimming about 1½in. (3.8cm) wide.

Cut out two cardboard circles 3in. (7.6cm) in diameter and two circles 3-1/8in. (7.9cm) in diameter. Glue the two larger ones together and the two smaller ones together to make a bottom and a top both double thickness. (To avoid warping, glue each of the two layers together with the "grain" of the cardboard running at right angles. An easy way to accomplish this is to mark "north" on each circle before you cut it out of the sheet. Then glue the two circles together so that north on one meets east on the other.) When the glue is

dry, sand the edge of the larger circle with very fine sandpaper to make it smooth and spread a thin coat of glue along the edge to hold it neatly.

Cut two strips of cardboard 1½in. (3.8cm) wide and 9-3/8in. (23.8cm) and 9¾in. (24.9cm) long respectively. Pull these strips between your fingers or over the edge of a table top so that the cardboard bends into a curve. (If you have trouble curling the cardboard, check to see that you have cut the strip from the sheet with the grain running in the proper direction. Cardboard bends more easily in one direction than in the other.) Overlap the ends about 3/8in. (.91cm) and join with Elmer's Glue-All used sparingly but evenly.

Be sure one ring fits easily inside the other. (To avoid leaving a ridge where the ends overlap, split the cardboard back about 3/8in. (.91cm) from both ends and remove the outer portion from one end and the inner portion from the opposite end. When the remaining portions of the ends are overlapped and glued together they make a single thickness with a smooth edge.)

Glue the smaller ring down to the base (which is the larger circle) centering it to leave a uniform rim around the bottom. Glue the larger ring onto the top (which is the smaller circle) fitting it exactly. When the glue is dry, sand the edge of the top to make it smooth.

Cut a piece of muslin or other tightly woven fabric 10½in. (26.7cm) long and 4in. (10.2cm) wide on the straight of the goods and sew the ends together with fine stitches to make a tube or sleeve to fit snugly over the top of the box. Glue this cloth sleeve over the top of the box so that the bottom edges are even. Make sure the cloth is glued securely at the top edge of the lid inside the sleeve. (Unless you do this, the sawdust may work down around the sides of the lid making it lumpy.)

When the glue is thoroughly dry, pack the top of the sleeve with sawdust. (You can get this from your nearest lumber yard. They used to give it away, but some now have a small charge.) When the sleeve is packed full, sew a draw-string with strong thread and gather the top together tightly. (Button and carpet weight thread is good for this.)

Glue some fancy trimming around the bottom edge of the lid, sew or glue the pincushion doll in place over the gathered ends of the sleeve, and put a powder puff inside the box. Add a pretty skirt decked with ribbons, lace or flowers, and you will have a lovely, useful gift.

Cut these pattern pieces from cardboard and construct box.
Cut piece of muslin 4in. x 10½in. (10.2 x 26.7cm) (on the straight of the goods) and seam it to make a tube to glue over top of box. Pack tube with sawdust, gather at top, and sew on pincushion doll.

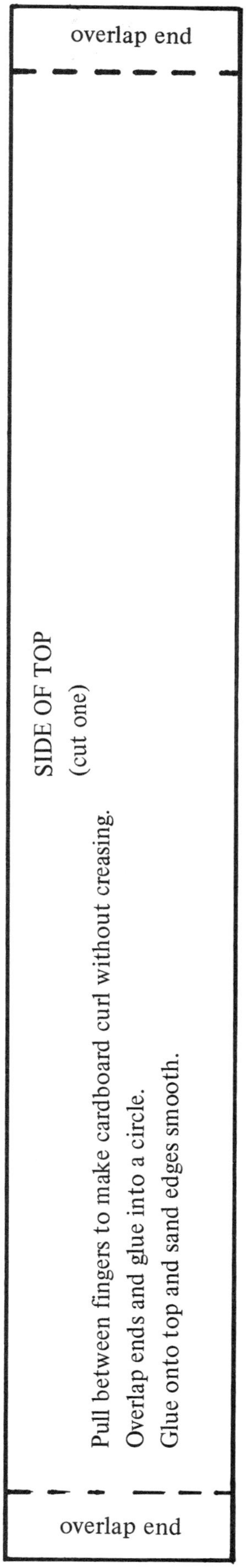

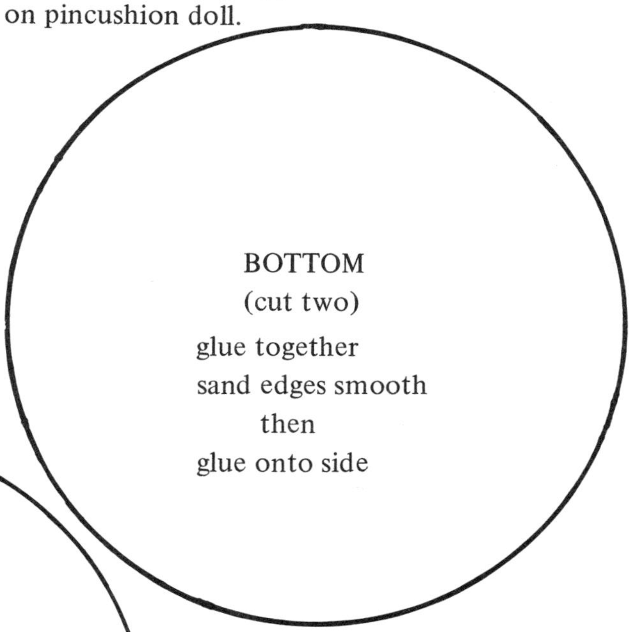

BOTTOM
(cut two)
glue together
sand edges smooth
then
glue onto side

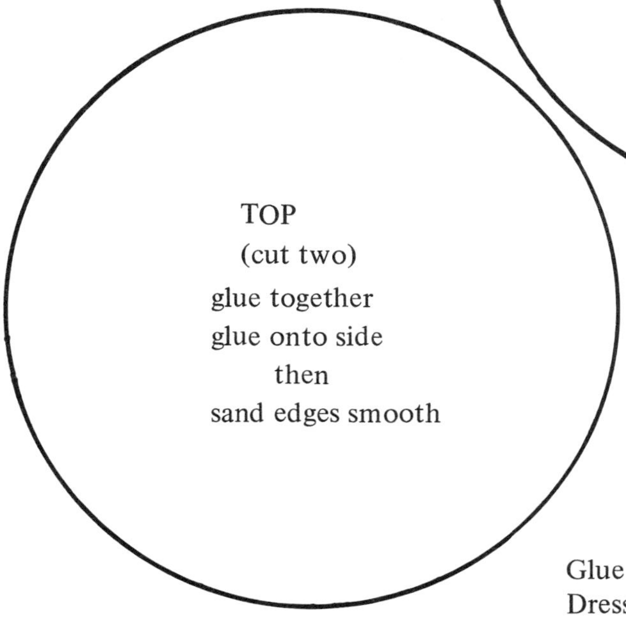

TOP
(cut two)
glue together
glue onto side
then
sand edges smooth

Glue lace at bottom.
Dress as desired.

BOTTOM

overlap end

SIDE OF TOP
(cut one)

Pull between fingers to make cardboard curl without creasing.
Overlap ends and glue into a circle.
Glue onto top and sand edges smooth.

overlap end

overlap end

SIDE OF BOTTOM
(cut one)

Pull between fingers to make cardboard curl without creasing.

Overlap ends and glue into a circle making sure it will fit inside the top circle.

Glue onto bottom leaving a uniform extended edge.

overlap end

Doll Costuming & Patterns

From *The Mary Francis Sewing Book* by Jane Eayre Fryer.

The Collector's Book of Dolls' Clothes

by **Dorothy S., Elizabeth A.,** and **Evelyn J. Coleman**

"COSTUMES IN MINIATURE 1700-1929"

The primary purpose of dolls' clothes has been to provide an instrument of learning, and for collectors today this is still a most important function. The clothes help to date the doll and to identify the age and sex represented and often the country of origin. Dolls' clothes are costumes in miniature and have been examples of contemporary fashions down through the ages. It is difficult to prove that a given doll was used primarily to display fashions but we know from many sources that dolls were used for this purpose. In the 19th century dressed dolls not only showed the mother the current fashions but they were also an educational toy for a child.

A small child could learn how to dress and undress a doll and how to care for its clothes. The many nightgowns for dolls show that it was important to change from a day dress into a night dress. The multitude of pinafores and aprons indicate the importance of protecting your clothes. As the child grew older the dolls' clothes began to teach more sophisticated things. The child learned the type of clothes that were proper to wear for each occasion. In an era of domestic help, social life was more complicated than it is today. One type of outfit was worn by dolly when she went for a walk, another type when she went calling, yet another when she went for tea and so forth. If dolly were fashionable she might have to change her clothes many times during the day. In the 19th century most women made the clothes for themselves and their children or supervised a seamstress who made them. Sewing for dolls was the way little girls (sometimes boys) learned not only how to sew, but also fashionable styles, selection of fabrics, blending of colors and related knowledge.

The importance of dolls as an educational tool for little girls was discussed in the 1878 *The Delineator:*

"She will have gathered for herself, while constructing dolly's pretty wardrobe, that knowledge of the subtle charm

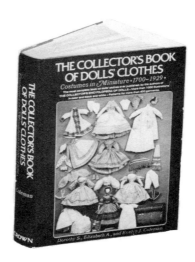

Illustration 1. The doll and its clothes shown on the dust jacket were sold at the 1864 Brooklyn Sanitary Fair to raise money for the predecessor of the American Red Cross. The china-head doll, 18in (45.7cm) tall, has a professionally-made trousseau and is in the collection of the Brooklyn Museum, New York. This type of doll was frequently called a "Flora McFlimsy" doll because of the character in the satirical book *Nothing to Wear* which had been published a few years previously.

of form, color, fabric and fashioning, by the application of which to her own period she may ... become a leader of style and a belle in the fashionable world.

"The models for dolly's attire are as skillfully designed, as carefully proportioned, and as exact in their adjustment, as if they were provided for the most elegant of fashionable costumers....

"As mama is dressing dolly, she can easily interest the child in the first lessons of physiology. Then the origin of the textures can be explained. Then may follow a description of the growth of cotton and flax; the production of silk and wool; the spinning, weaving and

dyeing of the textiles and threads; the geographical origin of materials; the primary colors from which all others are compounded; lessons in the geometrical proportions of flat surfaces; and a hundred other bits of interesting and instructive information, which lead on to other improving topics....

"The generality of sensible little girls prefer for their everyday bliss, a real doll infant...but for ceremonious occasions and for afternoons out, these feminine natures demand a superior being who is all bedecked in fashionable attire. It is upon the everyday dolly that sewing instruction is mostly given; and taste, discrimination and the realities of true elegance are found out by the little dressmaker while she is deciding and devising the costumes of this dear little bit of inanimate ostentation. The little girl enjoys...array[ing] Miss Dolly with her own tender hands for an afternoon outing in the park or for a visit to a neighboring mama of her own age."

Many collectors today delight in sewing for their dolls. The clothes that they make represent styles that appeal to the taste of someone living in the 1970s. These clothes are eminently suitable for dressing modern reproduction dolls and NIADA dolls, but should NOT be put on old or antique dolls. For these dolls original clothes are always the best. In many cases the original clothes can be freshened by laundering and a little mending. If the tears are more extensive, a backing of net can often hinder further deterioration. If a doll is naked or has been recently redressed improperly, the collector should seek a contemporary outfit or, as a last resort, make a proper costume.

Unfortunately prior to the publication of our new book, *The Collector's Book of Dolls' Clothes, Costumes In Miniature, 1700-1929,* few collectors were able to identify original clothes or to select proper contemporary outfits. Collectors, especially in America, often had access to a very limited number of dolls in original clothes for study. Early doll catalogs are rare and only a few have been reprinted. Some of the pictures accompanying old patterns have been published such as those in our book, *The Age Of Dolls*. But never has there been a detailed study of the changing shape of patterns through the years for various ages and sex represented. Our new book has patterns for nearly 500 garments, all taken from contemporary sources. This new book is a study in depth of original clothes, based on tens of thousands of dolls in original clothes, hundreds of contemporary catalogs and a vast number of contemporary patterns.

Heretofore in providing clothes for their dolls, collectors have usually relied on fashion periodicals such as *Godey's Lady's Book*, contemporary portraits or the study of people's clothes. None of these sources are satisfactory although they are the basis for most costume books. Fashion prints and portraits are subject to artistic license and do not show what people actually wore everyday as do many dolls in original clothes. People's clothes tend to be only the clothes that were saved for best and not representative of what people and dolls wore most of the time. People's clothes were usually altered to keep them in fashion but dolls' clothes were too small to bother to alter. It was easier to make a new outfit in the current style. None of these sources, -- fashions prints, portraits or people's clothes -- show a complete costume, what was worn together or how it was worn. Dolls' clothes do show a complete costume at a given period better than any other source and for this reason accredited museums in Europe and America usually have dolls in original clothes in their costume collections.

Original clothes, according to our definition, are those clothes worn by the doll during the childhood of its original owner. American collectors have not fully appreciated these original clothes because they lacked knowledge about them and in some cases these clothes have even been wantonly destroyed. It is hoped that the information in our new book will educate collectors to appreciate the original clothes and to cease dressing 19th century dolls in modern materials and styles. When the doll was new its clothes were its most important part. They usually cost more than the rest of the doll. They represented its primary purpose and they provided the greatest eye appeal. Somehow through the years their importance has dwindled because most collectors were unable to appreciate and recognize many of the old styles. This is not true in Europe. A recent publication of the National Education Museum in Paris states "Often [the

clothes] for the collector they are of greater value than the doll itself." We hope that thanks to the information in our new book this may one day be the case in America also. The study of dolls' clothes is fascinating and the effort to learn has tremendous rewards. For many collectors this is a whole new area in their field. One day we hope it will be as important to identify the clothes on a doll as it is now to identify the mark.

It cannot be denied that all collectors are interested in clothes for their dolls. A naked doll showing the contours of its articulation mechanism is attractive only to someone interested in the construction of a doll. When you go to an antique show or shop you seldom see many naked dolls, they nearly all have clothes. Dealers have learned that dolls must be dressed in order to attract buyers. Clothes transform the doll into a miniature replica of a person. Except for the small face and hands, the clothes are usually the only visible part. How often have you heard of people carrying a baby doll that was mistaken by onlookers for a real baby. In many plays the part of a baby is taken by a doll dressed as a baby. The realism and much of the appeal of a doll is in its clothes.

There has been considerable concern recently over the wide-spread reproduction of dolls. Collectors seek antique dolls and are willing to pay high prices for authentic ones. Yet most of the dolls bought on the market today and most of the dolls in collections are only partially antique. When you buy a redressed doll, you have only part of an antique. One of the most important parts of your doll, -- the clothes -- are modern. This is also true if you redress the doll yourself. No matter how good a seamstress you are and how pleasing to modern eyes are the clothes, they are still modern clothes and you do not have a real antique doll, only part of an antique doll. That is, only the framework on which the clothes were placed. The same collectors who avoid reproduction dolls like the plague will try to reproduce their dolls' clothes, one of the most important parts of their dolls. Unfortunately in many instances even the so-called reproduction clothes do not resemble even remotely the clothes actually worn by dolls originally.

Many books on the market today claim that they provide information on how to dress your doll "authentically." Most of the authors of these books and patterns, use the word "authentic" in the limited sense of its being a genuine doll's garment. Technically this is correct since they are clothes for dolls, even though they are modern ones and they are often appealing to modern taste but have little if any historical accuracy. Very

few so-called "authentic clothes" resemble those that dolls actually wore when first purchased or played with. Only patterns that were contemporary with our dolls or made from known original clothes on similar dolls can be called historically authentic. Some authors do base their patterns on those published long ago or on actual original clothes to start with, but later become carried away with their own creativity and make changes that modernize the costumes. The collector then becomes confused and often thinks she has an authentic reproduction of original clothes for her doll when actually she has only the author's modern interpretation of an original garment.

Unfortunately many collectors have the *Godey's* and *Peterson* syndrome. These are the best known of the fashion magazines and therefore the ones to which collectors turn most frequently for ideas in redressing dolls. If you compare the clothes on people in old photographs with the fancy drawings in these fashion periodicals, you will see very little resemblance in attire. Few if any people or dolls wore what the *Godey's* artists dreamed up. There were very few patterns published in *Godey's* and *Petersons* for people to copy either for themselves or for dolls. When our ancestors wanted patterns for clothes they went to *Harper's Bazar, The Delineator* or *Demorests*. These periodicals gave patterns for both people's and dolls' clothes. Only a few books have referred to these sources.

Often collectors see a period play or movie and would like to copy the costumes seen in the show. However, they should realize that theatrical costuming is a separate field from historical costuming. The theatrical costume must blend the styles of the period in the play with modern styles to make them pleasing to today's audience. This is more or less the problem with most redressed dolls. It is very difficult to divorce yourself from current concepts of beauty which you must learn to do if you want really authentic costumes.

Most collectors are not yet sufficiently knowledgeable to appreciate the styles of the original clothes and this is the chief reason why so many original clothes are discarded. Of course we hope that our new book on original dolls' clothes will help to educate collectors so that they will appreciate the old clothes and be able to identify them.

All too often collectors try to argue that the old clothes were soiled and torn. This may be true in some cases but many dolls can still be found with original clothes that need only a little gentle washing, preferably with Ivory Snow and a little bleaching in the sun, -- no chemical bleaches, please. Tears can often be mended, seams sewed together, lace whipped on again and the garment is thus restored to its original appearance. Never do any restoration to a doll or its clothes that cannot be easily undone. This is a museum precept that should be followed by conscientious doll collectors. Speaking of museums, most museums are far more interested in an antique doll's clothes than in the rest of the doll. The clothes are the most important part of the doll from a historical point of view.

Few dolls with wardrobes of clothes are on the market today, yet most dolls originally had several garments. When a doll is purchased from the original owner or her descendants, there are usually several outfits available but unless you ask for them specifically they are often forgotten and thrown away. Let us begin to ask dealers for the extra clothes and by our demands make it worthwhile for dealers and pickers to go to the extra work of getting all the garments that originally went with the doll. As collectors become more aware of the importance of dolls' clothing and their appreciation increases, I am sure more original clothes will appear on the market. Alas, reproductions may also become more difficult to detect. You will need to study our new book very carefully so that you can distinguish between actual original clothes and reproductions.

Let us try to upgrade our collections with whole not just parts of antique dolls. Remember that garments contemporary with the doll is the next best thing to its original clothes and with an antique outfit you have a wholly antique doll. Many of our old and antique dolls have replaced antique heads which are difficult to detect and detract very little from their value. The same would be true for antique clothes from a similar type of doll. If you are forced to redress an antique doll, at least do it correctly in accordance with antique styles and materials of the same period and not in some modern or semi-modern attire.

Nearly all doll collectors fall into three categories. First there is the beginning collector who has just entered the world of antique dolls and finds it tempting and exciting. Second there is the sophisticated doll collector who already has a sizable collection but is still eager to upgrade her collection and cannot resist an unusual doll. Third are the collectors of modern dolls; that is, foreign ones, NIADA dolls or dolls recently and currently found in toy stores. Obviously there are no problems with either the dating or the dressing of modern dolls so we are primarily concerned with the first two groups of collectors.

The begining collector usually has limited knowledge and limited finances. Her first concern should be to learn about dolls and to become acquainted with the current prices so she will spend her money wisely. All too often a novice learns that hard way and regrets her first purchases. The best investment at the beginning is in books. The three Coleman books: *The Collector's Encyclopedia of Dolls; The Collector's Book of Dolls Clothes, Costumes in Miniature 1700-1929;* and *The Age of Dolls* should provide needed knowledge if studied carefully. No matter how much a collector knows about the dolls themselves she can make stupid purchases unless she has some idea of the current market prices. Current doll lists are helpful as well as up-to-date authoritative books on prices. The beginning collector will also need to keep systematic records of her dolls. These are needed not only for her own use but also for insurance and income tax purposes. Index cards can be used or if more elaborate information is desired, printed forms such as *Dolls' Pedigree* pages are available.

Let us suppose that the beginning collector after buying the necessary books has only $100 to spend on dolls. She looks longingly at the bisque dolls that she sees everywhere but most of them are out of reach financially. The French bébés and the German character dolls are far too expensive so she must pass them by. Perhaps some later and more opulent day she will be able to afford these dolls. Some of the German bisque head dolls with open mouths are within her price range but she knows from her studies that these are the most numerous of the collector's dolls and therefore she can readily purchase them at any time. Moreover, the $100 ones that she sees are not in original clothes which she has learned is a very important factor. She is more discriminating and would prefer older and more unusual dolls. She haunts antique shops, especially the "junque" type and one day she finds a wax-over-composition doll on a one-piece cloth body in original clothes for only $40. The doll is soiled and the wax is cracked, the hair is gone, the dress is partially tattered, but she has studied *The Collector's Book of Dolls' Clothes* and recognizes the clothes to be original. She cleans the doll and its clothes and places appropriate hair in the slit on its head. A few strands of hair imbedded in the wax tells what color and type of hair the doll had originally. The lace on the dress is sewn on where it has come loose, tears are mended over net. Nothing is done to the doll that

Illustration 2. Wax-over-composition head on a cloth body of the type purchased by the beginning collector in our story. A similar picture appears in *The Collector's Book of Dolls' Clothes*. These dolls were made at least from 1820 to 1860. The doll in this illustration has an earlier outfit than the one in the text. This doll wears a homemade pelisse of the 1820s from rural France. It is contemporary but not original to the doll.

cannot be undone but the cleaning and restoration will help to preserve this 1840s doll. The doll can be dated 1840s from its original clothes.

Next she finds a small all-bisque doll with the Limbach trefoil mark on its back. It is unstrung and without clothes so that she only has to pay $35 for it. For a few pennies she can purchase the elastic necessary to restring the doll and *The Collector's Book of Dolls' Clothes* tells her how to dress this doll properly. Since it was made in Germany probably 1890 to 1915, she chooses a German pattern for a girl doll of about 1900. It could have been dressed in a French or American style of clothes since many of the German dolls were dressed and sold in other countries. She also has to decide whether she wants it to be dressed in clothes that resemble commercial ones, professionally made or homemade clothes. If her preference had been for a boy instead of a girl she could also have found suitable patterns and information in *The Collector's Book of Dolls' Clothes*.

This leaves only $25 of our collector's allotted sum and few desirable dolls can be found today for this amount. But, she is persistent and one day at a country auction, a Mme. Hendren doll with composition head and limbs on a cloth body, all in original clothes came up. She was able to purchase it for $25. The Mama doll type body is marked "Madame Hendren" and the clothes, including an adorable bonnet, are of the Mama doll era (1918 to 1928). Mama dolls with their chubby bodies are not appreciated as yet by collectors and therefore are often "sleepers" when in excellent condition and all original clothes.

Our beginning collector with her waxed doll of the 1840s, the all-bisque doll of circa 1900 and the Madame Hendren composition doll of the 1920s has the start of a worthwhile collection upon which she can build in the future without regrets and without exceeding her financial limitations. Two of her dolls are in original clothes and the third has accurately reproduced clothes which she properly labels as reproductions made in 1975. (Note: The dolls described above were actually available at these prices in 1975.)

The sophisticated doll collector has a large library of books on dolls which she has studied carefully. She has considerable funds to spend on dolls and attends the doll conventions and antique shows where she can choose from a remarkable array of rare dolls. Nevertheless, she wants to spend her money wisely and to add real treasures to her collection.

Despite having collected dolls for many years this collector knew relatively little about the clothes on dolls until she purchased *The Collector's Book of Dolls' Clothes*. In fact, when she first saw some dolls in original clothes she thought them very peculiar looking and took them off, redressing the dolls to look like those of many other collectors. Gradually by visiting accredited museums which displayed only dolls in original clothes and by studying *The Collector's Book of Dolls' Clothes* she became aware of the real beauty of original clothes and began to appreciate them. The original clothes were then cleaned, mended and put back on the redressed dolls from which they had been removed.

Let us now examine some of the ways in which *The Collector's Book of Dolls' Clothes* has helped our sophisticated collector with her recent purchases of dolls. First in her all-wooden doll with gesso covered face, glass pupil-less eyes and dots for eyebrows, the type often referred to as a "Queen Anne" doll. This doll has to be redressed and the information on correct attire can be found in the 1790 to 1840 periods. Contrary to previous opinion, the dolls of this type are primarily found in original clothes of 1790 or later. Those dressed earlier usually have the carved wooden faces.

The second doll has a bisque head on a lady-type kid body and is accompanied by a trunk full of clothes and accessories. The clothes date this doll and studying *The Collector's Book of Dolls' Clothes* the collector can also discover the occasions for which many of these clothes were originally meant to be worn. These clothes thus become more meaningful and the appreciation of the doll increases. Upon careful examination a few of the garments and accessories are found to be later additions. If these later items are all of a period 20 to 40 years later, they could be second generation additions, but if they are of various periods they may be spurious and probably were added recently.

The third doll is a French bébé in original clothes. The collector is surprised and pleased to find that the dress could be that of a boy doll, since boy dolls are usually considered to be especially desirable.

The fourth doll is a German character doll that has been redressed in unsuitable attire. Thanks to the information in *The Collector's Book of Dolls' Clothes*, the collector knows the proper style for this doll and is fortunate in finding a dress contemporary with the doll and of the correct size.

The last doll is a large Lenci, some of its clothes are original and some have been replaced. The collector can verify which ones are original after a little study. Of course proper records are kept of the findings of this collector and these records will be transmitted with the dolls when she or her family dispose of them.

Part of the fun of collecting dolls for both the beginner and the person who already has a collection is the challenge of learning more about their dolls. Formerly clothes have been relatively neglected but now the collector can learn and appreciate not only the facts about this important part of a doll, but also the many things that the clothes tell us about the doll itself. This wealth of information about our dolls is available to beginner and sophisticated collector in *The Collector's Book of Dolls' Clothes, Costumes in Miniature 1700-1929*

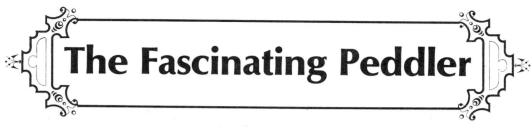

The Fascinating Peddler

by **Susan Sirkis**

For many generations the assembling of a peddler doll has been an amusing challenge enjoyed by the fair sex. In the old days, before supermarkets and plastic bags were invented many wares were hawked from house to house by peddlers, each of whom often had a distinctive cry to advertise his goods. Peddlers popular with doll collectors included flowers, ribbons and laces, pots and pans, sewing notions, and even fish. Please use this basic early 19th century peddler costume and your own imagination to enjoy the challenge of creating your own peddler. This pattern will fit a 10in (25.4cm) doll.

PANTALETS: Make of white lawn or batiste.
1. Sew seams AB in each leg.
2. Hem edges AC.
3. Hem bottoms.
4. Make narrow casing in top of each leg. Run narrow tape through casing.

PETTICOAT: Make of white lawn or batiste.
1. Cut a piece 19'' (48.3cm) wide and 6½in (16.5cm) deep.
2. Sew back seam together.
3. Make ½in (1.3cm) casing in bottom.
4. Make a narrow casing in top. Run narrow tape through top. Draw up to fit doll.

DRESS: Make of dark cotton print.
1. Sew shoulder seams.
2. Gather sleeves on dotted lines to fit armscyes. Sew to armscyes.
3. Make a narrow hem in sleeve bottom.
4. Sew under arm seams.
5. Cut skirt 32in (81.3cm) wide by 7in (17.8cm) deep. Gather to fit bottom of bodice. Sew to bodice.
6. Hem placket. Leave about 1in (2.5cm) on skirt for placket.
7. Work buttonholes (Whew!) for four small buttons to close front.
8. Sew skirt center front seam.
9. Bind neck edge with self bias strip.

APRON: Make of white lawn or batiste.
1. Cut apron 12in (30.5cm) wide and 6½in (16.5cm) deep. Make a narrow hem in two short sides. Make a ½in (1.3cm) hem in bottom.
2. Gather top to 2½in (6.4cm). Sew to waistband and sash ¾in (2cm) wide and 32in (81.3cm) long.
3. Cut pockets 1¼in (3.2cm) square. Hem ¼in (.65cm) along tops. Baste seam allowance on other three sides under. Blindstitch to apron.

SHAWL: Make of fine black yarn. Cast on ten stitches and work in garter stitch until piece measures about 12in (30.5cm). Loop 1in (2.5cm) long pieces of yarn through stitches at each end to make fringe.

MOBCAP: Make of white lawn or batiste.
1. Roll a narrow hem around outside.
2. Run a gathering thread around dotted lines. Draw up to fit doll's head.

BONNET: Make of black felt.
1. Sew crown back seam AB.
2. Sew brim to crown on dotted lines.
3. Cut 5in (12.7cm) Piece of black grosgrain ribbon 1in (2.5cm) wide. Taper both ends. Pleat to dotted line of brim and crown.
4. Sew top of crown in place.
5. Trim with middy braid ¼in (.65cm) wide.

NOTE: My peddler is poor but neat, so, no lace -- you may have a more successful merchant and she may want some lace trim.

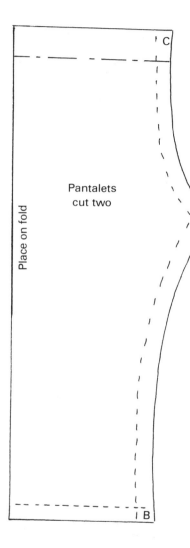

Pantalets
cut two

Place on fold

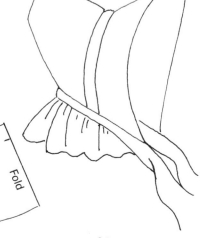

Bonnet
Brim
cut one

Fold

Bonnet
Top of Crown
cut one

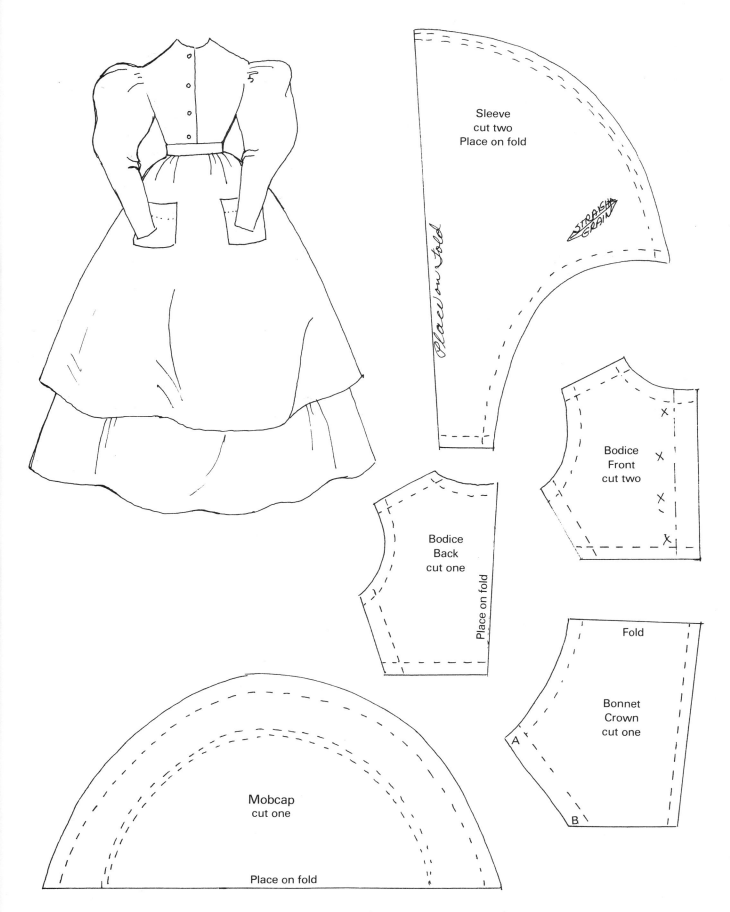

Sleeve
cut two
Place on fold

Place on fold

STRAIGHT GRAIN

Bodice
Front
cut two

Bodice
Back
cut one

Place on fold

Fold

Bonnet
Crown
cut one

A

B

Mobcap
cut one

Place on fold

65

Two-Piece Outfit for a French Fashion Lady

The original of this dress came to me quite a few years ago as a gift. It is made of well-washed batiste with a white background sprigged with tiny gray flowers. The ribbon bows appear to have originally been blue, although they are very faded now. This dress may be made much more elaborate by the addition of cuffs and a train. I prefer it simple, just like the original. It will fit a 15in (38.1cm) or 16in (40.6cm) doll, although by lengthening the waist and skirt length it will also fit a larger doll.*

TOP

1. Dress should be lined with cotton satin. Cut and sew dress and lining together, handling them as one piece of fabric.
2. Sew darts in front. Sew side back seam in bodice back to dots.
3. Sew center back seams. Form pleats by bringing solid lines together to meet at dotted lines.
4. Sew shoulder seams.
5. Sew underarm seams.
6. Sew sleeve upper sections to lower sections. Trim bottoms with lace.
7. Slightly gather sleeve tops and set sleeves into arms eyes.

8. Sew collar sections together, wrong sides facing. Turn, and sew collar to dress.
9. Trim all edges with ¼in (.65cm) lace, slightly gathered. Use three rows on bottom as shown.
10. Sew double looped bows at x's on the right side of front opening.
11. Close with snaps under bows.

SKIRT

Sew four gores together. Slash placket opening in center of back panel only. Face placket. Gather surplus on either side of placket and draw up to fit doll's waist. Mount on waistband. Close with snaps. Trim with three rows of lace along bottom.

*Note: Always try any pattern in muslin or tissue before cutting into good fabric.

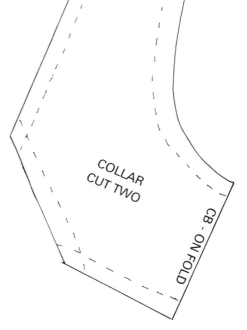

COLLAR
CUT TWO

CB - ON FOLD

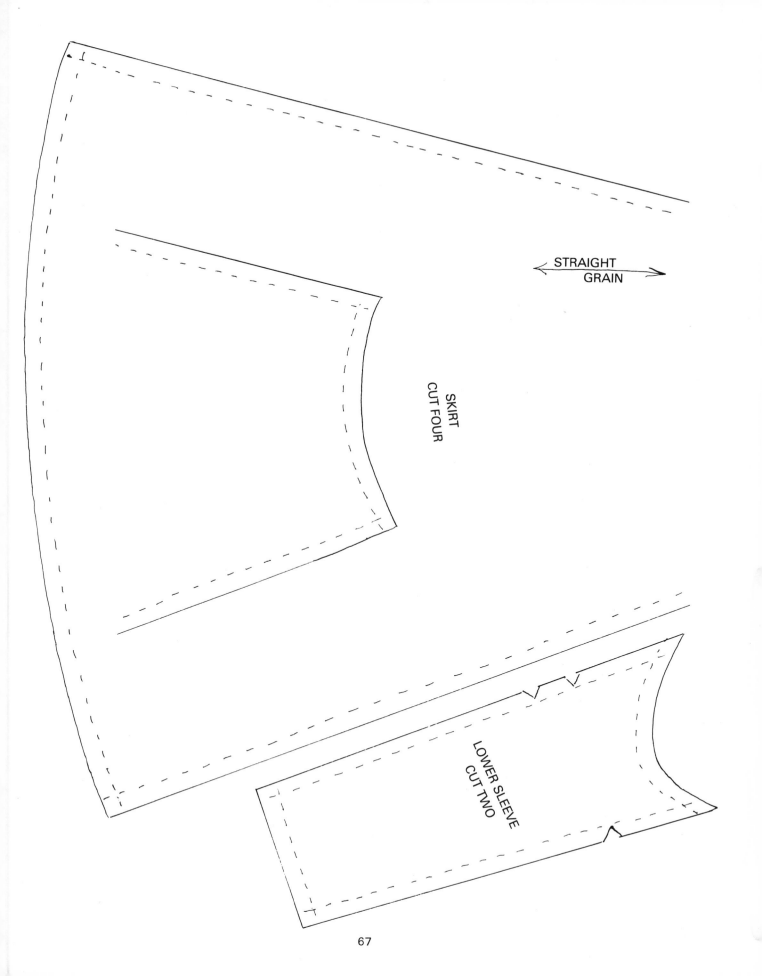

STRAIGHT
GRAIN

SKIRT
CUT FOUR

LOWER SLEEVE
CUT TWO

67

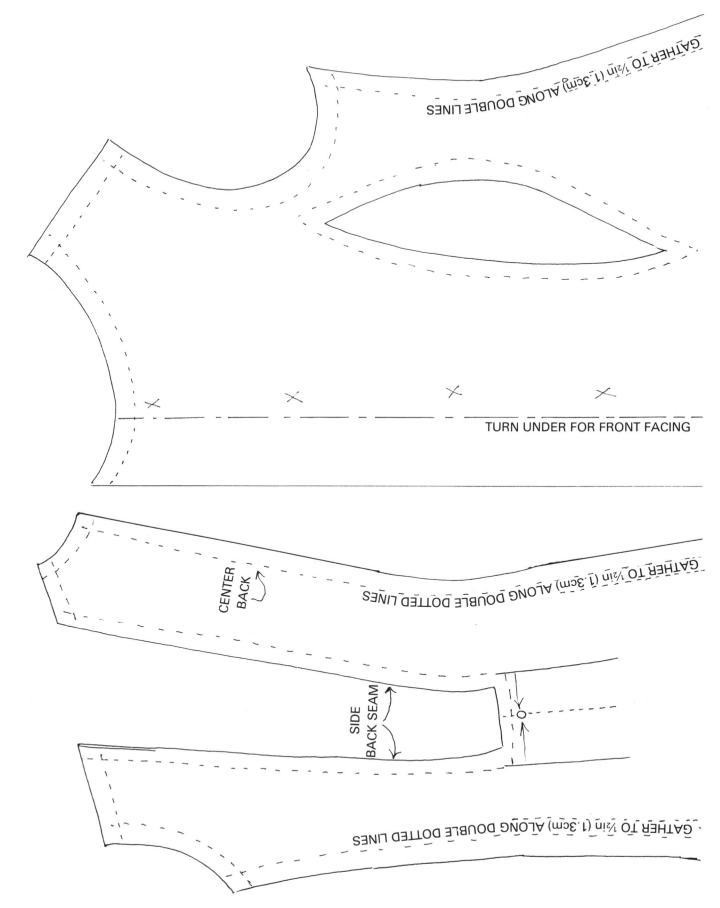

GATHER TO ½in (1.3cm) ALONG DOUBLE LINES

TURN UNDER FOR FRONT FACING

CENTER BACK

GATHER TO ½in (1.3cm) ALONG DOUBLE DOTTED LINES

SIDE BACK SEAM

GATHER TO ½in (1.3cm) ALONG DOUBLE DOTTED LINES

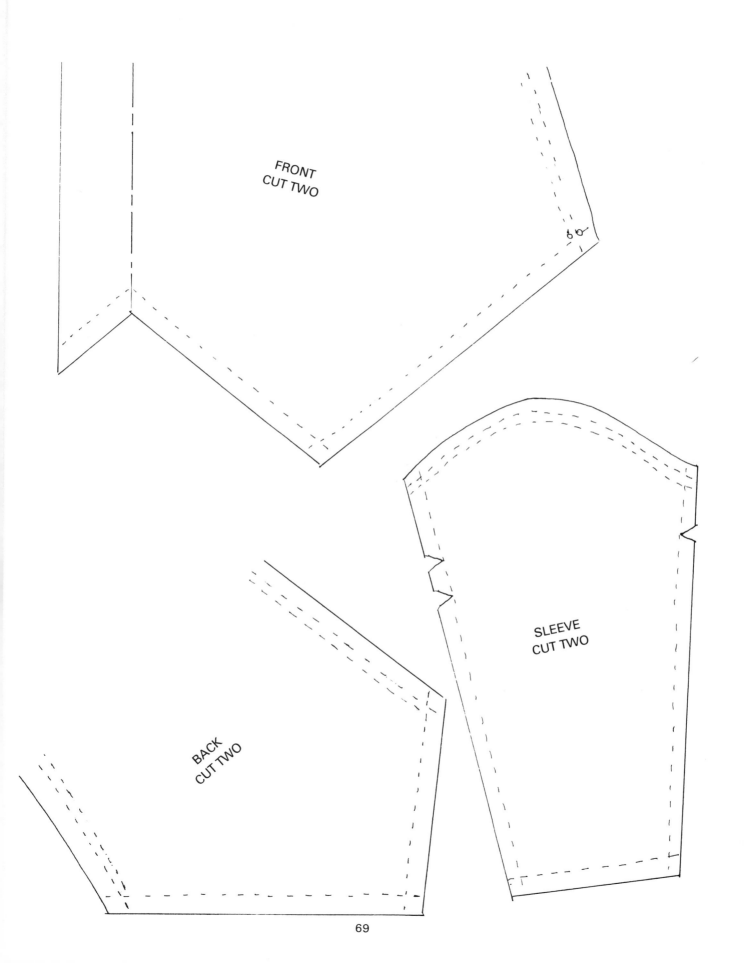

FRONT
CUT TWO

SLEEVE
CUT TWO

BACK
CUT TWO

69

Dressing an 18in (45.7cm) China Head Doll

by Sandy Williams

crinoline

We have had so many requests for patterns for large dolls that I chose an 18in (45.7cm) reproduction china head doll to dress. With her center-parted, black curly hair drawn back into a chignon, she is reminiscent of the 1850 to 1860 period. The well-dressed woman of that time wore a multitude of undergarments. The newest and most welcome garment of that time was the crinoline which replaced most of the bulky petticoats -- but created quite a few problems! Sitting or getting through doors gracefully were only a few. The patterns included here (and in order of placement on the doll) are drawers, chemise, petticoat, corset and crinoline. Due to the large size of the patterns, we had to overlap them --so trace them onto thin paper. Since china head muslin bodies vary from doll to doll, the patterns here should be used as a guide. Finish one garment before you measure your doll for the next garment. Set your sewing machine for ten stitches per inch. Use ¼in (.65cm) seams unless noted; press after each step. Use extra fine thread for lightweight fabrics for sewing the garments.

DRAWERS: Cut two drawer patterns from white batiste and a waistband 1¼in (3.2cm) wide by doll's waist measurement plus 1½in (3.8cm). Mark the two tuck fold lines; press on fold lines; stitch ¼in (.65cm) in from fold lines to make tuck. Hem drawers and blindstitch ½in (1.3cm) wide lace to this edge. French seam each inner leg seam. Sew the two leg pieces together from CF waist to dot; narrowly hem each crotch seam. Gather waist of drawers to fit waistband (waistband overlaps waist about ½in [1.3cm] on each end.) Attach waistband, tucking in ¼in (.65cm) twill tape as you sew. Place drawers on doll; pull tapes; wrap tapes around doll's waist and tie ends in small bow.

CHEMISE: Knee length, off-the-shoulder. Fold white batiste twice so that shoulder and CF/CB edges are on folds. Mark tucks. Sew each tuck with tiny backhand stitches; make each ¾in (2cm) long. Tightly gather front chemise between * and triangle. Gather back chemise between triangles to fit doll. Cut

a bias strip of white batiste ¾in (2cm) wide by the desired neckline width plus ½in (1.3cm) (I needed ¾in [2cm] by 10¼in [26.1cm]). With right sides of bias strip and chemise neckline together, sew a ¼in (.65cm) seam; trim to ⅛in (.31cm). Turn bias strip to wrong side of chemise and turn in ⅛in (.31cm); blindstitch closed. Hem sleeve and sew ½in (1.3cm) lace to sleeve edge. French seam side seams. Blindstitch chemise hem.

PETTICOAT: Calf length. Cut a piece of white batiste 10in (25.4cm) by 25in (63.5cm) and a waistband 1¼in (3.2cm) wide by waistline measurement plus ½in (1.3cm). Mark hem fold line ½in (1.3cm) from bottom edge; mark tuck fold line ¾in (2cm) above hem fold line; mark second tuck fold line ¾in (2cm) above first tuck fold line. Follow drawer's

directions for tucks, hem and lace edge. Sew a ¼in (.65cm) CB seam to within 3in (7.6cm) of waistline. Press seam open; turn raw edges of CB seam and opening in and blindstitch closed. Gather waist of petticoat to fit waistband; sew together. Close petticoat with tiny button and thread loop.

CORSET: Back-laced; white was the preferred color. Other colors were red, black and beige. Use silk, polished cotton, or other similar material for right side of corset and a firmly woven fabric for lining. Cut out the five pattern pieces: two each for right side and two each for lining. Sew right side of corset together matching pattern markings; repeat with lining. Trim seams and press. With right sides of corset and lining together, sew each CB seam together; trim to ⅛in (.31cm); turn right side out; press. Topstitch corset close to each CB edge and then ¼in (.65cm) in; topstitch on each side of each corset seam. Bind all edges (except CB) with a ¾in (2cm) wide bias strip of self material or with ⅜in (.9cm) wide ribbon. Attach five tiny eyelets on each CB edge (or tiny worked buttonholes). Trim corset as desired. Place corset on doll and lace corset with KNIT-CRO-SHEEN (J.&P. Coats crochet thread) to match corset. Pull laces tight and tie in a small bow.

CRINOLINE: The crinoline was a framework of whalebone or steel loops. It could be covered with material or it was merely steel loops attached to tapes that hung from the waist. Cut patterns from white muslin; mark casing lines (dotted lines) on wrong side of fabric. There are two side pieces for each side of the crinoline. French seam all seams except left CF seam. Turn seams to one side and topstitch down close to seam line. Sew left CF seam to dot; narrowly hem opening and seam. To make casing for "steel" loops: place the folded edge of "double fold bias tape" against casing mark line; topstitch close to each edge of tape. Repeat with each casing line. Turn up hem of crinoline ½in (1.3cm), tuck ¼in (.65cm) of raw edge in; topstitch hem down (leave small opening in which to insert "steel" loop). Cut a waistband from tape, taken from doll's waistline measurement plus ½in (1.3cm). Gather crinoline waistline (except CF section) to fit waistband: sew together. Close with button and thread loop. To make "steel" loops use No. 20 gauge soft copper wiring: with pinch nose pliers, make a tiny loop at one end of copper wire (so wire will not puncture fabric), insert into casing, straightening wire as you work; cut wire off at desired length, also making a tiny loop at this end; tack these two loops to crinoline; stitch casing closed. Repeat with each casing. Place crinoline on doll and shape each wire loop into desired round shape.

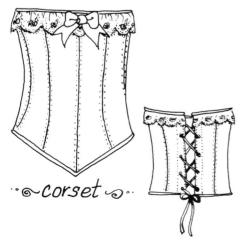

corset

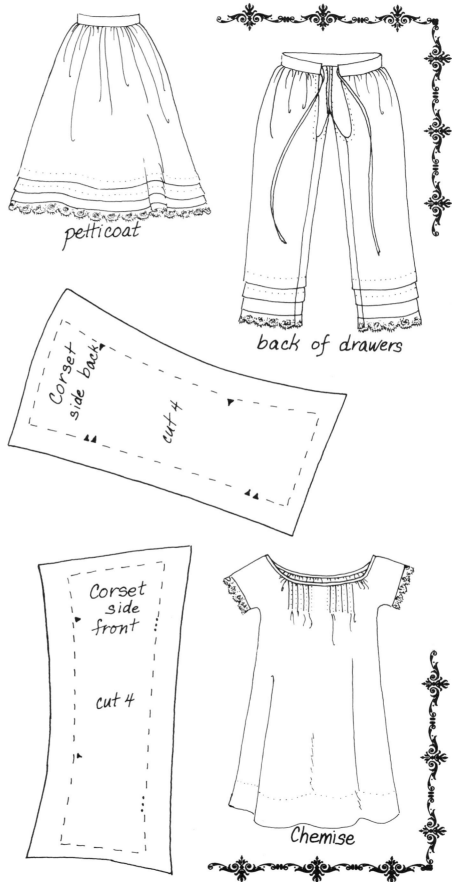

petticoat

back of drawers

Corset side back
cut 4

Corset side front
cut 4

Chemise

To complete the doll's 1850-60 period wardrobe of open drawers, knee-length chemise, petticoat, corset and wired crinoline, I have designed a pattern for a lace-trimmed dress. The silk dress has a tightly-fitted bodice, short puff sleeves edged with two rows of gathered lace and a deeply pleated attached skirt. I chose a thin pale blue silk to match her molded hair frill. The dress is fully lined with a thin white batiste.

Dresses of this period were quite full-skirted, enabling them to swing alluringly over the wide crinolines. Evening necklines were often quite low. Laces, ribbons, ribbon ruching, flowers, embroidery, braid, tassels and fringe were used lavishly as dress decorations. Use this basic dress pattern as a guide and trim your dress as desired -- just remember not to use too much decoration as it may overwhelm your doll.

Since china head muslin bodies vary from doll to doll, use the patterns as a guide. First complete the doll's underwear before starting on her dress. Then compare the doll's measurements against the dress patterns. Make whatever necessary alterations and then make the dress up in a thin muslin to insure a correct fit. Take this muslin dress apart and use it as a pattern for the silk dress. Set your sewing machine for ten stitches per inch or use tiny hand stitches. Use ¼in (.65cm) seams unless noted and press after each step.

MATERIALS NEEDED: Thin tracing paper, white batiste, thin colored silk material, extra fine thread for lightweight fabrics, 1½in (3.8cm) wide fine ecru lace, five tiny hooks and eyes, ¼in (.65cm) white twill tape.

BODICE: Sew darts in lining front. Sew side back bodice to back bodice. Sew shoulder seams of front and back bodice lining together. Repeat with silk bodice parts. Clip curves and press seams to one side. With right sides of lining and silk bodice together, sew a continuous seam from one CB waist edge around neck then back down other CB edge to waist. Clip curves and notch corners; turn right-side-out; press. Baste silk bodice to lining as one piece.

SLEEVES: Ease sleeve lining into bodice armhole so raw seam allowance faces right side of bodice. Turn up lining sleeve hem and baste two rows of gathered lace to this hem edge (one a little above the other). Sew sleeve underarm and side bodice seams in one continuous seam. Blindstitch raw edges of each lace flounce together. You may want to cover the raw bodice side seams with the ¼in (.65cm) white twill tape. Gather silk sleeve cap to fit bodice armhole and gather silk sleeve hem to fit sleeve

lining hem edge. Blindstitch silk sleeve to armhole, at bottom sleeve hem and stitch underarm seams together.

SKIRT: Sew CB seam of skirt lining from dot to hem, press entire seam open (also CB opening). Repeat with silk skirt. Blindstitch the silk skirt and lining skirt together at CB opening. Baste waist seams together -- treat the two skirts as one piece now. Press silk skirt hem up onto lining, slightly tuck raw hem edge in and blindstitch silk hem to lining. Press. Evenly space pleats from CB waist toward CF dot of skirt to fit bodice; blindstitch skirt and bodice together. Trim waist seam and cover this raw seam with twill tape.

Either leave the bodice plain or decorate with gathered lace (as shown) and ribbon ruching. Close the CB opening with five evenly spaced hooks and eyes.

Side Back Bodice
cut 2 - batiste
cut 2 - silk

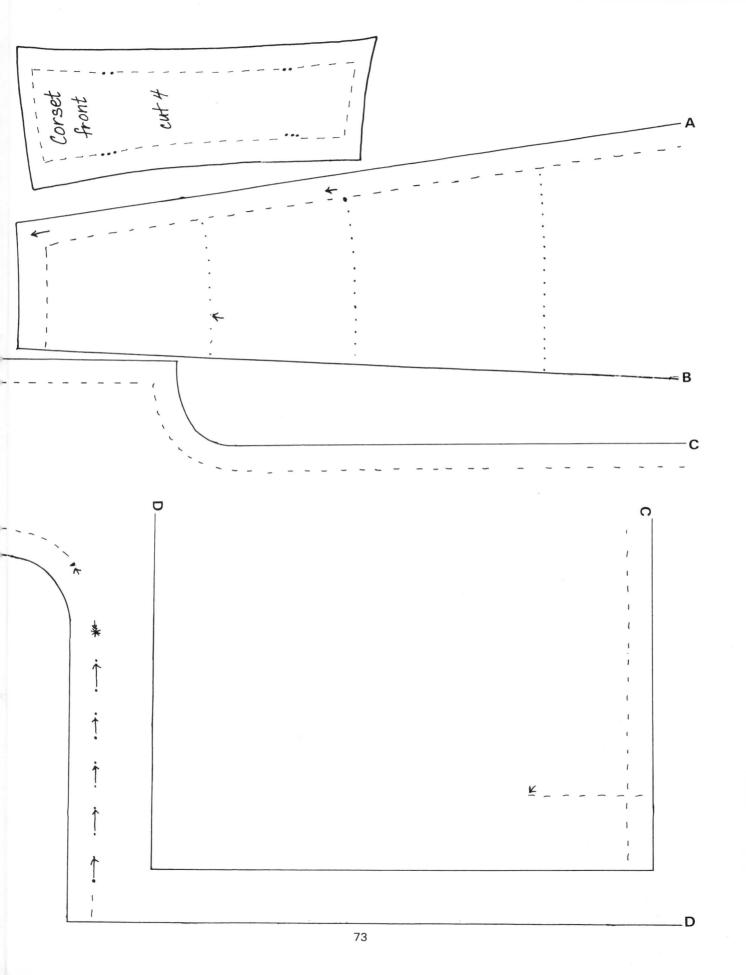

Corset
front

cut 4

A

B

C

D

C

D

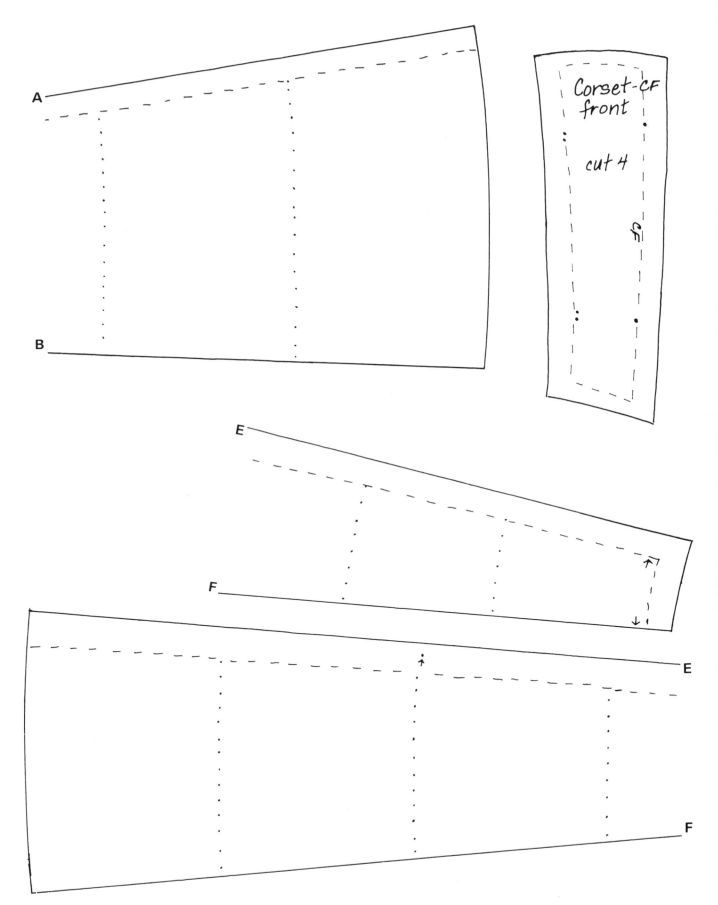

A

B

Corset-CF
front

cut 4

CF

E

F

E

F

74

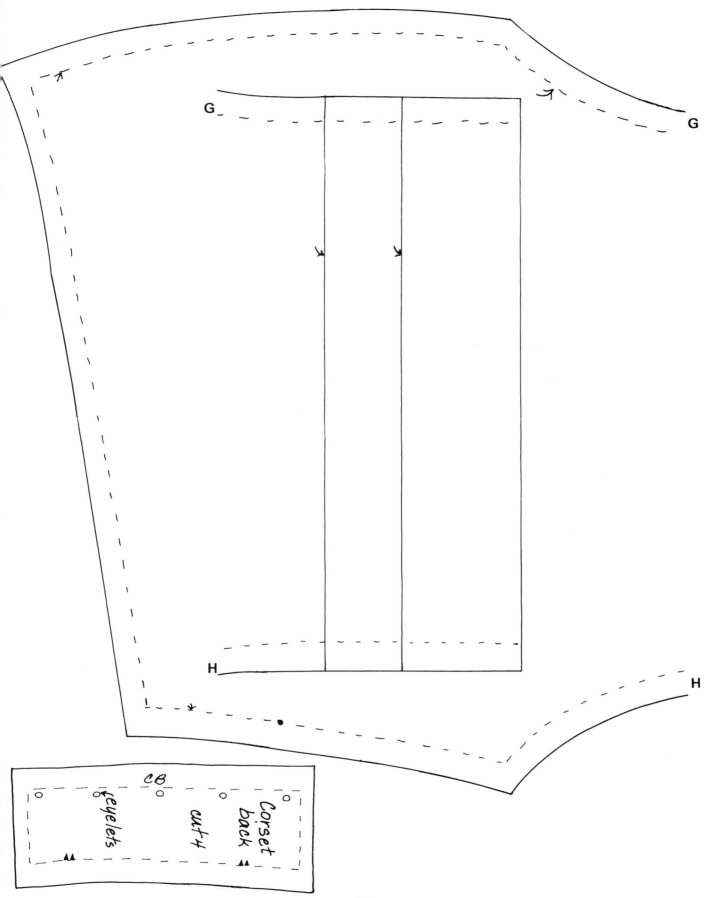

G   G

H   H

CB

eyelets

cut 4

Corset
back

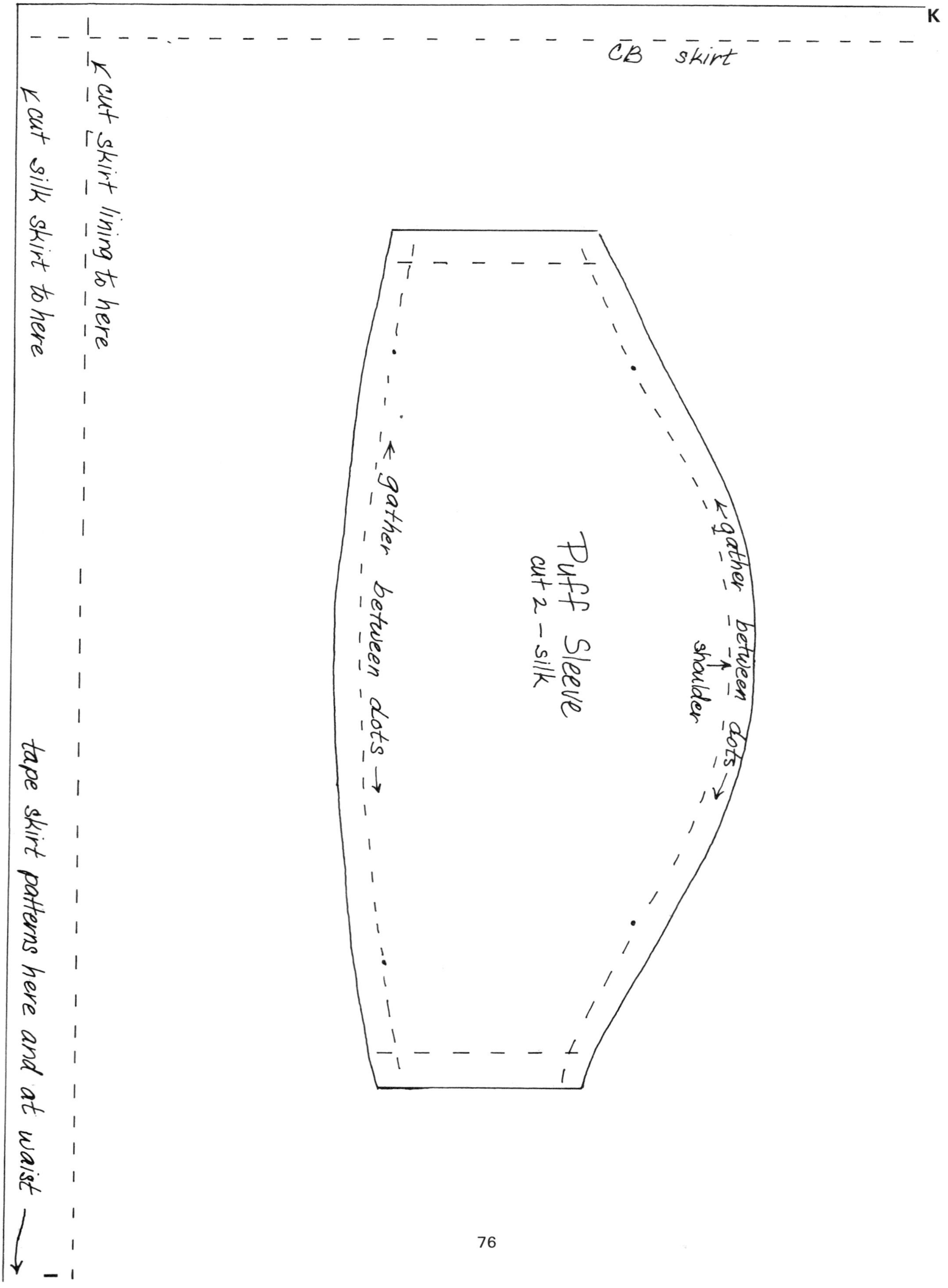

K

CB skirt

↙ cut skirt lining to here

↙ cut silk skirt to here

tape skirt patterns here and at waist ⟶

Puff Sleeve
cut 2 — silk

↙ gather between dots ↘
← shoulder →

← gather between dots →

76

K
- - - - - - - - - - - - . *leave open*

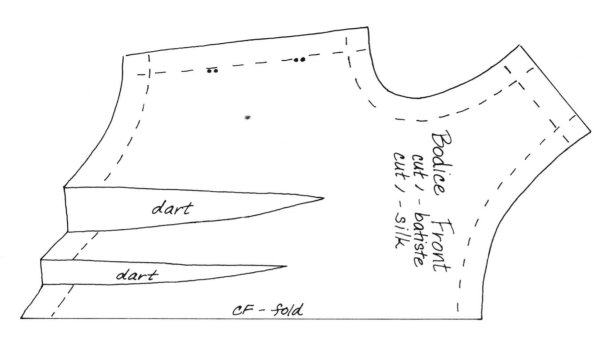

Bodice Front
cut 1 - batiste
cut 1 - silk

dart

dart

CF - fold

→ *arrange in pleats facing CF dots* →

Bodice Back
cut 2 - batiste
cut 2 - silk

· overlap CB
· approx. ¼"
· each side
· close with
· tiny hooks
· 4 eyes on
· dotted line

K Skirt pattern

77

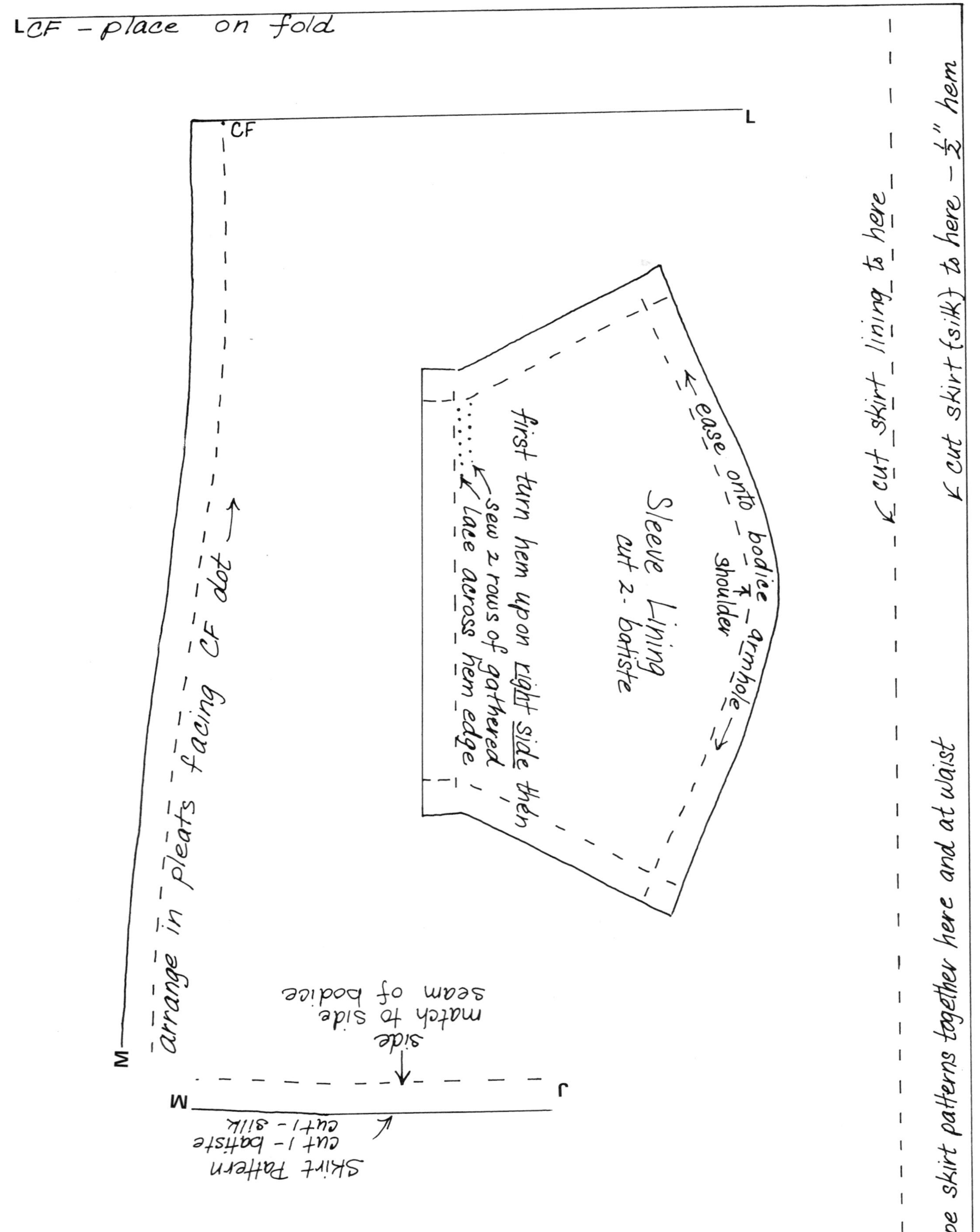

LCF - place on fold

CF   L

← cut skirt lining to here

← cut skirt (silk) to here — ½" hem

← ease onto bodice → shoulder ← armhole →

Sleeve Lining
cut 2- batiste

first turn hem up on right side then

← sew 2 rows of gathered

← lace across hem edge

arrange in pleats facing CF dot →

tape skirt patterns together here and at waist

M

side
match to
seam of bodice

M   L

Skirt Pattern
cut 1- batiste
cut 1- silk

78

LADY DOLL'S DRESS AND CAPE

The Designer - November 1898.

Illustration 1. Lady doll's dress and cape.

No. 4593. This handsome costume and dressy little cape would be exceedingly becoming to any young lady doll, and would undoubtedly be much admired by her little owner. The cloak is made of pink cashmere trimmed with silver braid. The dress as shown on the figure is made of taffeta brocade, decorated with ruching of pink satin ribbon. As shown in the front and back views it is made of blue cashmere with braiding of narrow black velvet.

The cape is circular and fitted on each shoulder by a dart. A two-piece graduated ruffle finishes the lower edge and fronts, and a flaring collar is attached to the neck edge.

The waist of the costume has a lining fitted by underarm and shoulder seams, also single bust-darts. This is overlaid to yoke depth. The back and fronts are shaped at the upper edges, and cut to display the yoke. The fronts are slightly gathered at the waistline, and the closing is effected down their center. The sleeves are one seamed, and the neck is finished with a binding. The skirt consists of two circular portions united by a center back seam. The fullness in the back is arranged in two backward-turning pleats each side of the seam. The two-piece flounce extends into the front panel. A narrow band finished the upper edge.

This pattern is cut in seven sizes, for dolls measuring 14in (35.6cm) to 26in (66cm) from crown of head to sole of foot. The 18in (45.7cm) requires for dress 1⅞yd (1.68m) of 22in (55.9cm) goods. Cape requires ⅝yd (.55m) of goods.

Bridal Dress and Morning Dress

From *Ladies' Cabinet of Fashion*, 1848.

BRIDAL DRESS

White silk robe. The corsage, made quite up to the throat, tight to the shape, and deeply pointed, is trimmed with a ruche round the top. Long sleeves, very full trimmed round the shoulders and hand with Mechlin lace. Two flounces of the same lace nearly cover the whole of the skirt. The hair is decorated with a bridal veil of Brussels lace, attached by a wreath of orange blossoms; a bouquet of the same ornaments the corsage.

MORNING DRESS

Lavender levantine robe. The corsage is made quite high and close. The sleeves a three-quarter length, with mancherons of a half-length: muslin under sleeves. The front of the corsage and skirt is trimmed with two rows of black lace. A knot of lavender ribbon ornaments the centre of the corsage, and a succession of them the front of the skirt; the mancherons are trimmed to correspond. Light green velvet chapeau. A round open shape, the interior trimmed with red roses without foliage, and green brides, the exterior with green ribbon, and a tuft of tetes de plumes on each side.

HOW TO DRESS A DOLL

Editor's note: This is a reprint of *Godey's Lady's Book* and *Magazine* which started in the April 1860 issue and continued in subsequent issues.

Having a special love for our young readers -- especially the female portion of them -- we have provided something for their amusement and instruction; and, to show them how we like them, we give them a seat in our own "Arm Chair." Let us say a word to mothers, also: The same patterns enlarged will answer just as well for children of a larger growth than dolls.

HOW TO DRESS A DOLL

This is not only pleasant employment, but it is extremely useful; to be able to make your own doll's clothes, you will acquire the knowledge of making your own dresses when you are older. Every little girl is fond of dolls, and to dress one neatly requires some experience. Young ladies too often depend upon others to make their doll's clothes; but with the practical illustrations we propose giving for making each article of dress separately, we trust all our young friends will be enabled to make their own things. Sewing is particularly a lady's accomplishment, and it cannot be too early practiced or encouraged. Cutting out requires more art and skill, but in making doll's clothes experience may be gained, and a little practice will soon enable any one to make them neatly and properly; so that you will thus gratify your own taste, and afford amusement to your juvenile companions and friends.

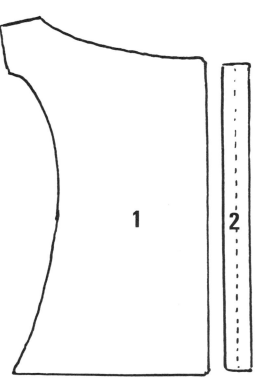

Illustration 2. Chemise patterns.

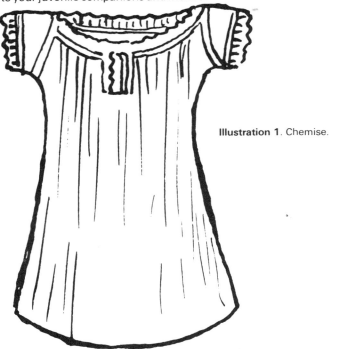

Illustration 1. Chemise.

CHEMISE (See *Illustration 1*.) Take a piece of fine white calico, the size you require for your doll. Double it once, then fold it in half again, and cut it out to the shape of No. 1. When opened out, you will find the two sides both alike, making the back and front. Put the four seams together, and tack them on both sides, run them a little way from the edge, fell these down very neatly, and hem the bottom round. Before you commence it, take a piece of card the width you require the hem, and cut it to the size, tack it along, and afterwards hem it down. Then run the tops of the sleeves together a little way from the end of the calico. Separate these, and fold them down as if you were going to hem them, keeping it even, turn the chemise to the right side, and also turn down the sleeves and backstitch them. Do the same to each side of the small seams at the top of the sleeves. You will require a band to put the chemise on to, and for that, get a strip of calico. This must not be too wide. Measure it round the shoulders of your doll, and cut it to the required length, lay it flat upon the table, and turn it over at the dotted line (No. 3). Backstitch it a short distance from the dotted line. Then take the chemise and cut the front a little way down, so as you can put it on the doll without tearing it. Make a narrow hem on the right side, and afterwards do the same with the left, only making it about as wide again. Double the broad one over the narrow, and stitch it just at the end of where you have hemmed it. Then take a long needle and thread and gather the top round, beginning at the small opening in front. When you have come to the other side, pull the thread out of your needle and measure the width of the band on the chemise. When you have got it, pin it to keep it in its proper place, twine the thread you have left round the pin. Then take the band on the right side which is stitched, and lay it down on the same side of the chemise, and stitch it there. When done, turn the band up and hem it down on the other side. Sew a small linen button on the end of the band, and, at the top of the narrow hem on the opposite side, make a small buttonhole. This completes the plain work of the chemise, but, to make it more finished, you can trim it with a narrow piece of embroidery, sewing it all round the neck and sleeves, as in *Illustration 1*.

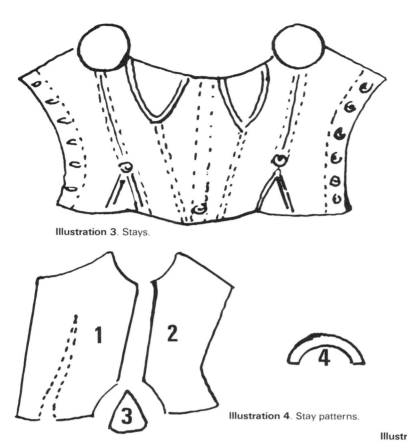

Illustration 3. Stays.

Illustration 4. Stay patterns.

wish to be added, and hem it down, and do the same with the other leg. For the band, take a plain piece of calico, and measure it round the waist of your doll. Make a buttonhole in the middle and one at each end, and sew it on to the drawers in the same way as already described for the chemise.

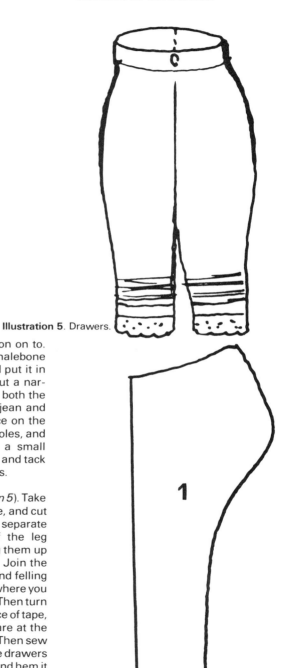

Illustration 5. Drawers.

Illustration 6. Drawers patterns.

STAYS (See *Illustration 3*.) Take a piece of jean, double it once, and cut out the pattern (No. 1), which is the front. For the backs fold another piece, and cut it out as No. 2. Fold another piece for the gussets, and cut them out as No. 3. Then take the front, open it out, and backstitch in the sides, as in dotted lines in No. 1. Stitch it twice down the middle of the front, as in *Illustration 3*, leaving a small space between each. Then take one of the backs, and backstitch it to one of the sides of No. 1 down as far as it is cut off for the gusset, and do the same on the other side. Stitch in the gussets (No. 3); take a piece of stay binding, first separating the seams, and sew it over them, doing the same with the gussets. Then bind all round the stays with the same material. For the shoulder straps take a piece of binding, and form it to the shape of No. 4, and sew each of the ends on to Nos. 1 and 2. Backstitch a little way from each end of the backs, as the dotted line in *Illustration 3*. Make as many buttonholes as you require, taking care to keep them at equal distances, and between the stitching and the ends. To fix on buttons, place the two backs together, and put pins through the buttonholes, which will enable you to get them exactly in the proper places. Sew them on strongly -- one in front (*Illustration 3*), also one above each gusset, for the petticoats and drawers to button on to. Take a rather broad piece of whalebone for the center of the front, and put it in between the stitching. Then put a narrower piece of whalebone into both the seams in No. 1, between the jean and the binding. Sew another piece on the inside, just behind the buttonholes, and also behind the buttons. Put a small piece of bone up each of them, and tack them in at the ends of the stays.

DRAWERS (See *Illustration 5*). Take a piece of calico, double it twice, and cut out the pattern (No. 1). Then separate them, join up the seams of the leg separately, running and felling them up as far as the end of the slope. Join the two fronts together, running and felling them about half way down, to where you left off sewing up the drawers. Then turn them to the right side, get a piece of tape, and turn in the edges which are at the top of the back part of the legs. Then sew over the tape and the part of the drawers which you have turned down, and hem it on the inside. Tack down a hem as wide as necessary. Before doing so, measure it with a piece of card to get it the even distance. Do the same between the hem and the tuck, and again with the width of the hem above that. Tack it down, and run it, and so on for as many tucks as you require. Then put the work which you

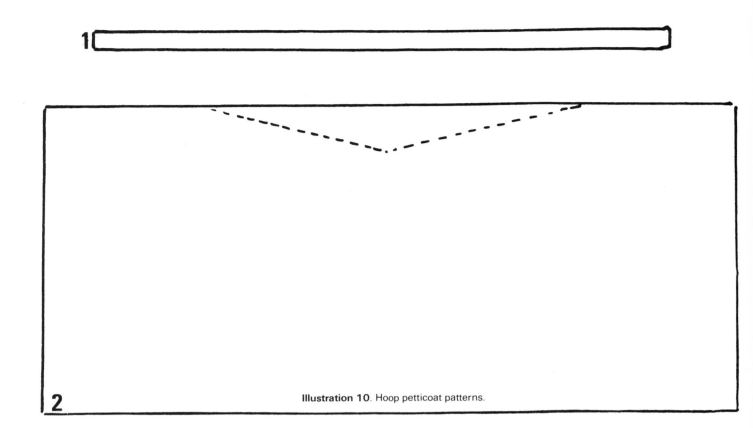

Illustration 10. Hoop petticoat patterns.

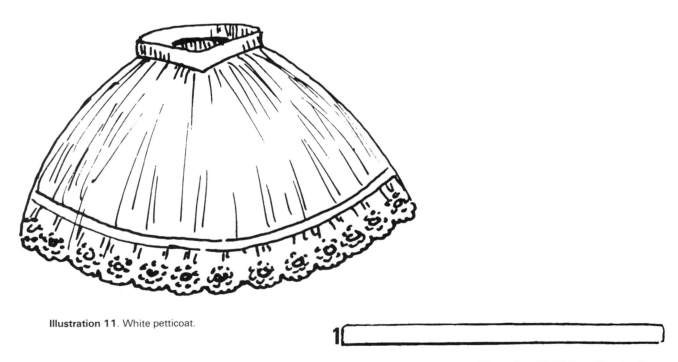

Illustration 11. White petticoat.

Illustration 12. White petticoat pattern.

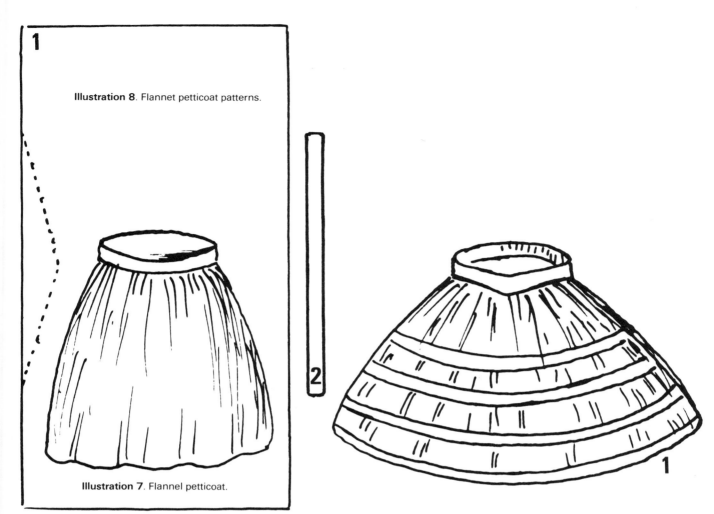

Illustration 8. Flannel petticoat patterns.

Illustration 7. Flannel petticoat.

Illustration 9. Hoop petticoat.

FLANNEL PETTICOAT (See *Illustration 7*). Procure a piece of nice fine flannel and cut it to the shape of No. 1, and the size of your doll. Then take the two ends, and run them together nearly up to the top, but leaving a piece undone for the placket hole; herringbone the seam down very neatly. Take a piece of flannel binding and hem it on to the wrong side all round, then turn a small piece over on the right side, hem that down also. Slope it out a little in front as in the dotted lines in No. 1, and bind round in the same manner the placket hole. Now take a long thread in your needle. Begin at the middle of the flannel, gather it up, also on the other side, and make a band, No. 2, the same as you did for the drawers, only of a little coarser material.

HOOP PETTICOAT (See *Illustration 9*). Take a piece of stout white calico, and cut it the shape of No. 1 of the flannel petticoat, and the size you require it; hem the two ends together, leaving enough for the placket hole. Do that also in the same manner as you did the opening in the chemise. Then take some binding the proper width and the same length as the petticoat (No. 1). Just turn the bottom in, and sew it to the petticoat at the end, and hem the binding at the top on the wrong side. Then hem two more pieces of binding on in the same manner, at an equal distance apart. Gather the top up, and slope it in the same way as you did No. 1 of the flannel petticoat. Also make a band of the same sort, only of a little finer material. Now put in the steel, which should be very narrow; run in the bottom one first, not gathering it up in the least. Then sew a small piece over to keep it firm, and do the same in fastening in all the others, gathering them gradually in, to make each one smaller than the one under, till you get a proper shape.

WHITE PETTICOAT (See *Illustration 11*). This is also made of white calico, but of much finer quality. Run the two sides up together, leaving a small piece at the top for a placket hole, and hem it in the same manner as you did in the hoop petticoat. Tack down as in the drawers, and also tuck in the same way. When you have done as many as you require, hem in some nice work at the bottom, and for the sloping of it do it a little more than in the other petticoat (as shown in *Illustration 10*, No. 2), and turn it in a little at the top. For the band No. 1, take a piece of the same material, and cut it a little longer than the other. Take it in a little in front, and make the buttonholes the same as before. Turn the band in at the bottom, and tack it, to keep it in its place. Gather the top of the petticoat as you did before, only, as you have it turned in, you will find it a little more difficult. Sew on the band strongly, and take the tacking threads out of it.

83

Lady Godey Dresses a Doll

by **Clara H. Fawcett**

between 1840 and 1860 and was made from the mold in papier-mâché, china and parian type bisque. Those in papier-mâché often had glass eyes. However, glass eyes are seldom seen in the china heads, hence their popularity as collectors' items. The costume dates from 1858. The bodice was fashionable at that period and was formed in points -- one in front, one at back and one on each hip.

BELOW: Illustration 3. *Rachel,* a fashionable body. *Peterson's,* 1858.

Illustration 1. *Avalena,* a typical china-headed china-limbed doll of the mid 19th century. This type was used from about 1830 to 1860. Dress dates 1858. Sketch above is a simplified version of the same dress pattern.

Avalena is one of the most interesting of the mid- 19th century china-headed china-limbed dolls. The corkscrew ringlets continue around the back of the head, and the narrow-waisted cloth body is typical of the period. The dress dates from 1858. The one shown here was made of white jaconet, trimmed with needlework and white braid. In the front of the waist there is a large bow of jaconet, with long, rounded ends edged with needlework, which falls over the apron trimming in front of the skirt. This dress would also be very beautiful when made in Marseilles.

Rachel, a glass-eyed papier-mâché head doll is so named because she is similar to Rachel shown in the Index of American Design, National Gallery of Art in Washington, D.C. The doll was popular

1. Half the front.

3. Side-body.

2. Half the back.

Illustration 2. *Rachel,* a glass-eyed papier-mâché-headed doll of the mid 19th century. Costume, 1858.

Illustration 4. *Mary Todd,* a mid 19th century china-headed doll with gold colored hairnet and bows of self-material. Marseilles jacket and skirt of 1859.

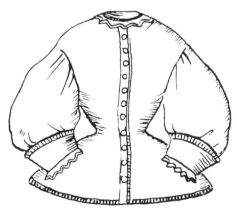

Illustration 5. Marseilles Jacket of white pique or Marseilles, with half-tight sleeves, just allowing the hand to pass; the bottom of the sleeve is embellished with a festooned trimming, as is also the collar. *Peterson's,* 1859.

Illustration 6. *Ninette,* a papier-mâché-headed doll of about 1860 with contemporary child's costume.

Mary Todd, a mid 19th century china-headed doll. It is said that the hair dress is in the style worn by the wife of our beloved Civil War President, Abraham Lincoln, just before her marriage. The black hair is beautifully modeled in china. The bows and hair net, which covers the curls at the back of the head, are also of self-material and are gold-colored. The jacket, which dates from 1859, shown here is Marseilles, but could also be of white pique. It has half-tight sleeves, just allowing the hand to pass. The bottom of the sleeve is embellished with a festooned trimming, as is also the collar.

Ninette, a papier-mâché-headed doll of about 1860, with contemporary child's costume. *Ninette* is similar to *Nina,* the doll that was used to smuggle morphine and quinine across the border during the Civil War. The hollow head was divided into sections to hold the medicine. Both have a papier-mâché head and a homemade cloth body. *Nina* who was formerly owned by the niece of General Anderson, Polatka, Florida, now helps entertain visitors at the Confederate Museum, Richmond, Virginia. The dress is half high and round, and worn with a band and buckle. It is cut square back and front (at the neck). The decoration consists of narrow velvet bands. It has a long, loose sleeve with jockey (over the sleeve).

Miss Prim, has a wax-over-papier-mâché head, molded hair of self-material, wax arms, wooden legs and feet and glass eyes. She is wearing a "Surplice" dress body of 1859. This graceful dress body first appeared in Paris and then in American fashion magazines. In the pattern diagram, No. 1 is half the front, No. 2 front of pelerine, No. 3 half the back, and No. 4, back of pelerine.

Fashions of 1854 with a china head of the same period. The girl in *Illustration 13* with the hat is wearing a frock of sky blue silk. The corsage is drawn in easy fullness and cut rather low round the neck, with the top of it trimmed with three bias folds of poplin. The sleeves consist merely of two small epaulettes, one falling over the other. The under-sleeves are of white cambric or jaconet muslin, loose demi-long, and trimmed at the ends by frills of open needlework. There is a muslin chemisette to correspond. The trousers are edged with needlework. The large garden hat is of leghorn, with a white feather waving around the crown, and strings of ribbon fastened at the ears by rosettes, also of white ribbon. She wears coral bracelets on her arms, while the boots are of gray cashmere tipped with black.

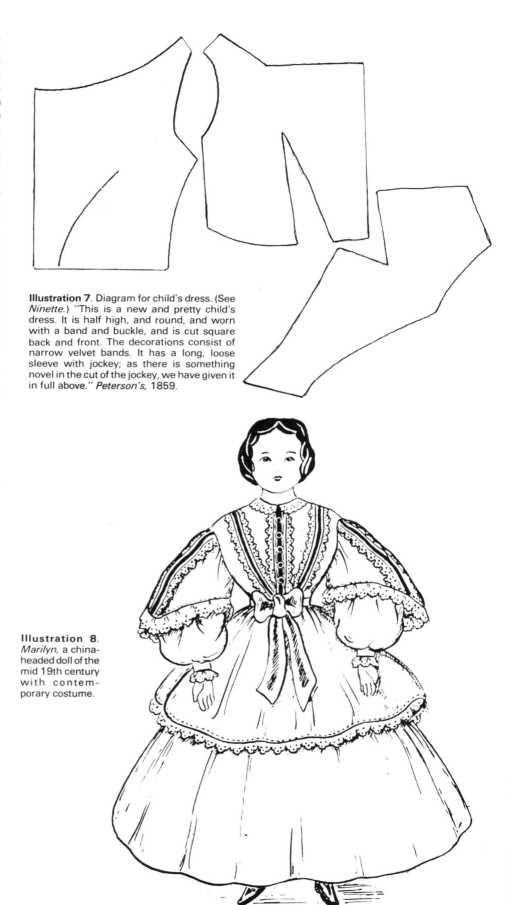

Illustration 7. Diagram for child's dress. (See *Ninette.*) "This is a new and pretty child's dress. It is half high, and round, and worn with a band and buckle, and is cut square back and front. The decorations consist of narrow velvet bands. It has a long, loose sleeve with jockey; as there is something novel in the cut of the jockey, we have given it in full above." *Peterson's,* 1859.

Illustration 8. *Marilyn,* a china-headed doll of the mid 19th century with contemporary costume.

Illustration 9. The surplice dress body. (See *Miss Prim*). "This graceful dress body has just appeared in Paris, where it is very popular; and accordingly we have had it engraved for "Peterson," and a diagram prepared by which to cut out a paper pattern. Such a pattern can be made, by any subscriber, by enlarging the diagram" No. 1. Half the front. No. 2 Front of pelerine. No. 3. Half the back. No. 4. Back of pelerine. *Peterson's*, February 1859.

Illustration 10. *Miss Prim*, a wax over-papier-mâché doll head, cloth body, hair of self-material; mid 19th century. 1859 Surplice dress body.

Illustration 11. *Sarah*, a "Greiner's Improved Patent Head, 1858." Papier-mâché head with cloth body and kid arms; contemporary dress.

Illustration 12. *Miss 1854*, a parian type doll head with hair and hair ornaments of self-material. Costume is the latest style in 1854. The dress is of plain white cambric, skirt full and plain. The basque is very deep and trimmed with a worked cambric ruffle. The sleeves are finished in a corresponding style. The bonnet is of straw, ornamented at the sides with bouquets of wild flowers. A wreath of wild flowers trims the face of the bonnet.

Illustration 13. Fashions of 1854.

Illustration 14. Court costume of 1854.

The little girl in *Illustration 13* hanging on the arms of the larger one has a white muslin dress with basque slit up at each side. The boots are of green cashmere and stocking of Lille thread. A wreath of scarlet geranium, roses and white heath encircles the head.

The court costume shown in *Illustration 14* has a train of pink moire antique, lined with white satin and edged with pink feather trimming, interspersed with gold berries. The petticoat is of white tulle over white satin, trimmed with rows of tulle puffings, arranged in three graduated groups. Between each row of puffings are placed small bows of gold ribbon. The corsage is trimmed with blonde and bows of gold ribbon similar to those on the skirt. The sleeves are in two small puffs. The hair is in full bandeaux at each side of the forehead, with one small flat curl just below the temple. There is a plume of pink marabous at the back of the head. The necklace and bracelets are of diamonds and pearls, and she carries a Watteau fan.

Illustration 15. *Inga*, an English doll of the early 1860s has natural hair, with head, arms and legs of wax. The dress, made in America, is in the everyday style of the period, simple white cambric with tucks in the skirt.

Illustration 16. *Eugenie* is the name given by doll collectors to the head shown on the right. The dress, styled in 1858, was called "The Eugenie" in honor of the French Empress. This is only one of the costumes named in her honor, as she set the fashions of the times for both Europe and America. The dress shown here has both flounces and side trimming. Either flounces or side trimmings by themselves would be sufficient. The sleeves, new at the time, were considered quite pretty. Either the berthe with sleeves or the fichu pelerine sketched could enliven a plain dress. In January, 1859, *Peterson's Magazine* had this to say about one of the Empress Eugenie's costumes: "A Costly Dress. -- The Empress Eugenie has just purchased the dress in point d'Alencon given by the city of Rouen to the aunt of Louis XVI, or her visit then with Louis XV. The Empress has paid the sum of ten thousand dollars for the dress, which has a train of two yards and a quarter in length, and is covered with birds, and trees, and emblematical figures of all kinds. We have seen lace dresses, at weddings in this city, worth five or six thousand dollars; but ten thousand, as yet, is a figure above republicans."

Illustration 17. Fichu pelerine.

Illustration 18. Berthe with sleeves.

Illustration 19. A fancy sleeve and a chemisette.

Illustration 20. Here is a dress of white cashmere with two skirts. The lower skirt is trimmed with two bands of blue cashmere, and the upper skirt is edged with the same blue cashmere. The body is made with a basque laid in full plaits (pleats) behind, and trimmed down the side seams with white silk buttons. A row of the same buttons ornaments the front. The sleeve is full and set into a cap and trimmed with blue cashmere. The hat is of white beaver, trimmed with blue velvet and flowers.

89

Illustration 21. This is a child's sack or over dress designed by Demarest of New York City. The upper portion is made to fit the form by plaits in front and back which extend from neck to waist. The skirt is short, and the back forms a polka rounded up at the sides. The neck is finished with a collar which forms a point in the back and on each shoulder, the front forming a lapel extending the full length of the skirt. A plain, flowing sleeve completes this pretty garment.

Illustration 22. Children's Dress circa 1860. The front and back views of a pardessus for a little boy of grey cloth trimmed with a band of cloth of a darker shade, with a long hairy nap upon it is shown here.

Illustration 23. China head, circa 1860.

Illustration 25. "For little girls...one of the newest styles of cloaks." 1858.

Illustration 26. China head of 1840 to 1860.

Illustration 24. Children's Fashions for January 1858. LEFT TO RIGHT: A dress for a little girl seven years of age. The frock is of blue silk, trimmed at the side with black velvet put on in diamond form. The coat is of black velvet, finished with a ball trimming. The little black velvet bonnet is trimmed with feathers. A baby's cloak of white cashmere, trimmed with rich silk embroidery in vandykes. The bonnet is made of white cashmere. A scarlet merino dress for a little girl four years of age. The body is cut square on the shoulders and has a full polka at the waist. It is profusely trimmed with black velvet ribbon and buttons. The undersleeves are of cambric, and the spencer is formed of cambric and insertions.

During this period dresses of velvet were much worn by small boys. They were longer than previously. A ruffled pantalette came below the dress, and a cloth gaiter kept the limbs warm. Round capes were sometimes added for the street dress. The caps were usually of velvet with a tuft of cock's plumes. For larger boys cassimere pantaloons, with a closely-fitting jacket of the same material, were popular.

Illustration 27. Petticoat body.

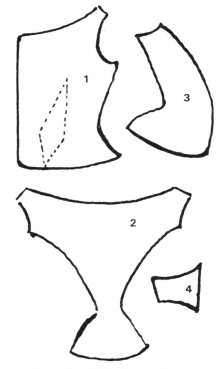

Illustration 28. Petticoat body patterns.

Illustration 29. Girl and doll in the fashions of the day.

PETTICOAT BODY. Take a piece of white calico of the same material as the white petticoat, and cut out two fronts of the shape of No. 1; then cut out part of the back, No. 2, double the calico again, and cut out two other parts of the back to the shape No. 3. Backstitch on the wrong side of the dotted lines in the two fronts, No. 1; stitch together the sides and the middle of the back, Nos. 2 and 3. Now take one of the fronts, No. 1., and backstitch it to one side of the back and do the same to the other front. Stitch the top of the armholes together. When you have finished all the seams, cut off the rough edges, sew them over, or, if you wish to make them look still neater, turn the edges in the same way. Then double a piece of calico, and cut out a sleeve to the shape of No. 4. Cut out another one exactly the same, and sew them up as the seams, turn the fronts in, and, if you

have not a selvage, turn it in and hem it neatly. Make as many small buttonholes as you require, and the other side sew on the buttons as already explained in the stays. Cut some pieces of calico on the cross, and take some cotton cord and put it between and backstitch it on the right side all around the jacket-piece, also around the neck. Turn the binding on the wrong side, and hem it neatly. Take another piece, cut on the cross, and put the cotton cord in the same as before. Tack it around the armholes, hem the bottom of the sleeves on the wrong side, stitch them in, cut off the rough edges, and sew it over. To give a finished appearance, sew on a piece of narrow embroidery around the neck and sleeves.

FROCK (See Illustration 30). This can be made of jaconet. Take the size you require, double it, and cut out to the shape of No. 1. Fold another piece, and cut out two parts of the back to the shape of No. 2. Do the same again, and cut out two more parts of the back to the shape of No. 2. Backstitch on each side of the dotted lines in No. 1 and the same again for the two pieces of the sides, No. 3, on to each side of the two parts, No. 2. Then stitch the back and front together on each side, cut the rough edges off the seams, and sew them over. Cut some of the same material on the cross, and take some fine cotton cord, sew it round the

bottom of the body and neck, as in the petticoat body. Cut some more jaconet on the cross, put some cord inside of it, and tack it around the armholes. Double the stuff, and cut out two sleeves to the shape of No. 4. Hem them neatly at the ends, and sew them up the same as the seams, and stitch them into the arm-holes. Take a piece of embroidery, and trim it around the neck and sleeves, as shown in Illustration 30.

SKIRT. Take a piece of jaconet the size you require, fold it once, and cut it to the shape of No. 5. Stitch the two ends together, leaving enough for the placket hole, and do this as before described for the petticoats. Make rather a broad hem around the bottom, measuring it with a card to keep it even, and then hem it. Trim it with wider work, but of much the same patterns as the work on the body, forming either a double skirt or flounces. Slope out from the dotted line, turn it in a little, gather it up, and sew it on to the body, and it will come the same as shown in Illustration 30.

CAPE (See Illustration 32). Fold a piece of Marcella once, and cut out a back the shape of No. 1. Fold it again, and cut out two fronts the shape of No. 2. Backstitch firmly together the two fronts on to each side of the back, putting the narrow sides together. Cut off the rough edges, and sew them over. Procure some fine plain braid, and bind around

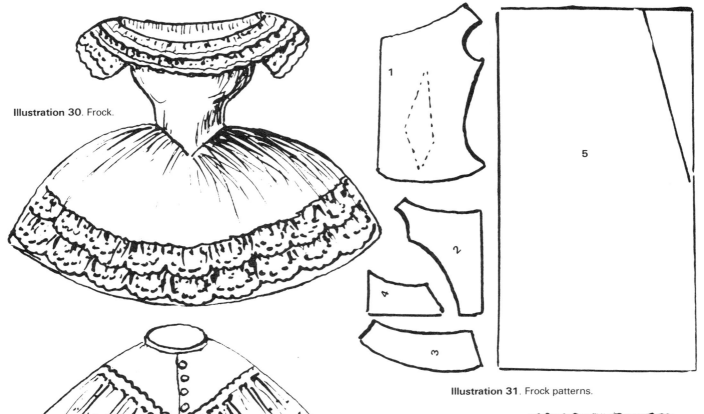

Illustration 30. Frock.

Illustration 31. Frock patterns.

Illustration 32. Cape.

Illustration 33. Cape patterns.

Illustration 34. Pinafore.

the bottom neatly. Turn in the two fronts, and make three buttonholes, or four if the doll be large, and the same number of gilt buttons on the opposite side. Then bind around the neck neatly. Take a wide strip of embroidery, the proper length from the shoulders, gather it up, and sew it on to the bottom. Get some white bally fringe, and sew it neatly all around the bottom of the shoulder pieces.

PINAFORE (See *Illustration 34*). Cut out a piece of fine diaper, double across

once to the shape of No. 1. Run and fell in a piece of insertion between the top of the shoulders. Hem the bottom and backs neatly, and also the top. Run a piece of tape through it, and sew on a small button, with a corresponding buttonhole about the waist. Sew on a narrow piece of embroidery around the armholes, and your pinafore will be finished.

HAT (See *Illustration 35*). The shape may be made of black stiff net and black wire; cut it out as No. 1 for the crown, and cut through the four straight lines up to the dotted one, and bend the latter down. Then make into a round by creasing the sides where they are cut through, and tack them together with black thread. Procure a piece of black silk velvet, and cut it the size of the round of No. 1, and it will form No. 2. For the brim, cut out of the same net the shape of No. 3, and cut out the round hole for the crown, and through the black lines at the top and bottom, turn up the dotted lines, and tack around inside of them a thin piece of wire. Then fold over the top and bottom, where it is cut through, and sew the sides together. Cut a piece of black

silk velvet on the cross, and shape it from the dotted lines to the circle in the middle of No. 3, and tack it under the brim of the hat. Cut another strip of the same velvet on the cross, and bind the whole of the edge of the brim very neatly. Put in the crown, and fix it to the brim by sewing it all around, and the rough edge with a small piece of sarsnet ribbon, lining the inside of the crown with Persian silk, and it will form No. 4. Get a small white ostrich feather, rather long, and tack it inside of the brim on the top of the hat. Carry it to the back, fasten it there, and allow it to hang over a little. Cut some more strips of black silk velvet on the cross, and make up a nice large bow upon black net, and ends of the same.

Illustration 35. Pinafore pattern.

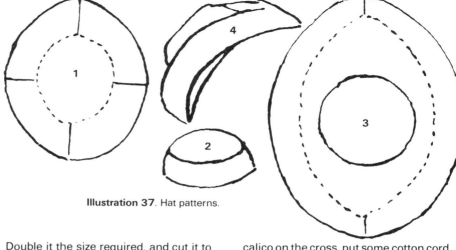

Illustration 37. Hat patterns.

Illustration 36. Hat.

Illustration 38. Nightdress.

Double it the size required, and cut it to the shape of No. 1 for the front. Double another piece for the back, cut to the shape of No. 2, and cut down as far as *a*. Then cut out two bell sleeves and the shape of No. 3, run and fell the sides of back and front together up as far as the armholes, and the same upon the shoulders. Do the placket hole the same as in the skirt of the frock, and make a rather broad hem around the bottom. Now run and fell up the sleeves, gather them up neatly at the ends. Make a band large enough to slip over the hands of your doll, backstitch it, and put the gatherings into the band, No. 4. Do the same to the other sleeve. Cut some calico on the cross, put some cotton cord in the inside of it, and tack around the armholes. Then backstitch in the sleeves, putting them rather further in than usual, and hem them inside the nightdress. Gather the top up, and make a band the size of your doll's neck. Put the gathering in as you did the sleeves. Get some narrow embroidery, and put it around the neck and sleeves, placing it both at the top and bottom of the band, and sew some tape on for the strings around the neck. Then make a wider band, long enough to tie about the doll's waist, and round it at each end. Make a frill of work around each end, as in No. 5. Then backstitch it to the middle of the front.

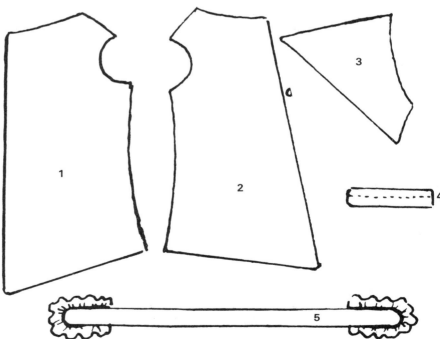

Illustration 39. Nightdress patterns.

Before making up the velvet, it should be hemmed all around. The strings must be pink ribbon; the rosettes can be made of pink and black velvet arranged upon black net.

NIGHTDRESS (See *Illustration 38*). This is made of calico, but it need not be quite so fine as the white petticoat.

Dressing Pincusion Dolls

by **Sandy Williams**

Not all pincushion dolls were meant to be sewn on a pincushion. Some of their other uses were to cover telephones, lamps, powder boxes, candy boxes, tea cosies and perfume bottles. Pincushion dolls were quite popular in the early 1900s and passed out of popularity by the 1930s. The dolls were usually manufactured in Germany but at the end of their popularity were made in Japan. To hide telephone and lamps, the dolls were mounted on wire frames. In the December 1922 issue of *The Ladies Home Journal* an article titled "Even the Grown-Ups Cry for Dolls This Christmas" states:

Illustration 1. 1922 doll lamp.

"Do it with dolls" would seem to be the season's motto, if it is anything from lampshades to laundry bags one is giving for Christmas. Doll lamps may be had in great variety. Those with silken skirts serve mainly as a decorative spot of color, but through chiffon skirts the light shines brightly enough for reading in bed. *Illustration 1* shows a 1922 doll lamp. My lady's gown is of rose taffeta and gold lace. The lamp is 11in (27.9cm) high; the spread of skirt of the bottom is also 11in (27.9cm). For the lamp in the center of the page (not shown here), orchid chiffon is lined with rose, shirred, and trimmed in front with ribbon roses. Both height of lamp and spread of skirt are 12in (30.5cm). *Illustration 2* is a sewing doll for the guest room, whose lovely colonial gown of pink and gold changeable taffeta has upturned hem pockets for needles, thread and scissors. The doll is 12in (30.5cm) high; skirt spread, 10in (25.4cm).

"If one is far from shops that show such lamps, dolls' heads may be bought and the lamps made at home, the voluminous skirts kindly concealing any discrepancies in the wire framework. City shops sell the frames with or without dolls' heads."

A good source book for pincushion dolls, dressed and undressed, is *China Half-Figures Called Pincushion Dolls* by Frieda Marion.

My half dolls have molded bodices so the following patterns are only for their skirts. If your doll does not have a molded bodice, you can easily make a pattern for one by draping pieces of paper towel directly on your doll in the style you desire.

Illustration 2. 1922 sewing doll lamp.

Since wire frames and pincushion forms are no longer available, I have given directions for making two pincushion forms. The basic concept is to make a muslin skirt pincushion. First, figure out how tall your completed doll should be: measure the length of your doll's head (do not include hair); multiply this measurement by seven. To get the height of your pincushion form: measure how tall your half-doll is; subtract this figure from completed doll's height. Add a ¼in (.65cm) bottom hem. The width of the skirt is the same as the circumference of cardboard base plus a ¼in (.65cm) center back seam. Sew center back seam. Glue the hem of the skirt onto the bottom of a circular lightweight cardboard base. The circumference of the base is just wide enough to keep the doll from

toppling over. The muslin skirt is now filled with about ½in (1.3cm) of aquarium gravel to give a firm base to the doll. Next is added sawdust, sand or kitty litter to keep your needles sharp (pack firmly). Tightly gather waist seam so no filler can escape; knot ends. A felt circle is glued onto the bottom of the cardboard base to hide the raw edges. Since the doll's skirt will most likely hide your doll's markings, copy the marks onto a paper label; glue label onto base of doll. The doll is now sewn onto the pincushion and dressed. Any soft thin fabric (silk or other similar material) may be used. A simple and often-used method of dressing these dolls is a gathered silk underskirt and a gathered lace overskirt (see *Illustration 4*).

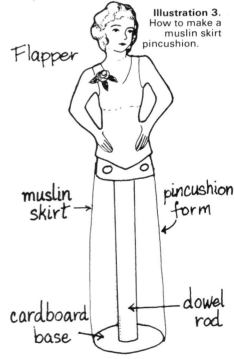

Illustration 3. How to make a muslin skirt pincushion.

1850 to 1860 Style Pincushion Doll: My 3¾in (9.6cm) tall delicately tinted half-doll looks ready for a ball. Her bodice and hair decoration are a pale lavender. She carries a bouquet of orange and yellow flowers. She has quite a wide range with two sew holes. Her hair style and dress are reminiscent of the 1850 to 1860 period when the neckline of a ball gown was off the shoulders and trimmed with flounces. Skirts were wide and gathered at the waist and sometimes

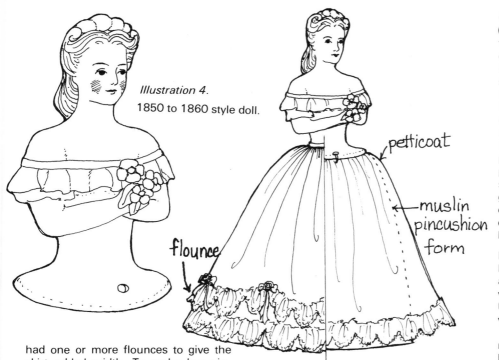

Illustration 4.

1850 to 1860 style doll.

flounce

petticoat

muslin pincushion form

Cut muslin skirt 5¼in (13.4cm) by 4½in (11.5cm). Follow the 1850 to 1860 directions for making her pincushion form except glue waist seam to doll's hips. Cut out skirt patterns. Sew center back seams together. Make the three tucks in the direction of arrows. Sew side darts. Make rolled hems where indicated. Using drawing of doll as a guide, glue waist of skirt to doll. Make a ribbon flower and leaves and tack over tucks. Pin tucks in place, spray with hair spray; let dry. Flapper half-dolls were also dressed in the simple gathered silk underskirt and gathered lace overskirt. If you prefer to dress your flapper in this style, make the cardboard base and muslin skirt slightly larger.

Powder box pincushion doll: If you're lucky enough to have a powder box with a slip-on lid (do not use a screw-on lid), you can convert it into a powder box doll. Use *Illustration 6* as a guide in making your doll.

Measure the length of doll's head; multiply by seven, this will give you the height of the completed doll. Measure height of half-doll and of box bottom; subtract this from height of completed doll. The resulting figure will give you the height of the pincushion form. Follow the directions of the 1850 to 1860 pincushion form except use the box lid as the base of the pincushion and glue the hem of muslin skirt to the sides of box lid. Measure the circumference of the box lid; add a ¼in (.65cm) back seam allowance -- this is width of muslin skirt. Cover sides of powder box with skirt material. Hide raw edges by gluing gold or silver braid to box edges (See *Illustration 6*). Dress doll in a simple gathered silk underskirt and a gathered lace overskirt.

had one or more flounces to give the skirt added width. To make her pincushion form: cut lightweight cardboard and white felt 4in (10.2cm) in diameter. Cut muslin skirt 6½in (16.5cm) by 13in (33cm). Sew a ¼in (.65cm) center back seam. Glue ¼in (.65cm) skirt hem to bottom of cardboard circle, let dry. Glue felt circle and mark label to bottom of cardboard base; let dry. Fill muslin skirt with ½in (1.3cm) of aquarium gravel; fill remainder of skirt with your choice of filler. With a double thread tightly gather waist seam so that no filler will escape; knot ends. To hide the bottom edge of the pincushion form, glue 1in (2.5cm) wide lace around entire edge.

Cut a petticoat out of a piece of white batiste 6½in (16.5cm) by 19in (48.3cm). Sew a ¼in (.65cm) center back seam. Narrowly hem petticoat hem; sew gathered ½in (1.3cm) wide lace to this edge. Tightly gather waist seam and tack onto muslin skirt closing. Center doll on top of pincushion. Sew doll on top of pincushion through sew holes (See *Illustration 4*).

Cut a skirt from a piece of lavender silk 6½in (16.5cm) by 28in (71.1cm). Sew a ¼in (.65cm) center back seam. Narrowly hem skirt. Gather waist seam to fit a waistband cut on the bias from the lavender silk 1in (2.5cm) by 4¼in (10.9cm). Finish off waistband and tack skirt closed around doll's waist. Trim skirt with lace flounces and lavender ribbon rosettes. Adjust folds in skirt; pin in place and spray with hair spray to control folds. Let dry and then remove pins.

Flapper: This haughty 3¼in (8.3cm) half-doll has blonde hair, a light pink

bodice and rose. Her head is 1in (2.5cm), so I made her to stand 7in (17.8cm) high. As flapper styles are straight and slim, I cut her cardboard base only 1½in (3.8cm) in diameter. Since her silhouette is so slim, she needs to have a dowel rod fitted in her waist (See *Illustration 3*). Saw dowel rod off at the point where the doll and rod together measure 7in (17.8cm). Glue one end of rod in doll and other end on center of cardboard base.

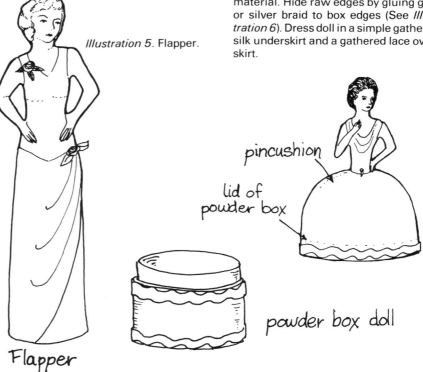

Illustration 5. Flapper.

Flapper

pincushion

lid of powder box

powder box doll

95

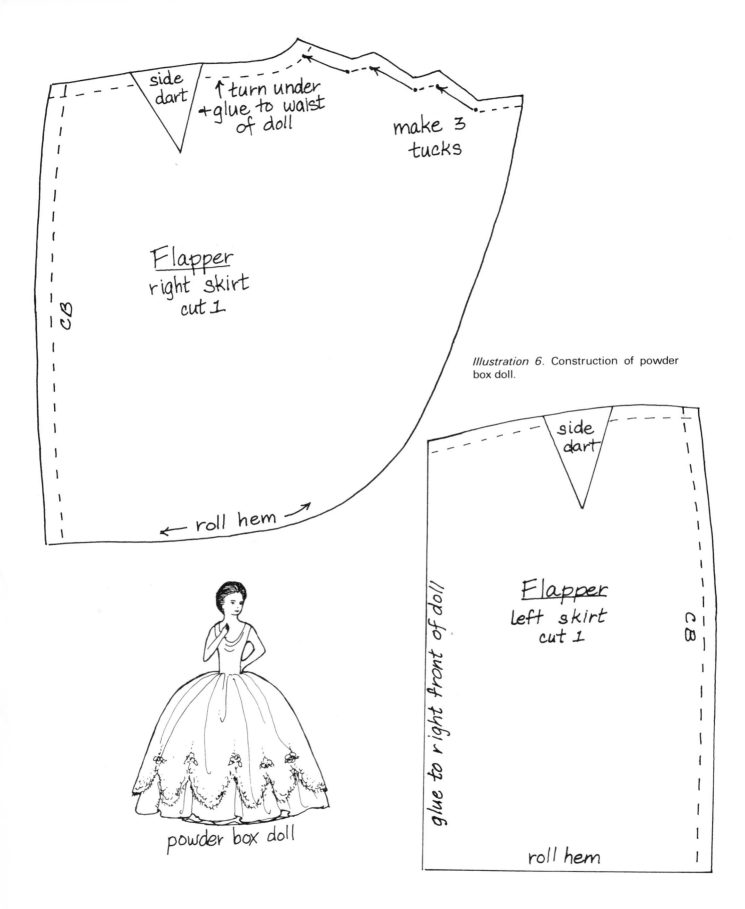

side dart

↑ turn under
+glue to waist
of doll

make 3
tucks

Flapper
right skirt
cut 1

CB

Illustration 6. Construction of powder box doll.

← roll hem →

side dart

Flapper
left skirt
cut 1

CB

glue to right front of doll

roll hem

powder box doll

Jacket Pattern

Including
Stocking Pattern and Hat

Submitted by Dorothy Coleman
and found in the collection of
Widener Library, Harvard
University

From *POUPÉE MODÈLE*, JUNE 1870
**For Doll Number 4 (17-18in. or
43.2-45.7cm)**

The following directions are given for making the paletot for doll number 4. In 1870 doll number 4 was about 45cm tall or 17-18in.

The little paletot with slits is made of white cloth trimmed with two rows of stitching or with a little chain of black embroidery twist. The cuffs and around the collar as well as the buttons are of black velvet. Other suggested trimmings are pleated ribbons or soutache braid. The hatched areas on the pattern represent velvet.

No. 3—One side of the front of the paletot

No. 4—Other side of the front of the paletot

No. 5—Half of the back of the paletot

No. 6 (A & B)—Upper sleeve and Under Sleeve. Sleeve has two lengthwise seams.

No. 7—Stocking for doll No. 2 (14-16in. or 25.6-40.6cm tall). Take an old cotton stocking, fit the pattern along the fold and just above the ankle. For doll No. 4 cut the stocking a little larger all around. How much larger should be determined by measuring the doll's leg.

No. 20—The new style round hat could be purchased at Mme. La-vallée-Peronne's shop, 21 rue de Choiseul, Paris, in the Summer of 1870. It was made of white straw tucked up behind and trimmed with blue satin. The bouquet on top is comprised of a little rose with its leaves and black berries (beads).

Additional Instructions

Before you cut out this pattern, measure your doll and compare these measurements with the pattern pieces. Add ¼in (6.3mm) seam allowance on all edges. Cut out the pattern from paper towelling. Scotch tape pieces together. Try this paper dress on the doll. Make any changes on the pattern pieces. Now cut out the altered pattern from your desired fabric. Good clothes of this period were lined with a glazed tan cotton. Use a thin, fine thread when sewing doll clothes; press each seam after sewing; clip all curves.

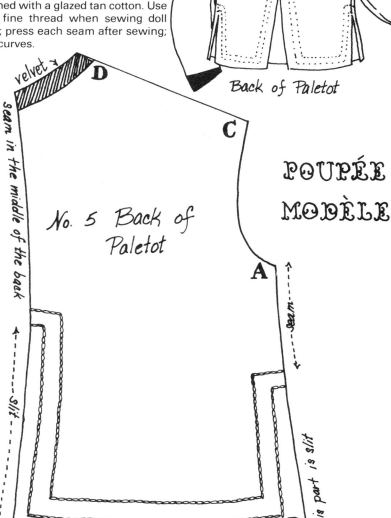

Front of Paletot

Back of Paletot

POUPÉE MODÈLE

velvet

No. 5 Back of Paletot

seam in the middle of the back

seam

slit

this part is slit

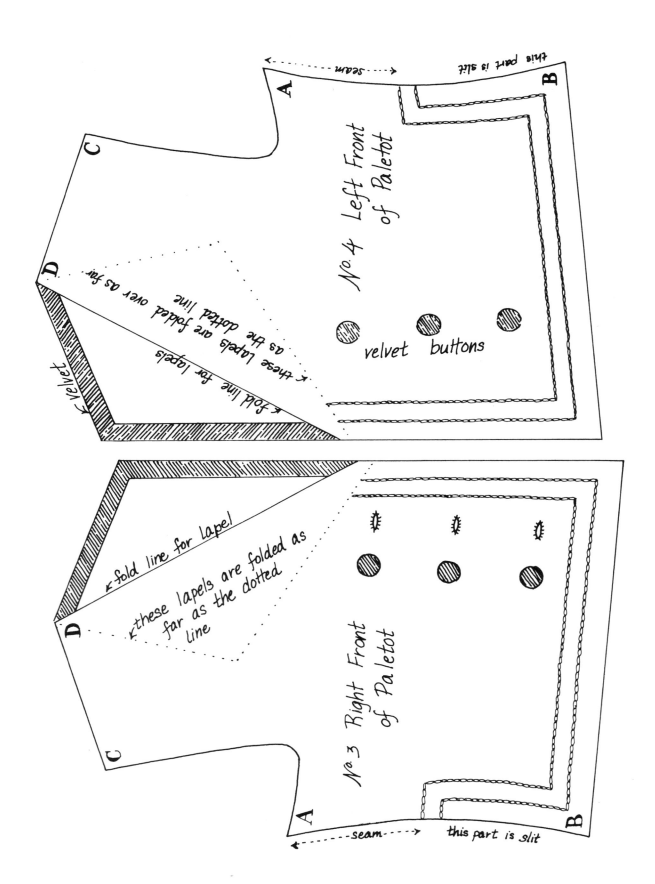

No. 4 Left Front of Paletot

this part is slit

velvet buttons

velvet

fold line for lapels

these lapels are folded over as the dotted line

seam

No. 3 Right Front of Paletot

fold line for lapel

these lapels are folded as far as the dotted line

seam

this part is slit

98

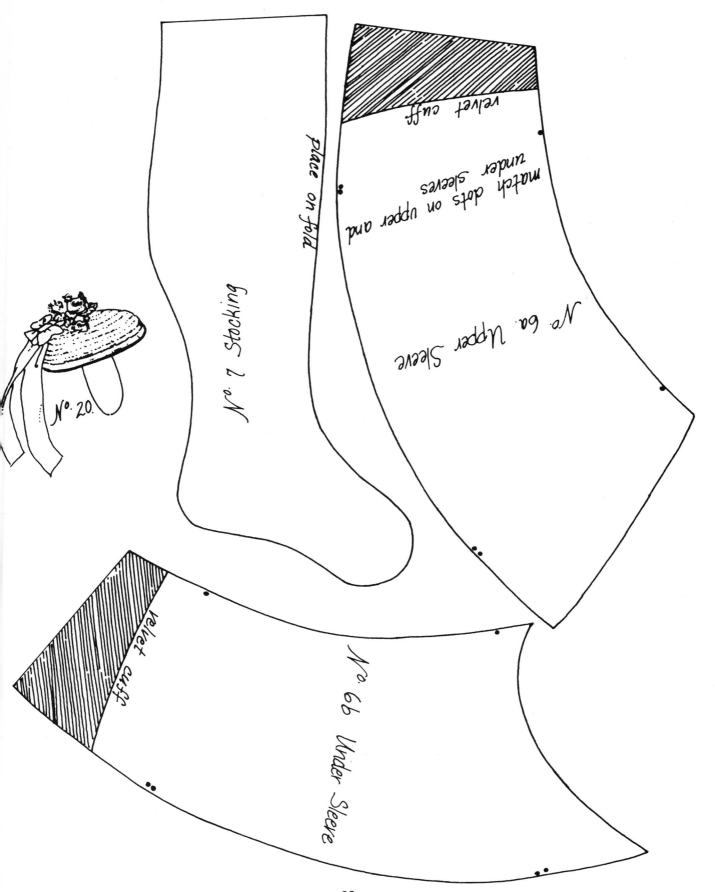

No. 20.

Place on fold

No. 7 Stocking

velvet cuff

match dots on upper and
under sleeves

No. 6a. Upper Sleeve

velvet cuff

No. 6b Under Sleeve

1886 Dress and Bonnet

by Sandy Williams

In the December 26, 1886 issue of *Harper's Bazar,* patterns for a dress and bonnet were featured for a 16in. (40.6cm) doll. The doll's outfit consisted of a "frock made from red cashmere, and the hood is of the same cashmere...Red stockings and bronze slippers" complete the outfit. The sleeve edges, front and back neck edges are shirred. Shirring means to make three or more rows of gathering stitches.

Fine soft and thin wools, silks, muslin, or challis may be substituted for the cashmere. A thin cotton material should be used for the lining. According to *The Mode in Costume,* "colors typical of the period were tender browns, olive, amber and vanilla." All patterns include a ¼in. (6.4mm) seam allowance. Use a fine thin thread and use small stitches. Press after each sewing step.

Dress: Fig. 28 Bodice—cut 1 of cashmere, and one of lining

Fig. 29 Shoulder Strap—cut 2 of cashmere, 2 of lining

Fig. 30 Sleeve—cut 2 of cashmere, 2 of lining

Fig. 27 Bodice Waist Lining—cut 1 of lining

Skirt—cut a 4¾in. by 36in. (12.1cm by 91.4cm) piece of cashmere

Sash—18in. (45.7cm) of 1in. (2.5cm) wide matching satin ribbon

With right sides of shoulder straps and their lining together, sew a ¼in. (6.4mm) seam from Nos. 64 to 61; turn right-side-out. Pin shoulder straps to front and back bodice matching numbers. With right sides of bodice and bodice lining together sew a ¼in (6.4mm) seam along one CB seam across neck edge of one back bodice; sew across neck edge of front bodice; then back across the other neck edge of back bodice then down remaining back CB edge; clip corner; turn right-side-out and press.

Shirr (machine gather) the front bodice between the Nos. 61 very close to neck edge, machine gather ⅜in. (9.5mm) down from first row of gathers three more times (total four rows of gathering); pull gathers to space of 3in. (7.6cm) across front bodice; machine-stitch over each gathering thread; remove gathering thread. Shirr the back bodice ¼in (6.4mm) in from center back edges to No. 64 following the front bodice shirring directions, except pull gathering threads

to a width of 1½in (3.8cm). Repeat with remaining back bodice.

With waist edges of bodice and its lining together, pleat X on • around bottom edge. Turn ¼in. (6.4mm) seams of back and top edges of Fig. 27 (lining) in and sew the remaining raw edge of Fig. 27 to bodice (Fig. 28) lower edge from Nos. 59 to 60; sew Fig. 27 and 28 together at *. Baste CB edges of Fig. 27 and 28 together.

With right sides of sleeve and its lining together sew bottom edges together; turn right-side-out and press. Shirr bottom edge of sleeve using front bodice directions except use only three rows of gathers and pull gathering threads so shirring is 4in. (10.2cm) wide. Gather sleeve cap between dots to fit shoulder straps and armhole; sew together. Trim armhole seams. Sew sleeve underarm seam together.

Cut a skirt of cashmere 4¾in. by 36in. (12.1 by 91.4cm). Turn up a 1in. (2.5cm) hem; box pleat the other long edge to fit bodice waistline. Sew bodice and skirt together using a ¼in. (6.4mm)

seam; sew CB skirt edges together. The back of bodice is fastened with buttons and buttonholes or snaps. A ribbon sash is tied around the dropped dress waistline and tied into a large bow towards the side of the skirt.

Bonnet: Fig. 31 Crown Lining—cut 1 of lining material

Fig. 32 Crown—cut 1 of cashmere

Fig. 33 Ruffle—cut 1 of cashmere 42in (106.7cm) of ½in. (12.7mm) wide matching satin ribbon

Pin and baste all pleats on crown and lining by placing X on •.

With right side of ruffle together (fold ruffle in half lengthwise), sew each end together; trim each seam; turn right-side-out and press; treat double thickness of ruffle as one piece of material. Make a total of eight box pleats across ruffle by placing X on • in direction of arrows; pin and baste pleats; press.

Match CF (No. 67) of ruffle to CF (No. 67) of crown by laying right side of ruffle on right side of crown. Pin and sew ruffle around front edge of crown (you may find it necessary to take up or let out each ruffle slightly). With ruffle in same position, place the right side of lining on right side of crown. Pin and sew lining to crown from Nos. 50 to 68 to CB (No. 69) to 68 to 50 on other side; trim seam and clip corners; turn right-side-out. Blind-stitch rest of front opening closed. Sew a 9in. (22.9cm) length of ½in. (12.7mm) wide satin ribbon tie to * edge of ruffle. Use about two 24in. (61cm) of remaining ribbon to make ribbon loops as pictured (with the two ends of loops straight up in the air) and tack to CF point of lining.

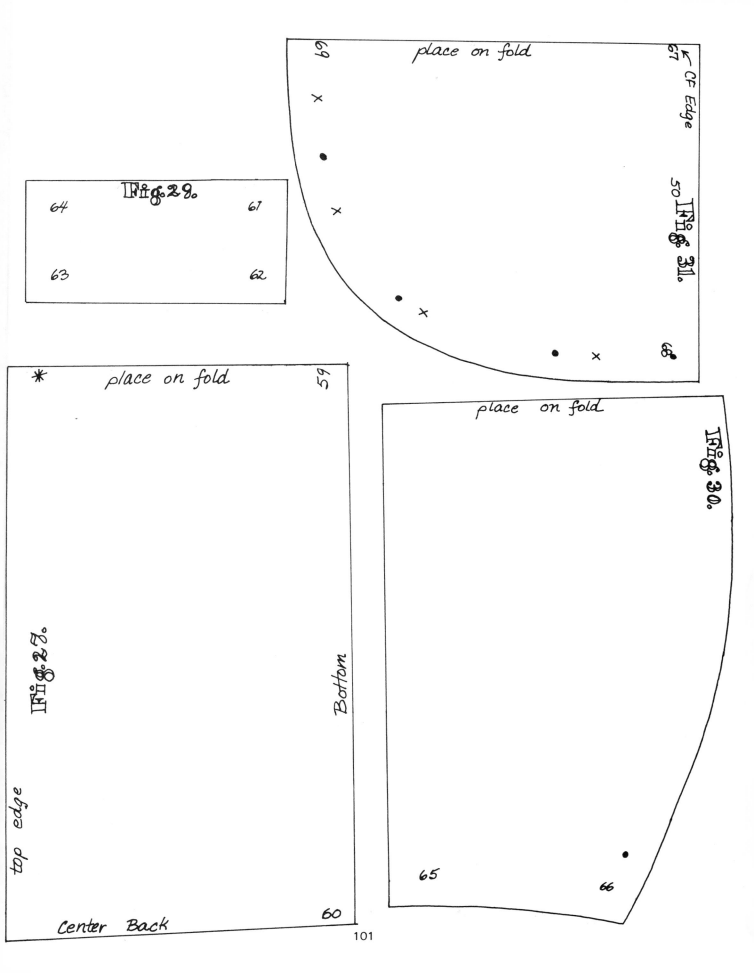

Fig. 29.

64   61

63   62

place on fold ← CF Edge

69

Fig. 31.

50

68

place on fold

Fig. 30.

65   66

* place on fold 59

Fig. 27.

Bottom

top edge

Center Back 60

101

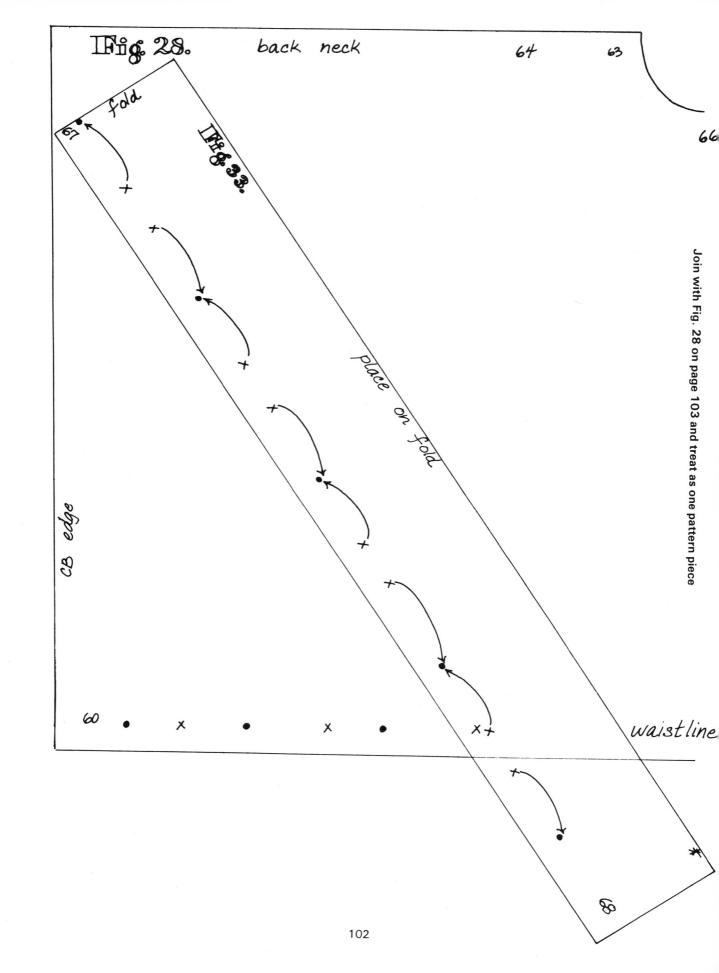

Fig. 28.

back neck

64

63

66

fold

Fig. 33.

place on fold

CB edge

Join with Fig. 28 on page 103 and treat as one pattern piece

60

waistline

68

62   61   front neck

place on fold — CF

Join with Fig. 28 on page 102 and treat as one pattern piece

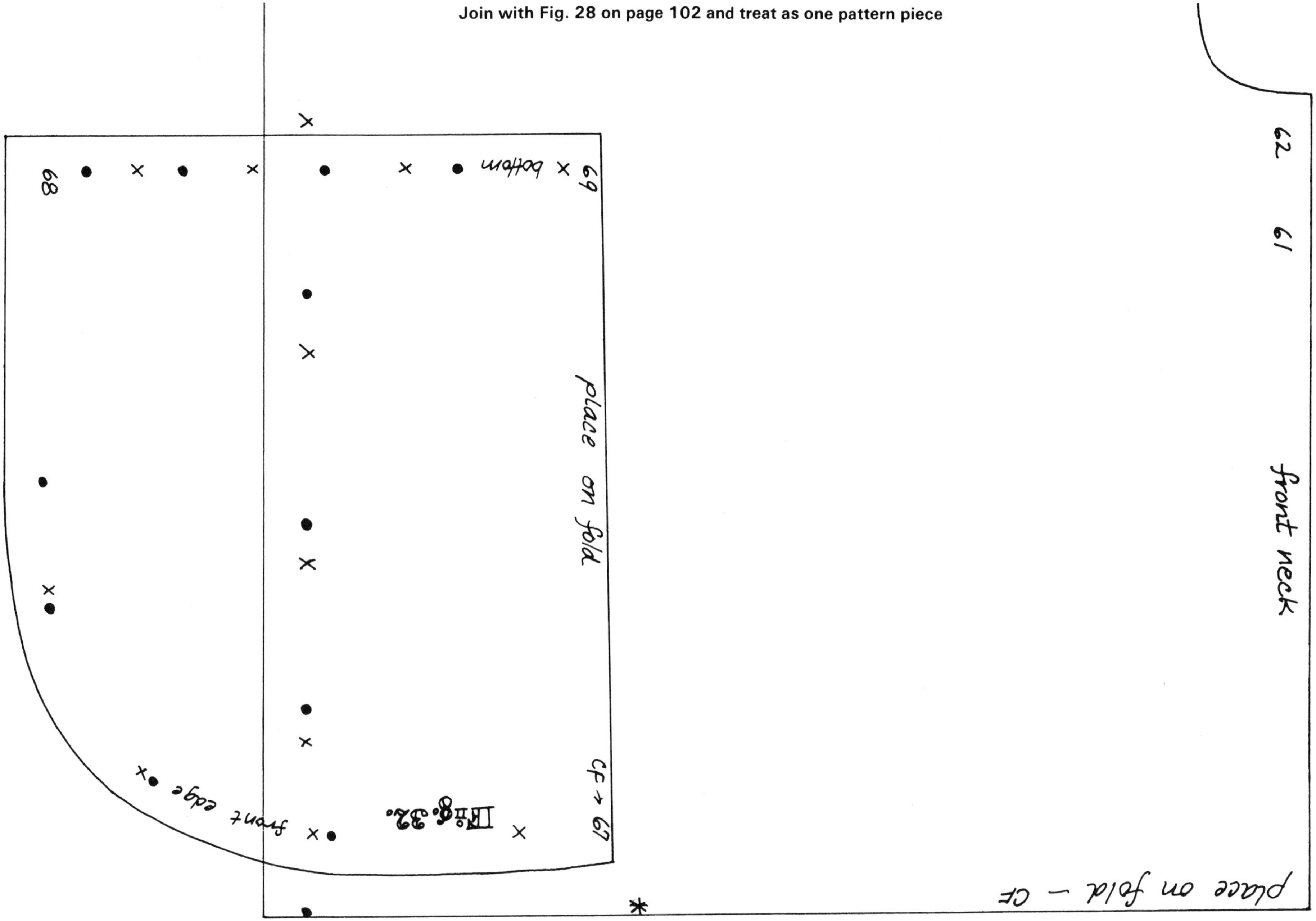

*

69   place on fold   CF → 67

× bottom

×

×

Fig. 32.

×

×

×

×   ●   ×   ● ×   ● ×   ×

front edge

×

×

×

68   × ●

Summer Costume Pattern

Submitted by Dorothy Coleman and found in the collection of Widener Library, Harvard University

From *POUPÉE MODÈLE*, AUGUST 1880
For Doll Number 4 (a 14-17-1/2" doll)

Directions for making a Summer Costume for doll No. 4 as given in *Poupée Modèle*, August, 1880. Doll number 4 is a lady or girl doll, size 4.

"This costume can be made of linen or cotton in blue, rose or gray. It can also be made with two colors combined or indeed it can be made of dotted swiss with the dots the same shade as the background. Another variation could be natural colored wool with bell shaped gilded buttons. On the cotton or linen one would put pearl or bone buttons.

"This simple little costume is in very good taste and will be becoming indeed to Miss Lily."

Miss Lily was the name given to Poupée No. 4.

Pattern No. 19. Front of costume for Poupée No. 4.

Pattern No. 19bis. Vest attached to the front.

Pattern No. 20. The small side piece of the costume.

Pattern No. 21. Half of the back.

Pattern No. 22. Half of the collar of the costume, fold on dotted line.

Pattern No. 23. Sleeve, front and back of sleeve, **sleeve has two length-wise seams.**

Pattern No. 24. Reverse of sleeve, cut double. This appears to be the cuff pattern and not the lining.

Pattern No. 25. Height and width of the pleats that form the skirt at the bottom of the costume of Poupée No. 4.

ADDITIONAL INSTRUCTIONS

Doll number 4 is a lady or girl doll—number 4 denoting a 14—17-1/2" doll.

Before you cut out this pattern, measure your doll and compare these measurements with the pattern pieces. Add 1/4" seam allowance on all edges. Cut out the pattern from paper towelling. Scotch tape pieces together. Try this paper dress on the doll. Make any changes on the pattern pieces. Now cut out the altered pattern from your desired fabric. Good clothes of this period were lined with a glazed tan cotton. Use a thin, fine thread when sewing doll clothes; press each seam after sewing; clip all curves.

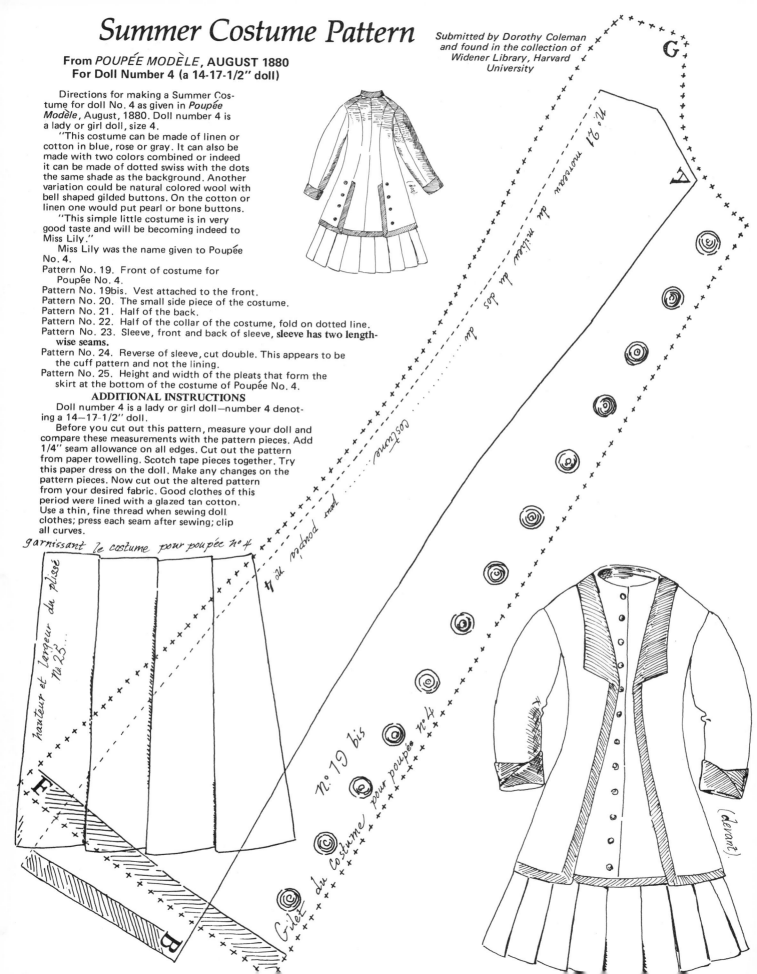

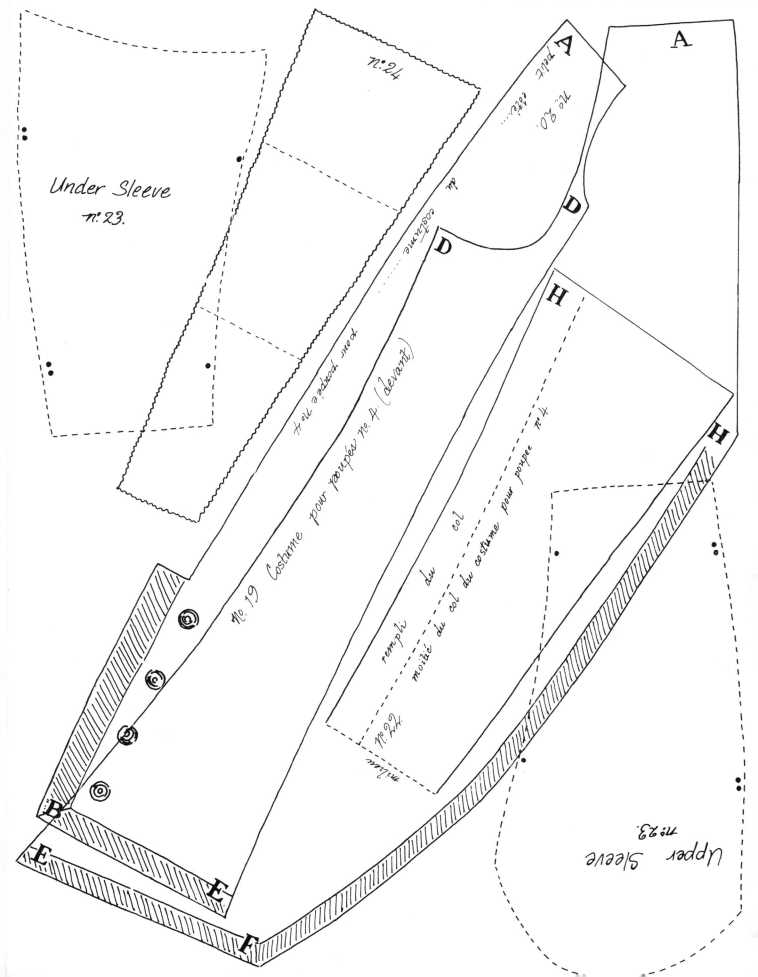

Under Sleeve
nº 23.

nº 24

A

nº 20 petit côté
du costume

A

D

D

H

H

nº 19 Costume pour poupées nº 4 (devant)

pour poupée nº 4

rempli du col

moitié du col du costume pour poupée nº 4

nº 24

Upper Sleeve
nº 23.

B

E

E

E

F

Editor's note: This is a reprint of the January 1881 "Styles for Dolls" section of *The Delineator*. They represent a very authentic source for doll costumers.

Illustration 1. Lady dolls' walking costume.

Illustration 2. Lady dolls' costume.

Lady dolls' walking costume.

Madamoiselle Dolly is here dressed very stylishly and looks as if she were perfectly conscious of it. There is no doubt but that she feels a little vain, and you can scarcely blame her, she is so prettily arrayed. Her skirt is four-gored, and is trimmed with a wide flounce below a narrow one, each laid in kiltplaits, and the top one stitched down close to its edge. You need not put so much trimming on the skirt unless you want to, as it is just as stylish with no trimming at all or with a very narrow one. The suit is made of cashmere, but the top flounce is of silk.

The polonaise is of the pretty princess style, and is neatly fitted, and draped high at the sides to form the side-points seen in the picture. The edge is trimmed with lace, which is headed by a tiny silk plaiting, while the wrist of the sleeve is finished to correspond. A dainty collar, also edged with lace, is about the neck and meets over a pretty cravat of ribbon.

The polonaise and skirt are separately shown in *Illustration 7* where you may see another method of making them up. The two models are in *Illustration 7* which is in seven sizes for dolls from 12in (30.5cm) to 24in (61cm) tall.

The lovely little bonnet is of velvet, trimmed with ribbon and an ostrich tip.

Lady dolls' costume.

Here is a doll who looks very matronly, and who knows but she heads a family of doll boys and girls? Anyhow, she is dressed just as your mamma is and has a long skirt of plain silk daintily trimmed with a narrow plaiting of the same. To this skirt are attached a shirred and plaited side-drapery, and a straight back-drapery with deep scallops at the bottom. The side-drapery is prettily trimmed with fringe, and the back-drapery is crossed by a strap of the brocade to hold it in place. There is a part of the front-gore between the two draperies that may be left plain, or you can cover it with rows of fringe, lace, plaiting, puffing, and so forth.

The basque has a short front and a pretty coattail back, and is as snugly fitted as you could wish. Its edges are finished with under-facings, and the neck and wrists are bordered with ruffles of lace.

You can use all one material or two or three fabrics in making up this costume; and by referring to *Illustration 5*, you will see another pretty way of decorating the garments. The patterns to both basque and skirt are to be found in *Illustration 5*, which is in seven sizes for lady dolls from 12in (30.5cm) to 24in (61cm) long.

Girl dolls' slip costume

A baby girl or boy always looks very cunning in a short, full slip with a gay sash of silk or ribbon, and so does the dolly whom you play is a baby or a very little girl or boy. There is nothing elaborate about the making of the garment, as there are only two yoke portions and two skirt-and-body portions gathered to the yoke, and neat little sleeves finished with lace and insertion. The joining of the yoke is also concealed by a frill of lace and a row of insertion, and there is a jaunty little bow of ribbon at the throat. The slip is trimmed at the bottom with two frills of lace and a row of insertion, and you may add a few tucks if you like.

Cambric, Swiss, lawn or linen may be used for this little slip, which you can trim with white and colored lace or embroidery, or make perfectly plain. The model to this costume is found in *Illustration 9* in seven sizes for girl dolls from 12in (30.5cm) to 24in (61cm) tall.

Illustration 3. Girl dolls' slip costume.

Girl dolls' street costume

This charming and stylish little costume is made of flannel, and is very plainly completed. It consists of a skirt and basque permanently united, so that both garments are put on at once. The skirt is four-gored and is hemmed up at the bottom, while the top of its back-breadth is neatly shirred before the belt is added. A strip of material is sewed across the gores and turned up in the "washer-woman" style of drapery. The basque is fitted in the same way that all the dolls' basques are, having a dart at each side, a center seam and side-back

Illustration 4. Girl dolls' street costume.

seams. The back and side-back skirts are divided into two tabs, and each is plaited or gathered at the bottom and tacked to the skirt over the end of the drapery strip, a knotted and tasseled cord being fastened over the ends.

You may line the tabs, the drapery and the wrists of the sleeves with gay silk, and place a knot of the same at the throat, where the standing collar meets, if you want the costume to be a little showy. You may also place a narrow plaiting of gay satin under the hem of the skirt, if you like; and bows of gay ribbon may be used in place of the cord and tassels. If you refer to *Illustration 6*, you will see how pretty the suit looks made up of striped goods. The model to the costume will be found in *Illustration 6*, which also contains a cosy little dressing sack and a very dainty little apron. The set is in seven sizes for girl dolls from 12in (30.5cm) to 24in (61cm) tall.

The hat is of the Derby style and is made of felt.

Illustration 5. lady dolls' set consisting of a coat basque and demi-train skirt.

Lady dolls' set, consisting of a coat basque and demi-train skirt.

How fortunate for dolly that these pretty patterns are ready just in season for the holidays, when all good dolls and good girls have pretty things sent to them. The costume comprised in this set is composed of a coat basque and a demi-trained skirt, and will be suitable to wear to any festivities to which dollies are invited.

Lady dolls coat basque.

The material represented is suit goods of the blue tint you see in peacock's feathers, and the trimmings are little gilt buttons and silk pipings. The closing edges of the front are turned under in straight hems and are slightly pointed at each side below these hems. There is a tiny dart in each side, and at the back are side-gores and a curving center seam, which perform the fitting. The center seam is not closed from a little below the waistline, and has narrow extra widths allowed on its edges, which are folded under for hems. The center and side-backs are a great deal longer than the fronts and fall in long coattails, which are made to look very pretty by having buttons arranged in rows upon the side-back seams. All the edges are piped with silk, and the pretty, coat-shaped sleeve is finished at the wrist with piping and decorated with three buttons. The collar is a straight band sloped off at the corners and edged with piping.

Lady dolls' demi-train skirt.

Perhaps you may think it is difficult to make this skirt, but it really is not. This is the way it is done. A front-gore, a gore for each side and a back-breadth are cut and joined together, and then the draperies are added. Upon each side there is a piece, which is laid up in plaits at its back edge and shirred twice about 1in (2.5cm) from the front. It is placed upon the skirt, with the tops of the parts even and its back edge over the side-back seam of the skirt, and is stitched there and along the shirring. The back-drapery is formed of a piece that is slashed through the center for a placket-opening in the same manner as the skirt and is shaped at the bottom in a broad tab between two narrower ones. It is sewed over the skirt so as to conceal the seam of the side-draperies as far as the second plait from the bottom in each of these; and all its edges, as well as the side-draperies, are finished with pipings of silk. The top is gathered, and so is the breadth of the skirt, and a belt is sewed to the skirt and draperies at once. Straps of the material, piped with silk, are

sewed just above the places where the seams end that join the back-drapery to the skirt, and the ends of these straps are pointed and fastened together with a buckle. Three pairs of ribbons are fastened under the shirred edges of the side-draperies and tied together in bows at the center, just as you see them in *Illustration 5*.

Now you see how easy it is to make the whole suit. *Illustration 2*, may be seen as another pretty illustration of this skirt and basque, as worn by dolly. You can put a tiny plaiting or a ruffle on the bottom of the skirt if you like, but it is just as fashionable to have it plain. Any kind of material is suitable for such a costume, but, of course, if you have a piece of silk or velvet or some other rich goods, so much the better. If you have only enough for the basque, you can use it for that, and make the skirt of something else, and it will also be very fashionable.

This set is in seven sizes for lady dolls from 12in (30.5cm) to 24in (61cm) tall. Of material 22in (55.9cm) wide, 1⅝yd (1.46m) are needed in making the costume for a lady doll 22in (55.9cm) tall.

Girl dolls' set, consisting of a walking costume, dressing sack and apron.

It seems as if the dolls' dressmaker was doing her best to design charming styles for the girl dollies, and many of the most beautiful ones she has provided are like those furnished for yourself. Of course, it pleases you to have dolly's toilettes like your own.

Illustration 6. Girl dolls' set consisting of a walking costume, dressing sack and apron.

Girl dolls' walking costume.

This costume is really composed of a skirt and a long basque, but the two are tacked permanently together, so that they are both slipped on or off Miss Dolly at once. The material selected for the dress is striped cambric, and pipings of cardinal cambric and ribbon bows form the trimming. The skirt is composed of a front-gore, a gore for each side and a back-breadth. After the gores are joined together, the flat scarf-drapery you see is placed over them and run along its lower edge and then turned so that the seam cannot be seen, and the ends are sewed in with the side-gore seams. The back-breadth has six rows of gathering across the top at distances of about 3/4in (2cm) apart, and this forms what is called "gauging" and is very stylish. Very likely, some of your mamma's dresses are made this way. The left side seam is open for a short distance from the top for a placket, and the top of the skirt is sewed to a belt. The basque is folded underneath for hems at the closing and is closed with buttonholes and little porcelain buttons, and below the last button and buttonhole it is cut away diagonally. There is a dart in each side of the front, and the back has side-backs and a curving center seam, which fit it beautifully. The center seam is closed only to a short distance below the waistline, and the ends of each center portion and the side-back next to it are plaited in a long tab, which reaches far below the front of the basque and is fastened upon the skirt at the bottom of the scarf-drapery under a ribbon bow, showing the gauging very prettily. The sleeve is in coat shape, and the neck is completed with a little standing collar. The top of the scarf, the wrists of the sleeves, the collar and the edges of the basque are all piped with cardinal.

Either woolen or cotton materials make up nicely into dresses of this style, and if you have two pretty varieties of goods, you can make the skirt of one kind and the basque and drapery of another. If you prefer trimming on the skirt, you can add a tiny ruffle or plaiting under or over the lower edge, but much trimming is not fashionable upon such skirts, and, of course, you do not wish your dolly to be unfashionably dressed.

Girl dolls' dressing sack.

When Dolly wants to be comfortable in an "at home" sort of way, she needs a dressing sack, and here is one so pretty that it seems suitable for any occasion requiring her company. It is made of swiss and is fitted by seams upon the shoulders and under the arms, and a seam through the center of the back. The fronts are sloped away a trifle, and all the edges are finished with a row of lace headed by a row of swiss insertion, the same being continued about the neck. The center seam is concealed by a row of insertion between two rows of lace, and a little bow of bright ribbon is fastened at the throat. The sleeve is a shape that we sometimes call the "angel" sleeve, because it is so wide at the wrist. It has but one seam, and is trimmed with lace and insertion.

Nainsook, lawn, muslin, print, cambric and bright or delicately tinted flannels and cashmeres make up beautifully into dressing sacks of this style, and if you trim them with embroidery, narrow bands, lace, tiny ruffles or velvet, your dolly cannot fail to be pleased.

Girl dolls' apron.

"Such a cunning little apron," you will say, when you behold this charming little model. "Just what I need to make Dolly appear neat and tidy. "Well, it is very easy to make, and a small piece of nainsook will form a very pretty one. The top is shaped to form a heart-shaped bib, and the bottom is gracefully curved. All the edges are bordered with narrow lace edging, and ties of the material are sewed to the corners and buttoned at the back.

Lawn, swiss, muslin or plain or figured wash goods of any kind will make pretty aprons, and the only trimming they need is a narrow edging, a ruffle or a little band.

This set is in seven sizes for girl dolls from 12in (30.5cm) to 24in (61cm) tall. To make the costume for a girl doll 22in (55.9cm) tall, will require 5/8yd (.55m) of material 36in (91.4cm) wide. It will also require 3/8yd (.33m) of material for the sack, and 1/4yd (.23m) for the apron, each 36in (91.4cm) wide.

Illustration 7. Lady dolls' set.

Lady dolls' set consisting of a walking skirt and polonaise.

In this set there are two pretty and useful garments. The polonaise may be worn with any other style of skirt and the skirt with any other overdress. The material used in making them in this instance is white cashmere, and the trimming consists of ruffles of the same and black velvet ribbon.

Lady dolls' walking skirt.

A front-gore, a gore for each side and a back-breadth are used in making the skirt, and the front-gore is fitted smoothly, while the side-gores and breadth are slightly gathered at the top before being sewed to the belt. The placket opening is made at the center of the breadth. Three narrow bias ruffles trim the bottom of the skirt, each of them being gathered at the top, with the upper one just far enough from the edge to form its own heading.

Illustration 8. Lady dolls' set.

Lady dolls' polonaise.

The polonaise folds under in hems at the closing edges and has a dart in each side of the front, and its back is fitted by side-back seams and a center seam, all of which end just a little way below the waistline. There is some extra fullness at the ends of these seams, which is laid in plaits that make the back just full enough to be stylish and pretty. There are two upward-turning plaits folded in each back edge of the front, and two turning downward in each edge of the back; and tapes are fastened under them and tied together to hold the drapery gracefully about Miss Dolly's figure. Another tape is fastened to the plaits below the waistline at one end and to the skirt lower down at the other. The back of the polonaise falls in two deep points, and all the lower edges are bordered with a band of velvet ribbon, which continues up each side of the front to the shoulder seam. The sleeve is in coat shape and is trimmed at the wrist with a band of velvet ribbon, and the neck is finished with a little standing collar.

If you add a row of lace under the velvet, it will enrich the suit very much; but either one is a pretty trimming when used alone. Any material suitable for yourself or your mamma is advisable for a skirt and polonaise made by these models, and it is just as fashionable to make the polonaise of one kind and the skirt of another as to have them alike. Sometimes the skirt is made up perfectly plain and the polonaise is cut in scallops and bound with bright color. You can see just how your own Dolly may look in *Illustration 1*, in forming a pretty street toilette.

This set is in seven sizes for lady dolls from 12in (30.5cm) to 24in (61cm) tall. To make this stylish costume for a lady doll 22in (55.9cm) tall, will require 1¼yd (1.14m) of material 22in (55.9cm) wide.

Girl dolls' set, consisting of a yoke slip and jacket.

One of the prettiest dresses for either a real live girl or a girl dolly is a slip, and we are sure you will think so if you make a yoke slip like the one here illustrated.

Girl dolls' yoke slip.

The material is swiss, and the body of the slip is formed of the parts joined by seams under the arms. It is gathered at the top and sewed to a yoke, which has seams upon the shoulder and is open at the center of the back, where its ends are turned under for hems. The back of the slip is also open for some inches, and its overlapping edge is turned under for a hem. The yoke is made entirely of strips of swiss and lace insertion, and is edged with a row of lace set on under a tiny band. Upon the bottom of the slip is a

row of swiss insertion between two rows of lace insertion, and below is a row of wider lace. The sleeve is in coat shape and is trimmed at the wrist with a row of lace headed by two rows of insertion. Buttonholes and little pearl buttons close the back. A sash of pale blue ribbon is gracefully arranged low down about the slip, and is tied in a large, double bow-knot at the back.

Lawn, nainsook, plain or figured cambric, fine muslin or, indeed, any kind of dress goods makes up prettily in such slips for girl dollies, and embroidery, narrow ruffles, bias bands and other neat trimmings are pretty upon them. You can tuck a piece for the yoke, or you can make it of plain cloth, and in either event it will be pretty. Another pretty representation of this elegant little garment may be seen by referring to *Illustration 3*.

Girl dolls' jacket.

A comfortable jacket for dolly to wear upon cool mornings over her slip or any other dress, forms the remainder of this set. It is made of blue flannel, and is prettily fitted by seams under the arms and a seam through the center of the back. It is cut in deep scallops around the bottom and bound with white braid. The fronts turn under for hems and are closed with buttonholes and pearl buttons, and the neck is finished with a little sailor collar bound all around with braid. The sleeve is in coat shape, and is rounded off a little toward the outside seam and is finished with braid and daintily ornamented with a button at the end of the seam. Cashmere, silk, flannel of any color and a great many other materials are useful in making such

sacks as these, and as the model only requires a small quantity of goods, no doubt you will make your doll happy by providing her with two or three of different colors. Narrow lace, bias bands or pipings are pretty decorations for such a sack.

This set is in seven sizes for girl dolls from 12in (30.5cm) to 24in (61cm) tall. Of material 22in (55.9cm) wide, 1/2yd (.46m) is needed in making the jacket for a girl doll 22in (55.9cm) tall; 3/4yd (.69m) of goods 36in (91.4cm) wide will suffice for the yoke slip.

Illustration 9. Girl dolls' set consisting of a yoke slip and jacket.

DOLLS N' THINGS
Cape, Hat and Muff
by Sandy Williams

The cape, hat and muff presented here are designed to fit a slim lady doll 10in (25.4cm) to 12in (30.5cm) tall.

These winter outer garments are made in black cotton velvet and lined in a thin broadcloth or silk. I suggest sewing them with silk thread or the new very fine thread now put out to sew light-weight fabrics -- the regular thread is too bulky for very small doll clothes. Check the fit of the garments on your doll first by making them up in muslin, making the necessary adjustments and then cutting the patterns out in velvet.

Cape: The cape is lined except for the collar. The velvet cape is made separately from the lining so no raw seams can be seen when the cape is completed. The two sections are then sewn together in the final step. Sew shoulder seam of the front piece to shoulder seam of back piece. Gather sleeve tops between dots and star, pin sleeve to cape sides matching star and dots, pull gathers to fit cape shoulder, sew. With the right sides of velvet collars together, sew along top edge, turn right side out, press, baste collar to cape neckline. With right sides of velvet cape and lining facing each other, sew around entire edge of cape leaving the bottom back edge open, turn cape right side out through this opening, blindstitch opening closed, press. Sew a hook and eye on inside of cape at front neck to close cape.

Hat: For *each* pattern piece cut two out of velvet and one out of iron-on interfacing. Hat Brim 1: first, iron the interfacing to the wrong side of one velvet piece. With the right sides of the 1 Hat Brims facing each other, sew around the brim leaving a large opening through which to turn the brim right side out, blindstitch the opening closed. Follow the same instructions for each of the three remaining hat pieces. Each completed hat section is then blindstitched together to form the hat as illustrated except for A and B edges which are tightly gathered and then blindstitched together. The hat may be trimmed with fluffy white feathers and ribbon loops (use ¼in [.65cm] wide ribbon). Pin the hat on to the doll's head by using round-headed straight pins.

Muff: Gather velvet piece to fit lining. With right sides of velvet muff and lining together, sew along the two gathered edges, turn right side out. Turn the two raw end edges in and stitch closed. Blindstitch the two edges together to form the muff. Bend doll's arms so she has both hands in her muff. Since violets were so popular in the 1890s, pin a miniature bouquet of them to her muff or cape.

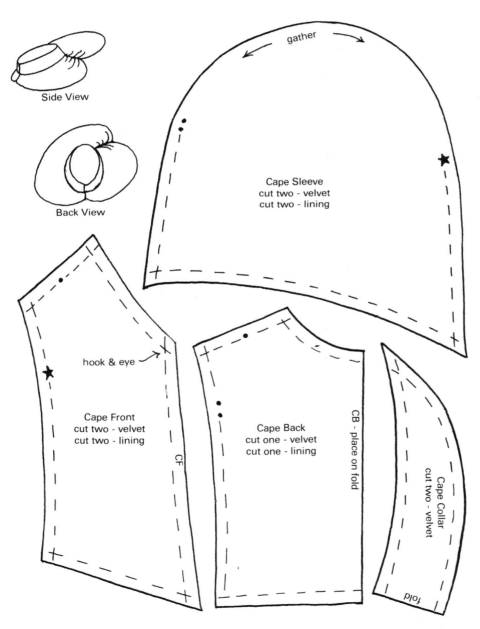

Side View

Back View

gather

Cape Sleeve
cut two - velvet
cut two - lining

hook & eye

Cape Front
cut two - velvet
cut two - lining

CF

Cape Back
cut one - velvet
cut one - lining

CB - place on fold

Cape Collar
cut two - velvet

fold

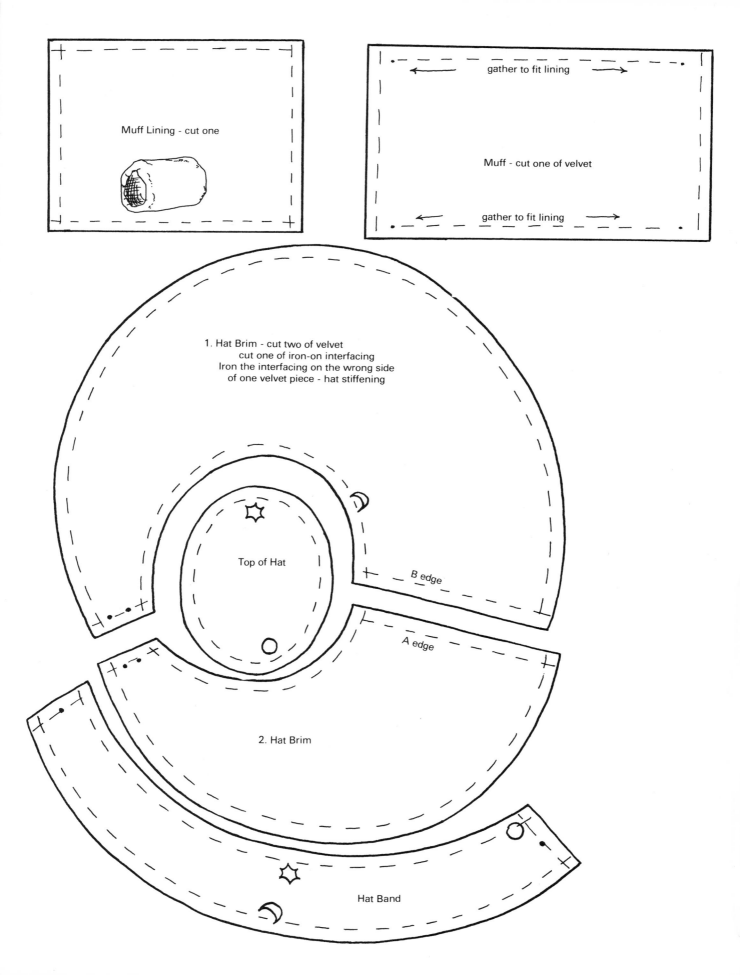

Muff Lining - cut one

gather to fit lining

Muff - cut one of velvet

gather to fit lining

1. Hat Brim - cut two of velvet
   cut one of iron-on interfacing
   Iron the interfacing on the wrong side
   of one velvet piece - hat stiffening

Top of Hat

B edge

A edge

2. Hat Brim

Hat Band

DOLLS N' THINGS

Doll's Shoes and Puritan Doll's Bonnet

by Sandy Williams

These two original patterns first appeared in the *Doll's Dressmaker Magazine:* the Doll's Shoes in the September 1892 issue and the Doll's Puritan Bonnet in the April 1892 issue.

The shoes fit a 14in (35.6cm) to 18in (45.7cm) doll. I made the shoes up in red satin, with red satin ribbon binding and a red satin rosette instead of the buckle and bow. You may make these shoes out of satin, felt, velvet, vinyl or as the magazine states "from a pair of mamma's old kid gloves, using the good part from the long wrists, or they look pretty made from chamois skin." It is easier to work with your fabric if you first back it with iron-on interfacing before cutting the shoe out -- this gives body to the shoe and keeps the fabric from fraying.

MATERIALS NEEDED: Scraps of satin, 24in (61cm) of 1/4in (.65cm) satin ribbon (30in [76.2cm] if you are also making the rosettes); iron-on interfacing, two 5/16in (.75cm) pearl shank buttons (perhaps old glove buttons); small piece of shirt cardboard (inner sole); leather (outer sole -- from old purses, clothes); white glue; paint for buckle and clear fingernail polish.

First, back the satin with the iron-on interfacing, then cut out the heel and band piece, the instep piece and the bow. Sew the heel and band piece to the instep piece where you see the numbers 1. Bind the shoe with the ribbon as indicated by the pattern or you may work a buttonhole stitch around the same area.

Next, cut an inner sole piece from the shirt cardboard and place it inside the shoe, slash shoe bottom to seam line around entire bottom and glue to the bottom of shoe sole. Dry. Cut an outer sole piece out of leather and glue to the bottom of the inner sole; hold in place until dry. When dry, sew a button on one end of the ankle band and cut a buttonhole in the other end of the ankle band.

With an X-acto knife cut the buckle out of leather or shirt cardboard. Paint the buckle gold, silver or black; and to give the buckle "shine," paint it with several coats of clear fingernail polish. Put the bow through the buckle and glue to front of shoe. You may wish to omit the buckle and make a ribbon rosette to replace it. To make a ribbon rosette, simply gather a 2 1/2in (6.4cm) length of ribbon along one edge and pull tight to make a flower rosette; tuck raw edges under and tack one rosette, to front of each shoe.

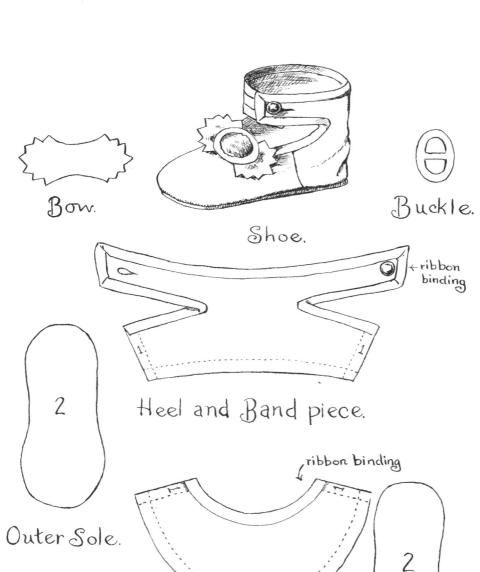

Bow.

Shoe.

Buckle.

← ribbon binding

Heel and Band piece.

2

Outer Sole.

ribbon binding

Instep piece.

2

Inner Sole.

3in (7.6cm) square

Side Head Piece.

cut two

nape of neck.

Doll's Puritan Bonnet.

5in (12.7cm) by 2in (5.1cm) wide

Center Head Piece.

cut one

nape of neck

The Puritan Doll's Bonnet fits a 12in (30.5cm) to 14in (35.6cm) doll. I made this bonnet up in red velvet with a red silk lining and trimmed it in white fake fur. A red satin ribbon ties the bonnet under the chin.

MATERIALS NEEDED: 18in (45.7cm) of ⅝in (1.6cm) red satin ribbon, scraps of red velvet and red silk and 14in (35.6cm) of ½in (1.3cm) wide fake white fur (perhaps cut from old clothes).

First, make the bonnet up in muslin, making the necessary adjustments to fit your doll's head. Cut two side head pieces and one center bonnet piece out of both velvet and silk. Sew the side head pieces to the center piece, easing to fit -- do this to both the velvet and silk. With the right sides of the velvet and silk bonnets facing each other, sew around the outside edge of bonnet, leaving 2in (5.1cm) open at nape of neck. Turn right side out through this opening, tuck raw edges in and blindstitch closed. Press. Cut the 18in (45.7cm) piece of ribbon in half and tack one to each front bottom side of the bonnet. Blindstitch the bottom.

LET'S MAKE A CHRISTMAS BONNET

FOR THAT SPECIAL DOLL

by DOROTHY NOELL

The Christmas season is coming upon us, and with it that happy festive spirit. Why not make a special hat for your favorite doll?

The pattern given is suitable for girl and children dolls from the late 1890s to about 1910. This was the hey-day of the German doll industry, and is the time period which most collectors of antique dolls are able to represent with several dolls in their collection. Hence, our choice. It is a very simple pattern, but quite becoming, too. This hat should not present problems to even the novice doll dresser!

Give careful consideration to your choice of fabric and trims; place the fabric against the doll's face to make sure it suits her complexion. Organdy, batiste, lawn, fine cottons, dotted swiss, china silk, silk broadcloth, silk taffeta or satin, and super sheer wool would be acceptable fabrics. If you edge the ruffles with lace, it should be no wider than 5/8in (1.6cm), and narrower for dolls 16in (40.6cm) and under. The pattern shown is for a doll with a 9in (22.9cm) head circumference, but is marvelously simple to adapt for a different head size, as follows:

1) Measure the circumference of your doll's head over the wig, add 1/2in (1.3cm) for seams, and another 1/2in (1.3cm) for ease. Cut a strip this length by 3/4in (2.0cm). This is the band.

2) Now take the measurement of the doll's head and multiply by two and a half. If the circumference is 12in (30.5cm), you will come up with 30in (76.2cm). This will be the length of the brim ruffles. The widest ruffle should be slightly wider than the radius of the diameter of your doll's head. Therefore, the diameter of a 12in (30.5cm) circumference would be almost 4in (10.2cm). So the ruffle should be 2-1/4in (5.8cm) wide; add 1/2in (1.3cm) for turning the raw edge under, and 1/4in (0.65cm) for the seam. So, cut a strip 30in (76.2cm) by 3in (7.6cm). Cut the upper ruffle 1/2in (1.3cm) narrower, therefore 30in (76.2cm) by 2-1/2in (6.4cm).

3) For the crown, we want approximately double the fullness. So for a 12in (30.5cm) head, allow 24in (61.0cm) around. Now, how do you get a 24in (61.0cm) circle? Divide by 3.14 to get the diameter, about 7-1/2in (19.1cm). Get your compass, set the radius for 3-3/4in (9.6cm), and draw your circle. Now add a 1/4in (0.65cm) seam all around. This is your crown pattern piece.

****

For the pattern shown, and for the instructions above allow 1/4in (0.65cm) seams. The hat can be sewn either by hand or by machine. I would suggest that the crown on heavier fabrics such as a sheer wool, or a crisp silk taffeta, could be lined with china silk. A lovely combination is a velvet crown with silk taffeta or satin brim ruffles! If desired, ribbon ties may be attached inside, to the band, to then tie under the doll's chin. Long streamers are authentic and quite lovely.

CONSTRUCTION:

1) Hem the edges of the brim ruffles. If you roll the hem by hand, trim 1/4in (0.65cm) off the width, as roll hemming takes less fabric. If sewing on the machine, allow a 1/4in (0.65cm) hem with a 1/4in (0.65cm) turn under.

2) If desired, stitch lace to the hemmed edges. Whip by hand or stitch close to the underneath edge by machine.

3) Lay the narrower upper ruffle on top on the wider lower ruffle, line up the upper raw edges, and stitch together 1/8in (0.31cm) from the edges with a basting stitch.

4) Draw up, to fit the band, pin ruffles right side to right side to the band, and stitch.

5) Place end edges right side to right side and stitch together. Trim the raw seam and finish it neatly by casting over it by hand.

6) Run a basting thread 1/8in (0.31cm) from the edge of the circular crown piece.

7) Draw up to fit the band, pin right side to right side, adjust gathers evenly, and stitch.

8) Turn the hat inside out. Turn the raw edges of the band so they face and overlap each other. Now stitch lace insertion over them, or take a piece of the hat fabric, iron raw edges under, and stitch this over the raw edges. This finishing of the band should be done by hand, and as neatly as possible.

9) If desired, now stitch the ribbon ties in place, to the band, on the interior.

10) Turn hat to the outside. You are now ready to start....

Trimming the Hat

The most obvious place to trim this hat is along the band. You should have 1/4in (0.65cm) showing. An ostrich feather positioned strategically is lovely, as are artificial tiny flowers. Satin or grosgrain ribbon may be placed about it; have the raw edges meet at the front, side or back, and cover them by stitching a large, loopy bow over them as shown in the illustration.

Viola! Now that you are finished, and your doll is dressed in her lovely new hat, why not make her part of your Christmas decoration? If your doll is the right size, she could be used very effectively in the center of the table, perhaps holding holly or mistletoe. Wherever and however your decide to display her, one thing is for sure - in her lovely hat, she should captivate all who see her!

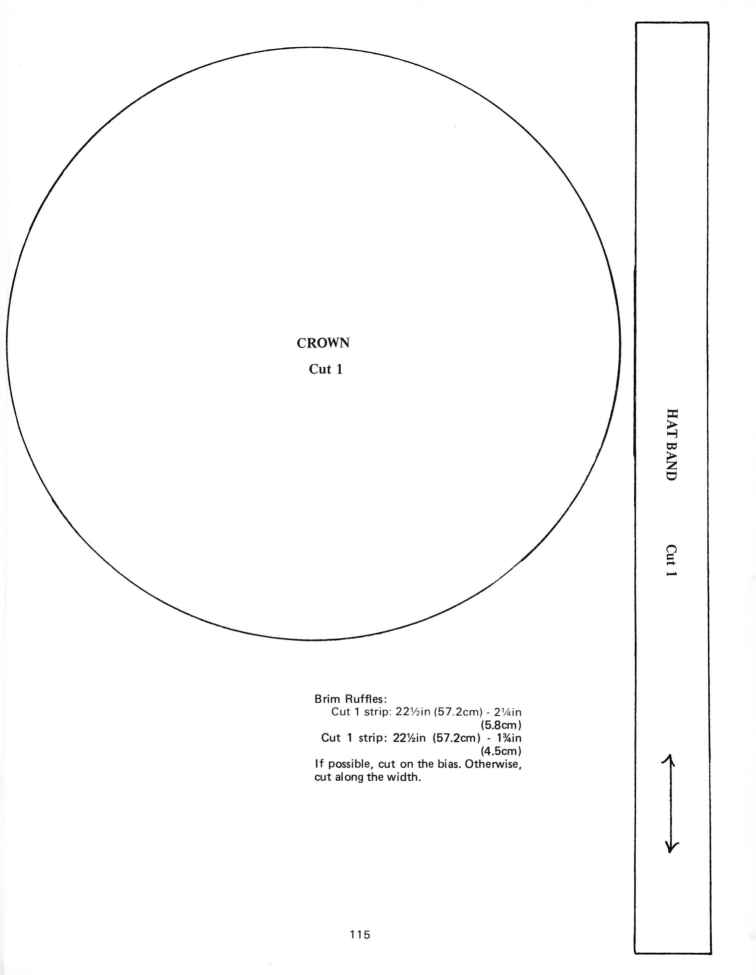

CROWN

Cut 1

Brim Ruffles:
    Cut 1 strip: 22½in (57.2cm) - 2¼in
                      (5.8cm)
    Cut 1 strip: 22½in (57.2cm) - 1¾in
                      (4.5cm)
If possible, cut on the bias. Otherwise,
cut along the width.

HAT BAND

Cut 1

THE LITTLE HOUSEKEEPER

Editor's Note: Some of the earlier dolls' articles depended entirely on a written explanation without the benefit of diagrams or pictures. Here are several items from *The Puritan* of 1899.

A Little Dutch Cap

The March winds are so bad for Miss Dollykins' hair that it is quite essential that she should have a hood or cap to wear instead of a hat. For certain occasions it is well enough to have a hood fastened to the top of a golf cape, but the most stylish cap this spring is modeled on the head dress of a Dutch peasant, probably in compliment to the new little queen in Holland. These little caps are extremely pretty, and the doll's dressmaker will find them very easy to make.

Pieces of silk or velvet or some bright woolen material can be used in their construction, and a pattern is not at all necessary.

The way to take the first measure is this: Lay the customer for whom the cap is intended on a table with the back of her head on a piece of paper; holding a lead pencil upright, draw a line from just below one ear around the top of the head to just below the other ear. This will give the shape for the back of the cap. Cut this out of a piece of velvet and bind the round edge with a narrow strip of silk, so that it will not ravel. Then measure from the upper part of the back of the head to the top of the forehead. Take a strip of silk or a ribbon twice as wide as this measure and as long as the round edge of the velvet. Overcast one edge of the velvet and the two ends of the ribbon with a very narrow little hem. Try the cap on to the customer and turn the front piece back not quite halfway, but so that it will come just over her hair. At the two lower edges of this fold sew narrow ribbons to tie under the chin. The fold that is turned back must be left loose and soft. Of course these caps can be lined, but a lining is always a troublesome affair, and while March is blustering it is not cold, so the little mothers will find that their children are very comfortable with just a single thickness of cloth over their heads.

Blazer Jacket

A little blazer jacket is another necessity in the summer outfit. This should be made of outing flannel, and needs for its trimming but four pearl buttons. The inside seams of this jacket must be carefully bound or overcast; otherwise they will fray out, and there is nothing in doll land that looks quite so untidy as frayed seams. For a small doll, the jacket pattern here given may be copied exactly; while a larger pattern may easily be cut with this as a model.

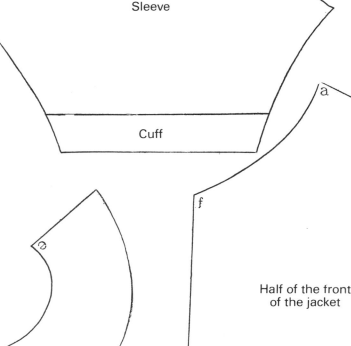

Half of the back of little jacket

Gather

Sleeve

Cuff

Half of jacket collar

Half of the front of the jacket

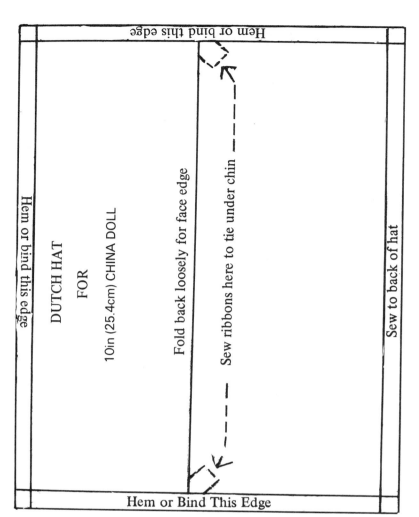

DUTCH HAT

FOR

10in (25.4cm) CHINA DOLL

Fold back loosely for face edge

Sew ribbons here to tie under chin

Hem or bind this edge

Sew to back of hat

Hem or bind this edge

Hem or Bind This Edge

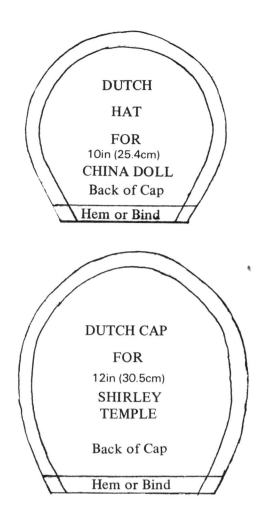

DUTCH
HAT
FOR
10in (25.4cm)
CHINA DOLL
Back of Cap

Hem or Bind

DUTCH CAP

FOR

12in (30.5cm)

SHIRLEY
TEMPLE

Back of Cap

Hem or Bind

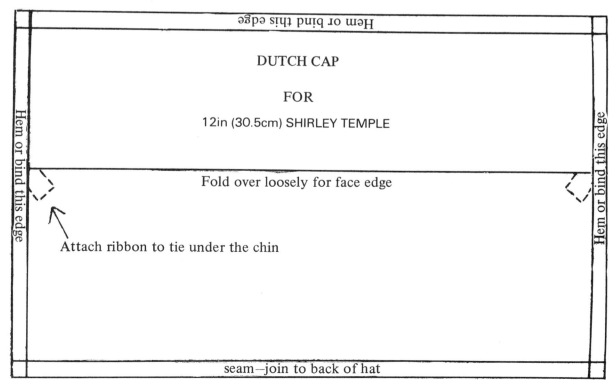

DUTCH CAP

FOR

12in (30.5cm) SHIRLEY TEMPLE

Hem or bind this edge

Fold over loosely for face edge

Attach ribbon to tie under the chin

Hem or bind this edge

Hem or bind this edge

seam—join to back of hat

117

1901
Russian Blouse Suit
for a 12in (30.5cm) to 13in (33cm) child doll

by Sandy Williams

One of the many children's dresses in the September 1901 issue of *The Ladies Home Journal* was a "simple Russian blouse suit fastening at the left side, trimmed with braid. Worn with patent-leather belt." The dress looks as if made in a soft fabric such as a figured challis. The bishop sleeves are also trimmed with braid. The belt gives the blouse a pouch waistline effect, one of the popular styles of that date. The separate kilt skirt has a box pleat at the center front while the side pleats face the center back seam.

I adapted this dress to fit a chubby 12½in (31.8cm) Heubach Köppelsdorf doll with bisque head and arms, kid body and cloth feet. The doll's underwear consists of white batiste drawers and slip petticoat; both have two tucks and are edged in narrow lace.

Challis, linen, serge, muslin, nainsook and cashmere were some of the early 1900s fabrics used to dress children. Any modern-day material which has the same feel and draping ability of the old fabrics would be suitable.

I made the blouse suit up in a dusty rose "super vino" material which has almost the same feel as challis. Always press the garments after each step. I find that silk or extra fine thread is best when sewing doll clothes as the thread seems to disappear into the fabric. Regular thread seems too bulky for such small garments.

Materials needed: White batiste, 1/4in (.65cm) wide white lace; tiny snaps or buttons, 1/4yd (.23m) dress material, 2/16in (.30cm) wide white tape (type used to sew china heads to cloth bodies), black dye, silk or extra fine thread to match materials, 1/4yd (.23m) of 1/2in (1.3cm) wide satin ribbon (color to match dress), black pearl cotton and embroidery thread, black patent leather (perhaps from an old purse), small gold buckle (make one from cardboard and paint gold), twisted string.

First, measure your doll for her underwear. Adjust patterns as necessary;

Illustration 1. Russian blouse suit.

Illustration 2. Drawers.

Illustration 3. Slip petticoat.

make underwear up. Do the same with the kilt skirt; then proceed onto the blouse. It is important to measure for the doll's outergarments only after you have made her underwear.

Drawers: Sew the two leg tucks, press. Turn up a narrow hem and sew lace to this edge. Roll side opening and blindstitch. Sew CF and CB seams. Sew inner leg seams. Turn right side out. Gather drawer's waistline to fit waistband, attach. Close drawers with snap or button and buttonhole.

Slip petticoat: Sew shoulder seams of front and back bodices together. Sew side seams. Finish neckline and armholes with narrow hems; you may wish to sew lace to these edges. Sew two tucks in slip skirt, press. Make a narrow hem and sew lace to this edge. Sew CB seam of skirt together. Gather skirt to fit bodice, sew together. Turn CB opening in and stitch. Close opening with snaps or buttons.

Kilt skirt: Finished skirt's waistline is 8in (20.3cm). Pleats start with a CF 1in

(2.5cm) box pleat and the other 1/2in (1.3cm) pleats are pressed toward the CB. The underfold of each pleat measures 1in (2.5cm). Turn up hem and finish. Mark the dotted and solid lines of pleats at waistline and at hemline with pins. To make a perfect pleat, place solid line on top of dotted line (follow arrow direction) and pin pleat in place at both the waistline and hemline; baste at these two points. Press pleats in place. Undo hem at CB point, sew CB seam, turn hem back up and press. Turn in back opening and finish. Sew waistband to skirt so there is a 1/4in (.65cm) overlap at each end. Close skirt with a snap or button.

Blouse: Dye narrow tape black. Trace design onto bodice and sleeves. Bind Russian opening with bias strip, press. Baste tape and pearl cotton on bodice and sleeves. Sew shoulder seams. Gather sleeve wrists to fit wristband, attach. Gather sleeve armhole to fit bodice armhole, attach. Sew undersleeve seam and side seam in one step. Make a narrow hem on blouse. Sew collar on. Close Russian opening with snaps. You may wish to do some black embroidery on collar.

Belt: Cut a piece of patent leather 3/16in (.45cm) by 9½in (24.2cm). Using the illustration as a guide: twist a piece of copper wire on buckle for "tooth." Cut one end of leather into a point. Pull blunt

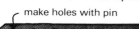
make holes with pin

copper wire tooth

end of belt thru buckle, make a hole (with a pin) where wire tooth will pierce belt, stick tooth thru belt and tack blunt end of leather to wrong side of belt.

Hair bow: Tie ribbon into a large bow and pin to hair as illustrated.

Jump rope: The jump rope is made from a twisted length of string dipped into a bath of strong tea or coffee to give the rope a tan color. The jump rope may be made in two ways. The simplest is to take a 20in (50.8cm) length of string, turn each end over 1in (2.5cm) to make hand loops, wrap thread around the base of each loop, glue. Or, take a 18in (45.7cm) length of string and glue each end into a hole dug out of end of a 5/8in (1.6cm) long dowel rod. Paint handles light brown.

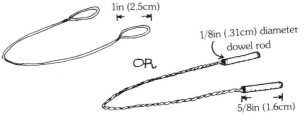

1in (2.5cm)

1/8in (.31cm) diameter
dowel rod

OR

5/8in (1.6cm)

Illustration 4. Jump ropes.

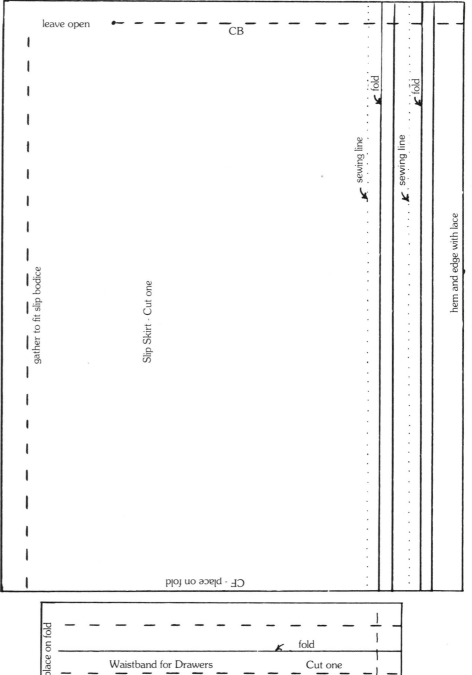

leave open

CB

fold

sewing line

fold

sewing line

fold

hem and edge with lace

gather to fit slip bodice

Slip Skirt - Cut one

CF - place on fold

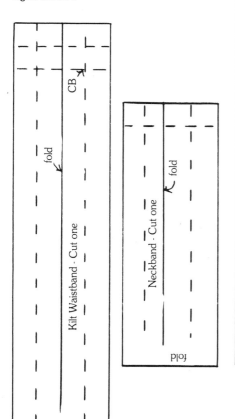

CB

fold

Kilt Waistband - Cut one

fold

Neckband - Cut one

fold

fold

place on fold

fold

Waistband for Drawers

Cut one

119

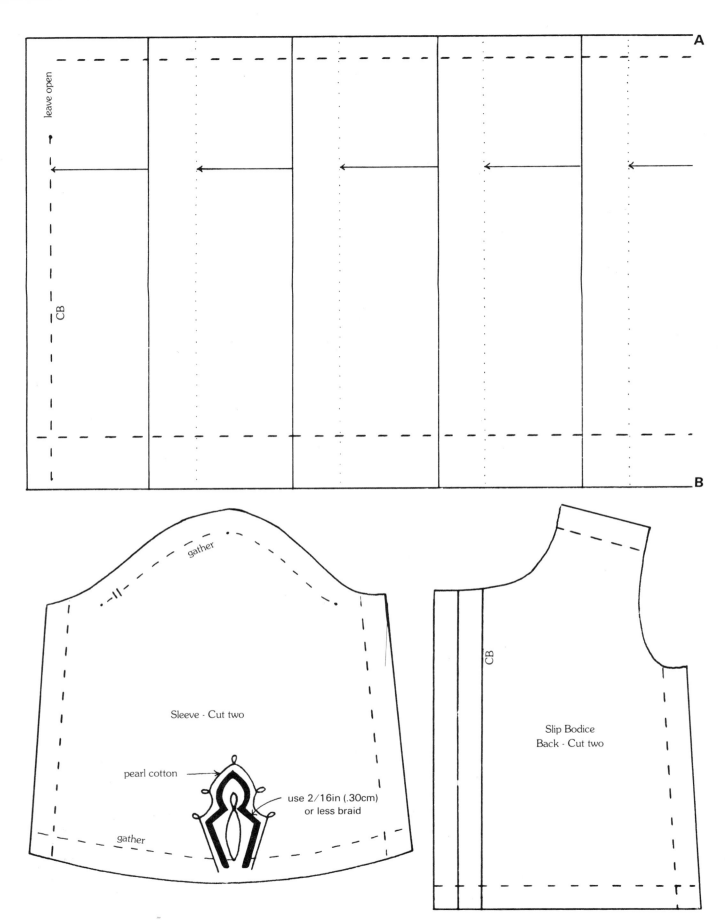

A

leave open

CB

B

gather

Sleeve · Cut two

pearl cotton

use 2/16in (.30cm)
or less braid

gather

CB

Slip Bodice
Back · Cut two

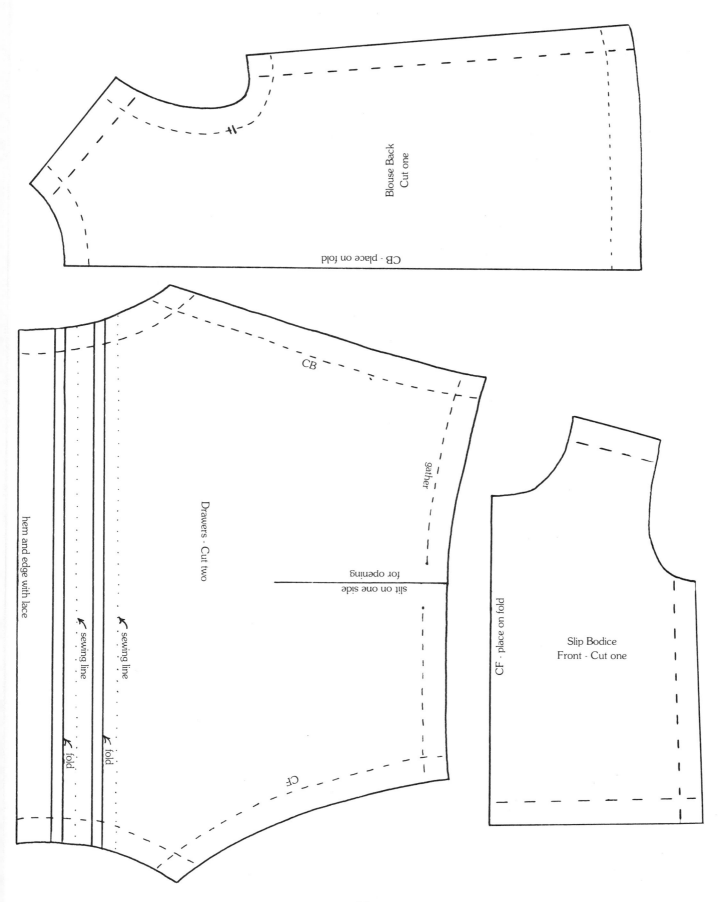

Blouse Back
Cut one

CB - place on fold

CB

gather

slit on one side
for opening

Drawers - Cut two

CF

hem and edge with lace

sewing line

sewing line

fold

fold

Slip Bodice
Front - Cut one

CF - place on fold

121

A

Kilt Skirt - Cut one

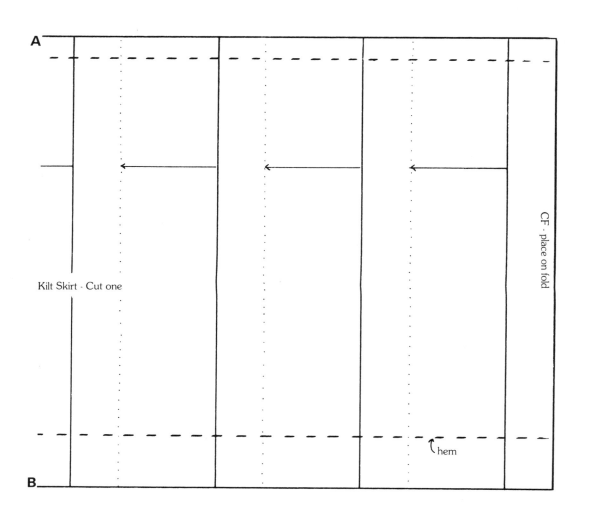

CF - place on fold

hem

B

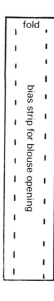

fold

bias strip for blouse opening

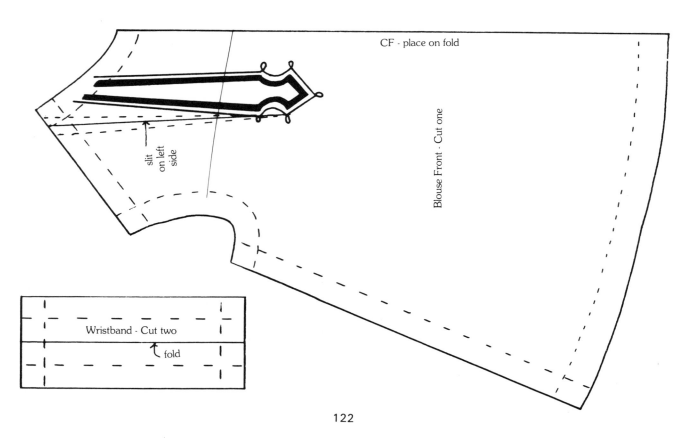

CF - place on fold

Blouse Front - Cut one

slit on left side

Wristband - Cut two

fold

Clothes for Christmas Dolls

by Anna Lent

2895

Illustration 1. 2895. All the underclothes for the little girl doll; a kimona and a nightgown, too. There are patterns in four sizes to fit dolls measuring 14in (35.6cm), 18in (45.7cm), 22in (55.9cm) and 26in (66cm).

(From *The Ladies' Home Journal,* December 1906).

These clothes for dolls have been designed with a twofold purpose: first, to please the little people, and then to assist the grown-ups who undertake the pleasant task of dressing dolls that will delight the hearts of the children at Christmastime.

The patterns contain few pieces, and this greatly simplifies the work. The wee garments are all cut like real babies' and children's clothes; for children find the greatest delight in the fact that Dolly's clothes are just like their own, and quite as easily put on and off.

Frequently the piece-box will supply the necessary materials for Doll's outfit; but sometimes it may be necessary to buy new. Lawn is suitable for the undergarments; it will also be pretty for the baby's dress, and, in combination with lace for the little girl's befrilled frock. Narrow lace will trim the underclothes. The dress of dotted material for the little girl doll is made by the same pattern as the frilled frock; lawn, dimity or challis with a tiny yoke of lace or embroidery is suggested for this.

For the same Dolly, cashmere or broadcloth will make a cute little coat, but I am sure Dolly's small mother would think a coat of taffeta or velveteen "perfectly dear."

DRAWN BY GRACE G. WIEDERSEIM   2894

Illustration 2. 2894. The dress, which may be made very simple or trimmed with frills of lace and ribbon bows; the cloak and the hat are for the little girl doll. Patterns for these little garments are made in four sizes to fit dolls 14in (35.6cm), 18in (45.7cm), 22in (55.9cm) and 26in (66cm). The hat may be made of material to match the coat, or of white or colored felt.

Illustration 3. 2892. A complete set of clothes for the baby doll. Flannelette is suggested for the "flannel" petticoat and for the little wrapper that is cut the same way as the nightgown; and, by the way, lap and pin the petticoat band -- also the shirt -- with tiny safety pins just like a real, live baby's clothes. Make the cloak of cashmere or challis, and the little cap of lawn or silk. The patterns for these doll's clothes are cut in four sizes to fit dolls 12in (30.5cm), 16in (40.6cm), 20in (50.8cm) and 24in (61cm) high.

2892   DRAWN BY GRACE G. WIEDERSEIM

STYLES FOR DOLLS 1904

From *The Delineator*, **November, 1904**

Illustration 1. No. 284 is a costume of rose pink lansdowne and valenciennes allover; No. 286 shows a bridal costume of mull combined with allover lace; the jaunty sailor suit, No. 287, is of blue flannel contrasted with white; No. 285 is a yoke dress of India lawn trimmed with lace, and is part of a set including a coat and bonnet.

Girl dolls' set (No. 285)

The yoke dress is illustrated in fine nainsook with lace. The square yoke, outlined by a bertha, is designed for square or high neck, the latter finished with a narrow band, and supports the full skirt, which is in one piece. The lower edge is turned up to form a hem, and the sleeves are of the conventional bishop type, confined at the wrists in narrow bands or cut off in three-quarter length. The dress closes at the back.

Tan kersey was selected for the coat, a box mode closed in double-breasted fashion with buttons and buttonholes. A back strap may hold the fullness in place, or a belt may be used if fancied. A shawl collar facing is a modish feature, but is not necessary, and the bishop sleeves are of generous proportions. The pattern makes provision for full or three-quarter length.

Girl dolls' costume (No. 284)

The frock pictured shows the characteristics of the prevailing styles. The guimpe blouse is of dotted silk, and the skirt and bertha suspenders are of rose—colored cashmere with applique lace. The former closes at the back and is gathered at the neck, the fullness at the waistline being regulated by a tape run through a casing. Bishop shaping is given the sleeves.

"Nun" tucks ornament the straight skirt, and a deep hem is allowed. Gathers adjust it at the top, where a belt confines it. Suspenders are attached to the bertha at each side of the front and back, but this feature is not essential.

Lightweight serge, nun's veiling, pongee, novelty goods and wash materials are adaptable.

Pattern 284 is in seven sizes from 14in (35.6cm) to 26in (66cm) in height. For 22in (55.9cm), the dress needs ¾yd (.69m) of material 44in (111.7cm) wide; the guimpe blouse, ⅝yd (.55cm) of material 36in (91.4cm) wide.

Illustration 3. No. 285 Girl dolls' set consisting of a yoke dress, with high or square neck and bishop or long elbow sleeves; a double-breasted box coat, in full or three-quarter length, with or without the back strap or a belt, and a brownie bonnet.

The bonnet is an attractive affair, becoming to any type of doll beauty, and was made of material like the coat. The only seam is at the top, where it forms a peak at the crown in true "Brownie" fashion. The slight fullness at the neck is taken up in backward-turning plaits at the back, and ribbon tie strings are added, fur at the edge affording decoration.

A dress of pink lawn trimmed with torchon lace, a coat of green broadcloth, and a bonnet of silk of the same color, trimmed with beaver, will be very pretty. Washable materials are always preferable for dolls' dresses.

Pattern 285 is in seven sizes from 14in (35.6cm) to 26in (66cm) in height. For 22in (55.9cm), the dress needs 1⅛yd (1.02m) of material 36in (91.4cm) wide, with ⅛yd (.11m) of allover lace 18in (45.7cm) wide for high necked yoke, 1½yd (1.37m) of edging 3in (7.6cm) wide for bertha; for coat, ⅝yd (.55m) wide; for bonnet, ⅜yd (.33m) 20in 50in (127cm) wide; for bonnet, ⅜yd (.33m) 20in (50.8m) or more wide.

Illustration 2. No. 284 Girl dolls' costume: Consisting of a guimpe blouse and a separate straight skirt having "Nun" Tucks, with or without the Bertha Suspenders.

Illustration 4. No. 286. Lady dolls' costume.

Illustration 5. No. 287 Boy dolls' suit.

The blouse closes in double-breasted style and may be finished with a "Buster Brown" collar and tie, or it may be made with an open neck displaying a removable shield, outlined by a sailor collar with pointed front ends. Bands finish the sleeves, which are of one seam shaping. Pattern 287 is in three sizes from 12in (30.5cm) to 16in (40.6cm) in height. For 16in (40.6cm), it will require ⅜yd (.33m) of material 44in (111.7cm) wide, with ¼yd (.23m) of contrasting material 27in (68.6cm) wide for sailor collar and shield, or ⅛yd (.11m) of contrasting material in the same width for "Buster Brown" collar.

Lady dolls' costume (No. 286)

Ciel-blue nun's veiling with lace is represented in the costume shown here. A lining serves as a foundation for the waist, which closes at the back and blouses stylishly all around. Three rows of tuck shirrings are employed in the body and sleeves, the latter being in full or three-quarter length and supported by two seam linings. A bertha may follow the round yoke, and provision is made for low or high neck.

Shirrings control the fullness at the top of the circular skirt. Sweep and round lengths are given, and three rows of tuck shirrings afford ornamentation. A sash is worn. Any soft, thin material, either silk or wool, will make up prettily. Pattern

286 is in six sizes from 16in (40.6cm) to 26in (66cm) in height. For 22in (55.9cm), it requires 1½yd (1.37m) of material 44in (111.7m) wide.

Boy dolls' suit (No. 287)

The smart little suit shown was made of blue serge contrasted with white, an emblem and braid in two widths being used for decoration in one instance. A center and inside and outside leg seams shape the knickerbockers, which close in a fly. They droop at the knees, where elastics confined the fullness. The back of the blouse is plain, and the fullness at the lower edge is regulated by a drawstring.

Dolly's Winter Clothes

from *The Delineator*, November 1907

The unusual interest in dolls' dress-making that is evident at the present time is due, in great measure, to the hundreds of Jenny Wren clubs that have been organized all over the world. The girls find it very pleasant to meet and sew together, and the natural desire to excel produces the spirit of competition that brings forth the best work. It is really marvelous how much has been accomplished in the knowledge of the use of patterns, and the development of good taste and practical ideas among the children. The consequence is that Dolly will be better dressed than ever before, and her wardrobe will be up to date in every particular. Time was when Dolly could go with her little mother clothed in any garments she might happen to possess, but now all that is changed and she must be garbed becomingly and suitably for every occasion.

There are many new designs a-dapted for her use, all showing the lines and details which stamp them with Dame Fashion's seal. The undergarments, dresses, coats, hats, caps -- even the shoes -- are closely copied from those worn by women and children, and the variety of this miniature wardrobe is limited only by the time and money devoted to it -- the former counting for more than the latter, for with the application of a little ingenuity the tiniest scraps and leftovers can be pressed into service. This need, in itself, is excellent training for the little dressmakers, and will be of the greatest benefit to them as they advance and take up more difficult work.

That dolls' clothes are made in such close imitation of those for "real people" is of benefit, for the problems that come up in dressmaking will be presented in miniature form, and overcome -- by studying out and strictly following directions -- at an age when knowledge is easily absorbed and impressed on the memory.

Not only in matters of dress does Dolly closely follow her prototype, but almost everything that is made for human kind is copied in reduced proportions for the doll world. All articles of adornment, including necklaces, rings, bracelets, watches, fobs, charms, lockets, chains,

combs, cuff buttons and links, fancy belts; toilet requisites, such as brushes and combs, manicure sets, powder puffs and boxes, tooth and nail brushes, curling-irons -- everything that can be conceived of is obtainable. All the newest furniture is copied, and all kinds of furnishings, portieres, lace curtains, draperies, couch covers, sofa pillows, hammocks, porch swings, lawn settees, lamps, candelabra, tableware and an infinite variety of bric-a-brac are on the market and ready for the holidays.

Dolls of high degree may ride in automobiles or carriages of the latest design, chauffeur, coachman and foot-man accompanying them, and steam, electricity or clock machinery providing the motive power. Tallyhos, trolley cars and all sorts of vehicles, including the lowly wheelbarrow, are placed at their services.

Domestic taste is fostered by the supply of household utensils: bathtubs and washtubs that may contain real water, a faucet near the bottom allowing them to be easily emptied. Clothes horses, wash benches, wringers, mangles, washing machines, flatirons and all laundry improvements are provided.

Nickel fixtures may be bought for the doll's bathroom, tiny towels, sponges, soap dishes, towel bars and mirrors; or, if her domicile boasts not a modern bath, she may have an enameled washstand, water pitcher, basin, slop jar, and all toilet accessories obtainable in larger size.

The tiny garden implements are attractive and practical. Lawn mowers and rollers are toys that give much pleasure. Even a rubber hose that will conduct real water, and miniature watering pots, are among the playthings the modern child may enjoy.

The trades, too, are represented, toy printing presses, looms, hods, bricks, sand screens, kilns, molds, dies and all sorts of tools being provided. It is safe to say that there is absolutely nothing that people use and enjoy that is not obtainable in dolls' size.

Illustration 1. Girl dolls' French dress, No. 311.

Girl dolls' French dress, (No. 311)

On account of the uncertain lines of the female doll's figure, the little dress of French style will be especially safe for reproduction. The body of the dress is attached to a square yoke, which may be high at the neck or in square outline; with the latter the sleeves are pretty when in short puff style. The bretelles can be made of the same trimming as the yoke, or they are left off if preferred; the skirt is attached to the blouse, the upper skirt section falling over the lower, giving the effect of a double skirt.

Sheer lawn, flowered dimity, China silk, crêpe de Chine, albatross and voile are suggested, and the design is one that can be developed plainly or made as fancy as desired.

Dress 311 is in nine sizes, from 14in (35.6cm) to 30in (76.2cm). For a 22in (55.9cm) doll, the dress with double skirt requires 1⅜yd (1.24m) of material 27in (68.6cm) wide, or ⅞yd (.77m) 44in (111.7cm) wide, each with ¼yd (.23m) of lace to cover yoke and bretelles; for dress with single skirt, 1⅛yd (1.02m) 27in (68.6cm) wide, with ⅛yd (.11m) tucking for yoke.

Batiste with embroidery French Dress 311

Linon with all-over

Lawn with net

Dolls' kimono wrapper or dressing sack, (No. 312)

Kimono or Dressing-Sack 312

Dotted French flannel, plain bands

Cashmere with silk bands

Of white albatross

Illustration 2. Dolls' kimono wrapper or dressing sack, No. 312.

The doll kimono is cut on the same lines as the ones for its little mistress, being seamed under the arms, and having either long or short frill sleeves. It can be made of lawn or challis, and the band fold is more attractive if of a different color; it is rolled over in shawl collar style about the neck, and extends to the lower edge. When a sack is desired, cut off at the necessary length.

A silk fold is pretty on light albatross or any soft wool fabric that may be found in the piece-bag; flowered dimity, lawn, challis, cotton crêpe and China silk are adaptable. This is an excellent design for a child to take up first, as it is very simple to make, and may be diversified in many ways. The edges are suitable for button-holing, or bands of contrasting goods might be feather-stitched.

Kimono 312 is in five sizes, from 14in (35.6cm) to 30in (76.2cm) in height. For 22in (55.9cm), the wrapper requires 1yd (.91m) of material 27in (68.6cm) wide, with ¾yd (.69m) 20in (50.8cm) or more wide for bands; for sack. ⅜yd (.33m) 44in (111.7cm) wide, with ½yd (.46m) of contrasting goods, will be needed.

Girl dolls' set consisting of a dress with guimpe, and a coat, (No. 313)

This little dress will be pretty made of colored linen or gingham, and the guimpe with puff or bishop sleeves of white lawn. The dress and frill sleeves are in one, the seams being on the shoulders and under the arms. The square neck outline can be trimmed with a bit of white needlework, and also the edges of the frill sleeves and the skirt of the dress. are in one, A sash may be used to draw the dress in at the waist, and the guimpe may be sometimes omitted. A dress of red China silk would be effective with a white lace guimpe.

The coat is on kimono lines, and seamed in the same way as the dress. The coat can be made of broadcloth, cashmere or any heavy silk, with bands and collar facing of contrasting material, and with braiding, binding or piping for elaboration.

Dolls' Set No. 313 is in nine sizes, from 14in (35.6cm) to 30in (76.2cm) in height. For a doll 22in (55.9cm) high, the dress requires 1yd (.91m) of goods 36in (91.4cm) or 44in (111.7cm) wide; the guimpe, ¼yd (.23m) of goods 36in (91.4cm) wide, with ¼yd (.23m) of tucking 18in (45.7cm) wide; for the coat, ½yd (.46m) 44in (111.7cm) or 50in (127cm) wide will be needed.

Coat of tan cloth with fancy braid

Set 313

Dress of linen with guimpe

Of cashmere with braid; open-necked guimpe

Illustration 3. Girl dolls' set consisting of a dress with guimpe and a coat, No. 313.

Dolls' set consisting of a long coat and a cap, (No. 314)

Illustration 4. Dolls' set consisting of a long coat and a cap, No. 314.

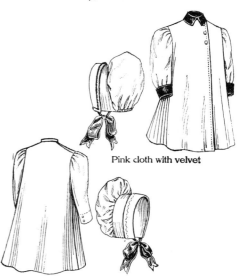

Pink cloth with **velvet**

Cream-white henrietta

This set consists of a plain coat in box style, buttoned to the chin slightly to the left side in military effect, and having a high turnover collar. The sleeves are of coat shaping or in bishop style with round cuffs. The cap will be pretty made of white plush or of white silk, the crown being quite full and gathered to the head piece; the latter has revers turning back from the face, and the edges are some-times trimmed with a bit of edging. The tie strings are of satin or of velvet ribbon. It can also be made of fine lawn, lace or linen, and the coat is adaptable to many kinds of material, linen, piqué, or cloth, serge, velvet or silk that may be left from the little girl's wardrobe. Any kind of trimming fancied may be employed to relieve the plainness of the coat.

Dolls' Set no. 314 is in nine sizes, from 14in (35.6cm) to 30in (76.2cm) in height. For 22in (55.9cm), the coat requires 1yd (.91m) of material 27in (68.6cm) wide, with ¼yd (.23m) of velvet for collar; the cap requires ⅜yd (.33m) 20in (50.8cm) or more inches wide.

Persian lawn with inser-tion; guimpe omitted

STYLES FOR DOLLS · 1908

Her Doll's Winter Clothes

from *The Delineator* Dec. 1908

Illustration 1. No. 290 portrays a shirt-waist costume of mixed cheviot; No. 288 pictures a Red Riding Hood set; No. 291 illustrates a pretty French mode in white lawn; Santa Claus is clad in a suit of red velvet trimmed with fur and braid; No. 289 is a box plaited dress of blue cashmere; No. 285 illustrates a set comprising a dress, box coat and brownie bonnet.

Girl Dolls' French Dress (No. 291). This pretty little dress was made of embroidered and plain lawn, and of fine linen with hemstitching. The full waist is gathered at the top to a narrow band decorated with fancy stitching, and closes at the back. Bretelles and shoulder frills are provided, and the short sleeves are shaped by one seam. The guimpe which is of plain lawn with a simulated yoke of tucking or allover embroidery is worn if fancied. It is shaped by shoulder and underarm seams, and the fulness at the waistline is regulated by a drawstring inserted in a casing. The sleeves are in bishop style, gathered into narrow bands, and a frill of edging finishes the neck. The skirt is gathered to the waist, and a sash is worn.

China silk makes pretty dresses for dolls, and nainsook or dimity may be associated with Valenciennes edging. India linen, muslin, soiesette and pongee are all suitable.

Pattern 291 is in seven sizes from 14in (35.6cm) to 26in (66cm) in height. For 22in (55.9cm), the dress calls for 1½yd (1.36m) of edging 7¾in (19.8cm) deep, with 2yd (1.82m) of edging 4¾in (12.2cm) wide for sleeves and bretelles, and 3/8yd (.33m) of plain lawn 36in (91.4cm) wide for front and backs; for guimpe, 1/2yd (.46m) of material with 1/8yd (.11m) of allover lace or tucking. Dolls' costume (No. 290). A smart costume is shown here in dotted albatross and in white linen. The skirt is in five gores and is tuck plaited all around with a panel effect at the front, the stitching of the plaits terminating at any yoke or flounce depth. Round length is given the mode.

The skirtwaist displays tucks at each side of the box plait in front, where the closing is arranged, and at the back from shoulder to waistline. The tucked sleeves extend to the neck, or terminate at the

armholes, as preferred, and the lower edge is gathered into a band. The neck is finished with a standing collar, and a narrow belt is worn.

Shot or plain taffeta, louisine, cashmere or velveteen may be used with good results, and lawn, gingham, sateen, pongee and cashmere are recommended.

Pattern 290 is in seven sizes from 16in (40.6cm) to 28in (71.1cm) in height. For 22in (55.9cm), it calls for 2¼yd (2.05m) of material 27in (68.6cm) wide, or 1¼yd (1.14m) 44in (111.7cm) wide.

Girl dolls' box plaited dress, (No. 289). There is distinctive style to this little dress, for the making of which blue cashmere was used, with reliefs of white. The body and skirt are in one, box plaits being stitched to body depth and falling free below. A large collar in shawl or sailor style may be added, and a standing band finishes the neck. A belt held in place by straps at the underarm seams is supplied for use when desired. Box plaits are laid in the tops of the bishop sleeves, and wristbands afford completion.

French flannel in an old rose tint will make up prettily, and small plaid or checked goods is recommended. Albatross, veiling, pongee, mercerized and washable fabrics are appropriate.

Pattern 289 is in seven sizes from 14in (35.6cm) to 26in (66cm) in height. For 22in (55.9cm), it will need 1⅜yd (1.24m) of material 27in (68.6cm) wide, or 1yd (.91m) 44in (111.7cm) wide, each with 3/8yd (.33m) of contrasting material.

Illustration 3. Dolls' costume, No. 290, in round length, with a shirtwaist, having regulation or epaulette sleeves, and a five-gored skirt with tuck plaits to any yoke or flounce depth.

Illustration 2. Girl dolls' French dress, No. 291.

Illustration 4. Girl dolls' box plaited dress, with body and skirt in one, with or without the sailor or shawl collar, No. 289.

Girl dolls' dress, Gretchen apron and cape (No. 288). A Red Riding Hood set would be an addition to Dolly's wardrobe, and the one illustrated is a suggestion of this type. Blue chambray was used for developing the dress, the waist of which is plain both at the back and front, the fastening being made in the former. The full skirt has a deep hem and is attached to the waist with gathers. The sleeves are of bishop shaping gathered into bands, and the neck is collarless and finished with a bias facing if fancied.

The quaint little Gretchen apron has a seamless body portion with straps extending over the shoulders and buttons at the back. The skirt portion is gathered to the body and is finished with a hem. White lawn was used in this instance.

The cape and hood were made of bright red cashmere, the cape being of circular shaping gathered in at the neck. The hood is also gathered where it is attached to the cape, and shirrings draw it into shape, a frill being formed at the edge.

Dimity, muslin and gingham may be used in making both the dress and apron, or woolen or silk fabrics for the former, and flannel, broadcloth, serge, cheviot and similar materials are usually employed in the construction of the cape.

Pattern 288 is in seven sizes from 14in (35.6cm) to 26in (66cm) in height. For 22in (55.9cm), the dress needs 7/8yd (.77m) of material 36in (91.4cm) wide; the apron, 1/2yd (.46m) in the same width; the cape, 1/2yd (.46m) 44in (111.7cm) wide.

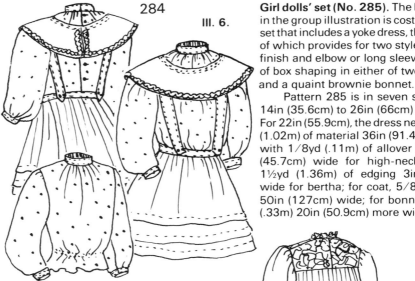

284

III. 6.

Illustration 6. Girl dolls' costume consisting of a guimpe blouse and a separate straight skirt having "nun" tucks, with or without the bertha suspender, No. 284.

Girl dolls' costume (No. 284). This is a pretty little costume of rose pink cashmere and fancy swiss. The costume is made with a guimpe blouse and a separate straight skirt with "nun" tucks at the lower edge, and with suspenders which are not always used.

Pattern 284 is in seven sizes from 14in (35.6cm) to 26in (66cm) in height. For 22in (55.9cm), the dress needs 3/4yd (.69m) of material 44in (111.7cm) wide; the guimpe blouse, 5/8yd (.55m) of material 36in (91.4cm) wide.

Girl dolls' set (No. 285). The last figure in the group illustration is costumed in a set that includes a yoke dress, the pattern of which provides for two styles of neck finish and elbow or long sleeves, a coat of box shaping in either of two lengths, and a quaint brownie bonnet.

Pattern 285 is in seven sizes from 14in (35.6cm) to 26in (66cm) in height. For 22in (55.9cm), the dress needs 1⅛yd (1.02m) of material 36in (91.4cm) wide, with 1/8yd (.11m) of allover lace 18in (45.7cm) wide for high-necked yoke, 1½yd (1.36m) of edging 3in (7.6cm) wide for bertha; for coat, 5/8yd (.55m) 50in (127cm) wide; for bonnet, 3/8yd (.33m) 20in (50.9cm) more wide.

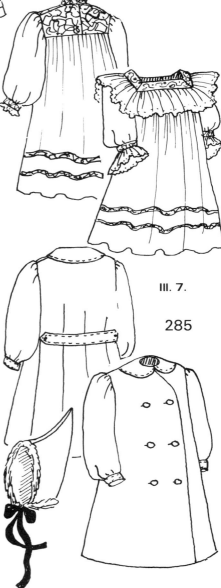

III. 7.

285

Illustration 7. Girl dolls' yoke dress, with high or square neck and bishop or long elbow sleeves; a double-breasted box coat, in full or three-quarter length, with or without the back strap or belt; and a brownie bonnet, No. 285.

III. 5.

288

Illustration 5. Girl dolls' Dress, with attached full skirt, Gretchen apron, and full circular cape, sometimes called the Red Riding Hood set, No. 288.

Styles For Dolls - 1908
Her Doll's Winter Clothes
From *The Delineator* December 1908

In dressing the little girl's doll for Christmas, it is well to get a set including the pieces that are intended for a certain style of outfit, such as this one (No. 324), which includes the dress, apron and cape. The dress has a short "baby" waist, and is gathered to a shallow square yoke. It can be made of sheer lawn, soft woolen fabric or China silk, or anything that is used for little children's dresses. The straight apron is gathered to a band yoke having straps over the shoulders, the top of the apron being cut out a little for the armhole. The apron can be made of lawn or flouncing. The full cape is either long enough to cover the doll's dress, or it can be a short affair, and a full hood gathered around the face is attached to the cape. The cape will be pretty of Scotch or French flannel, cashmere, or chiffon broadcloth, if this happens to be among the leftovers in the scrap-basket. To make the cape for a 22in (55.9cm) doll requires 1yd (.91m) of 27in (68.6cm) goods or 1yd (.91m) of 44in (111.7cm) goods, each with 1/2yd (.46m) of 20in (50.8cm) silk to line the hood. The dress can be made of a 1 1/8yd (1.02m) of 24in (61cm) goods or 5/8yd (.55m) of 44in (111.7cm) wide, with 2 5/8yd (1.93m) of insertion, and the apron needs 1 1/8yd (1.02m) of flouncing 11 3/4in (29.9cm) deep, or 3/4yd (.69m) of 27in

Illustration 2. Dress apron and cape, No. 324.

(68.6cm) goods with 7/8yd (.77m) of insertion. The set is in nine sizes, for dolls of 14in (35.6cm) to 30in (76.2cm) in height, measurement being taken from the top of the head to the sole of the foot.

Another important part of dolls' wearing apparel is a complete set of underwear (No. 326). It includes a gown, drawers, chemise and petticoat. The drawers are straight and rather full, opening at the side, and not unlike the design for misses described in this article. They can be made of lawn, cambric or nainsook scraps that are left from the family sewing, and to make them for a doll 22in (55.9cm) tall it requires 1 1/2yd (1.37m) of insertion for trimming; the entire set can be made out of 1 7/8yd (1.68m) of material 36in (91.4cm) wide. The petticoat consist of five gores, and may have a deep ruffle, and it requires 1 3/4yd (1.6m) of edging 4in (10.2cm) wide, a yard of beading, or 2 3/4yd (2.51m) of insertion. The chemise has a ruffle on the lower edge finished like the drawers and petticoat, and the shoulder seams are not sewed, but fastened with buttons and buttonholes. It requires 1 3/8yd (1.24m) of edging and 1 3/4yd (1.6m) of insertion. The nightgown is finished at the neck with beading and edging and may be drawn up a little closer about the neck if desired; it can have either the short frill sleeves or longer ones gathered into bands. It requires 5/8yd (.55m) of edging for the neck, 1/2yd (.46m) of insertion and 5/8yd (.55m) of beading. India linen, nainsook, lonsdale cambric, longcloth and lawn are suitable. The

design is in nine sizes, from 14in (35.6cm) to 30in (76.2cm) in height. In almost every family can be found enough material left over to make this set of underwear.

The dolls' Russian dress (No. 327) is a pretty design and can be made up in many different attractive ways. The body of the dress is tucked to waist depth and the closing is made in front under the wide tucks; short frill sleeves also tucked are inserted in the armholes of the dress. The neck outline is in V effect, and when the dress is made of white cotton repp, lawn or India linen, the top finish of the dress and the belt made of colored bands will be attractive, and also bits of needlework give a pretty finish, while cashmere, albatross or challis can have colored ribbon or satin folds for the neck. The guimpe that is supplied with the dress can be of lawn or lace, as preferred, and it may have elbow or long sleeves. So little material is required for the guimpe that any sheer white goods or net found in the family piece-bag can be utilized.

The dress is in nine sizes, for dolls that are from 14in (35.6cm) to 30in (76.2cm) tall. For a 22in (55.9cm) doll the dress can be made out of a 1 1/4yd (1.14m) of 24in (61cm) goods, or 3/4yd (.69m) of 44in (111.7cm) goods, with 7/8yd (.77m) of ribbon for the belt and to trim the neck, and 1/2yd (.46m) of goods 20in (50.8cm) wide for the guimpe, with 1/8yd (.11m) of lace 18in (45.7cm) wide for yoke facing.

The set of garments shown in *Illustration 5* for the doll is such as would be

Illustration 1. French flannel cape, No. 324, and white albatross dress, No. 327.

Illustration 3. Underwear set No. 326, of India linen with valenciennes insertion, edging, beading and ribbon.

Illustration 4. Back view of the dress, No. 327.

Illustration 5. Gingham rompers and nainsook dress, No. 325.

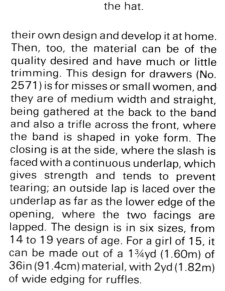

Illustration 6. Back views of rompers and dress in No. 325 and the hat.

worn by a little child when at play, and consists of a dress, hat and rompers (No. 325). The dress is cut entirely in one piece, without a seam on the shoulders, but it is seamed under the arm and at the inside edge of the sleeve, the latter being in full length or short puff style. The dress is straight across the top and is drawn up to the required size about the neck by shirring strings, the gathers thus formed being attached to a stay piece underneath; the sleeves are gathered and tucked in the same way. If the dress is made of flouncing, it will have a seam on the top of the sleeve and shoulders and it can also be made of lawn or any other material. The rompers are gathered to a square yoke or a square band yoke at the neck, and the lower edge is drawn up about the knee by elastic in a casing and a belt may be worn. These can be made of the same material as the dresses that children wear. The crown of the hat

is perfectly round and is fastened to the brim by buttons and buttonholes, so that it can be removed for laundering. The ribbon ties on the hat can match the dress or the doll's sash, and, as they can be fastened with small baby pins, may be changed to suit the costume worn. All of the articles in this set are simple to make, and it would be an excellent one for girls to undertake. The set is in nine sizes, for dolls that are from 14in (35.6cm) to 30in (76.2cm) in height. If the dress is made of flouncing it will require 1⅜yd (1.24m) 15in (38.1cm) deep, or 1¼yd (1.14m) of other goods 24in (61cm) wide; the rompers, 7/8yd (.77m) 27in (68.6cm) wide, with 1/8yd (.11m) of contrasting goods 27in (68.6cm) wide for yoke, belt and sleeve bands, and the hat 1/2yd (.46m) 20in (50.8cm) wide, for 22in (55.9cm).

It is such an easy matter to make undergarments that many prefer to select

their own design and develop it at home. Then, too, the material can be of the quality desired and have much or little trimming. This design for drawers (No. 2571) is for misses or small women, and they are of medium width and straight, being gathered at the back to the band and also a trifle across the front, where the band is shaped in yoke form. The closing is at the side, where the slash is faced with a continuous underlap, which gives strength and tends to prevent tearing; an outside lap is laced over the underlap as far as the lower edge of the opening, where the two facings are lapped. The design is in six sizes, from 14 to 19 years of age. For a girl of 15, it can be made out of a 1¾yd (1.60m) of 36in (91.4cm) material, with 2yd (1.82m) of wide edging for ruffles.

Illustration 7. Undergarments of long-cloth and nainsook with lace, No. 2571.

LADY DOLLS' DRESS

(From *Pictoria Review*, - "The Minaret Lady Doll").

Patented April 30, 1907.

Without lining, having sleeves combined with body and attached three-piece skirt with one-piece tunic, closing at center back.

Seven pieces: front (A), back (B), belt (C), peplum (D), right front gore (E), left front gore (F), the whole back gore (G). Cut one right front gore, left front gore and back gore; place on material as illustrated in guide, keeping right side of material up.

To cut. Avoid mistakes by laying out pattern on the material in accordance with *Cutting Guide.* Place pieces with edge marked by triple "TTT" perforations on a lengthwise fold, except belt which is placed on a crosswise fold and remaining pieces with line of large "O" perforations on a lengthwise thread of material.

To make. Waist: close underarm, sleeve and shoulder seams as notched. Turn hem in right back at notches. Gather lower edge of front and back between double "TT" perforations. Sew belt to lower edge, centers even, small "o" perforation at underarm seam.

Skirt: plait right front gore and back gore, placing "T" on corresponding small "o" perforations and tack. Slash back gore at center back (large "O" perforations indicate center back) from upper edge to small "o" perforation; finish edges for opening. Lap right front gore on left bringing single large "O" perforations near upper edges and single small "o" perforations near lower edges together and tack. Close seams as notched. Close back seam of peplum from large "O" perforation to lower edge, finish edges above for opening. Gather upper edge between double "TT" perforations. Adjust on skirt, centers even; stitch upper edges together bringing small "o" perforation to side seams. Sew to lower edge of belt, centers even.

Trim as illustrated or in any desired way.

MATERIAL REQUIRED: 3/4yd (.69m) 27in (68.6cm) wide or 5/8yd (.55m) 36in (91.4cm) wide.

Illustration 1. Lady dolls' dress, 18in (45.7cm).

Cutting Guide

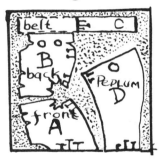

Illustration 3. Fold of 27in (68.6cm) material with nap.

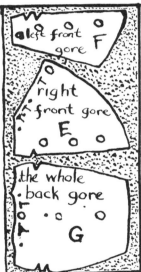

Illustration 2. Material open, (single) right side of material up.

Construction Guide

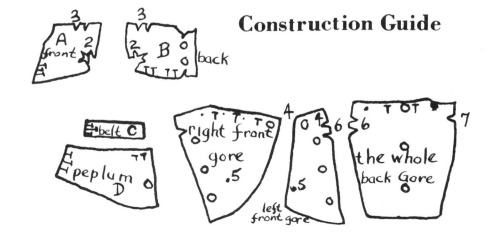

133

JUST FOR MISS DOLLIE

Every One Makes Dolls' Clothes for Christmas Presents

Illustration 1. Set of infant clothes consisting of a petticoat, a nightgown or slip, wrapper, dressing sack and little dress with a straight lower edge, No. 328.

Around Christmas time mothers and friends of children are busy making clothes for the little dollies, and truly there is a great deal of pleasure in doing sewing on this miniature plan. There is probably no set of clothes that so strongly appeals to the little one as the baby clothes, perhaps on account of the maternal or paternal instinct, as the case may be. **Illustration 1** (No. 328) shows a very complete set of infant clothes, consisting of a petticoat, a nightgown or slip, wrapper, dressing sack and little dress with a straight lower edge. These clothes are made of much the same material as is used for the real live babies. To make the dress for a doll 22in (55.9cm) tall, 1⅛yd (1.02m) of flouncing 23in (58.4cm) deep, with 1/4 yd (.23m) of nainsook 36in (91.4cm) wide for the sleeves, or 1½yd (1.36m) of nainsook 1yd (.91m) wide, with 1/8yd (.11m) of a yard of all over embroidery 18in (45.7cm) wide for the yoke, would be required. For the wrapper 2¾yd (2.51m) of flannel are needed or 5/8yd (.55m) for the sack. The slip is also designed for a nightgown, and it would take 1⅝yd (1.46m) of lawn 27in (68.6cm) wide to make this. Flannel is used for the petticoat and it would take 1⅛yd (1.02m) 27in (68.6cm) wide for this.

Every little girl who is the proud owner of a doll takes as much interest in making a suitable mátch for her as any of the society women of whom we read so much shows in making a match for her daughters. Another very important point in this matter is that the doll to be married should have a suitable dress, for doubtless in the next *Daily Dollette* a full account of the bride's attire will be duly chronicled. A dress designed especially for bride-to-be is shown in *Illustration 2, 3 and 4* (No. 330), though this design is equally desirable for the doll who is still enjoying a happy single life, when at receptions or making very formal calls. This semi-princess dress may be made with a full-length train or in round length as desired, with high or round neck, according to the purpose for which the dress is designed, and with the full-length or short one seam sleeves. Long sleeves are worn during the day, while short sleeves are more appropriate for evening.

Oftentimes these dresses may be made from remnants of dresses made for the woman, but when this is not the case exactly such materials as desired may be bought. For dresses on this order only soft materials, as crêpe de Chine and soft silks, are appropriate, as anything heavier would not drape gracefully. To make the dress for a 22in (55.9cm) doll with the train 2⅜yd (2.15m) of material 20in (50.8cm) wide, 1⅜yd (1.24m) 33in (83.8cm) wide or 1⅛yd (1.02m) 44in (111.7cm) wide would be required, with 3/8yd (.33m) of lace 18in (45.7cm) for the body and shorter sleeves.

Another girl dolls' set is shown in *Illustration 5* (No. 329), a set consisting of a semi-princess dress and a semi-fitting coat. Both of these models show the new features which are seen in the young girls' clothes at the present moment.

The semi-princess dress is made in the popular Moyen-âge style, with a plaited or gathered flounce according to the material used for its development. If very soft material is used for the dress, the gathered skirt would be more desirable, while made of firmer goods the plaited skirt would be better adapted to the material. This dress is one which may be developed very simply or elaborately as desired. The plainer model would be made without the bretelles and button trimming, while the more elaborate dress would be made with these and with the bretelles trimmed with a very narrow braid. A lightweight broadcloth would be very appropriate for this dress, or henrietta would be desirable. For the little yoke and collar, tucked lawn for the plain dress or allover lace for the dressy model would be pretty. To make this dress for a 22in (55.9cm) doll, 1⅛yd (1.02m) of material 27in (68.6cm) wide or 7/8yd (.77m) 36in (91.4cm) wide would be required, with 1/8yd (.11m) of lace or tucking 18in (45.7cm) wide for the yoke and collar.

Illustration 2. Doll in gown "almost ready to be married," No. 330.

The semi-fitting coat is made with the deep closing which has proved such a popular feature and is truly a very smart little model. If a three-piece effect is desired, the coat might be made of the same material as the dress, and broadcloth would be desirable for their three-piece suit. To make the coat, 7/8yd (.77m) of material 27in (68.6cm) wide or 3/4yd (.69m) 44in (111.7cm) wide would be required, with 5/8yd (.55m) of silk 27in (68.6cm) wide for the collar facing.

Every little baby seems to have a desire for a doll, almost as soon as it is large enough to hold one. It would seem

Illustration 3. Doll in gown with the long train, No. 330.

undesirable to give a mere infant anything at all breakable, for it is one of the chief delights of the youngster to throw everything on the floor that comes within its touch. A doll designed for just such use is shown in *Illustration 6* (No. 331), and this doll may be thrown clear to the other end of the room without being injured. Not only the mere infant, but the little girl, will like this doll the best to play with, as is seen every day in any family where there are children. The nice bisque doll is all right to show one's friends and dress up, but when it comes to real play it is the rag doll which is favored and is held close in some living little girl's arms at night.

This doll has all the good points of the bisque doll which may be bought, without any of its undesirable qualities. The arms and legs are made so as to bend, a feature dear to every little girl's heart, and the head of the doll may be painted in oil or watercolors or the features may be stitched with colored thread according to the lines in the pattern.

A strong muslin is the most desirable material for this doll, and cotton batting is used to stuff it. The doll is stuffed in sections and then stitched as to arrange for the joints in the legs and arms.

To make the 22in (55.9cm) doll 7/8yd (.77m) of material 27in (68.6cm) wide or 5/8yd (.55m) of material 1yd (.91m) wide would be required. Strong thread should be used for the stitching so as to stand the heavy strain.

After the little girl has had her doll for a while she usually wants to see it grow up, and the first step toward this is to put it in girls' clothes. The little girls' set shown in *Illustration 7* (No. 332) consists of a little dress, a box coat and a brownie bonnet.

The dress is very simple and is entirely appropriate for Miss Dollie to wear when she attends school or goes for walks with her mother. Cashmere would be a very good material for this dress for winter wear, and the skirt might be plaited or gathered as preferred. Of this material 44in (111.7cm) wide 7/8yd (.77m) would be required for the 22in (55.9cm) doll. Wash materials are also used a great deal for the dresses of dolls and linen and lawn are both satisfactory. The Dutch collar of the wash dress would be very dainty if trimmed with lace insertion and edging. To make the dress of 24in (61cm) material 1½yd (1.36m) would be required. Dark buttons would be used on the cloth dress, while for the wash model small pearl buttons might be used for the fastening, which comes in the front.

Illustration 4. Back of gown, No. 330.

The coat of this set may be made in either the full or 7/8yd (.77m) as desired, and with the fronts closed to the neck or rolled open. This last feature is one of the newest ideas in women's and girls' coats, so Mistress Dollie will doubtless appreciate it a great deal. To make the coat, lightweight materials, as serge or bedford cord, should be used, and for this model 5/8yd (.55m) 44in (11.17cm) wide or 7/8yd (.77m) 27in (68.6cm) wide would be required, with 1/2yd (.46m) of silk 27in (68.6cm) wide for the facings.

The bonnet might be made of white velvet or of material to match the coat, and trimmed with a pretty little frill as shown here. For this bonnet 1/4yd (.23m) of material 20in (50.8cm) or more wide would be required.

Illustration 5. Set of girl dolls' clothes consisting of a semi-princess dress and a semi-fitting coat, No. 329.

Illustration 6. Rag doll, No. 331.

Illustration 7. Set of girl dolls' clothes consisting of a little dress, a box coat and a brownie bonnet, No. 332.

Creative Collecting

by **Susan Sirkis**

Straw Bonnet

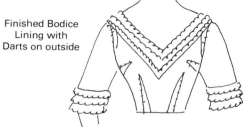

Finished Bodice
Lining with
Darts on outside

Illustration 1. The 20in (50.8cm) lady in her new dress and body standing with her original body. *Photograph by Rob Sirkis.*

Finished Dress

At sometime in the experience of each doll collector there is a basic decision which must be made. The necessity arises when one is faced with the problem of the dusty, dirty, unattractive specimens who arrive in one's collection clothed perhaps in their original if somewhat tattered garments.

I happen to be a purist -- I prefer my antique dolls to be dressed in original, or at least contemporary, garments as long as the garments are reasonably clean and well mended. If, however, the garments are murky with grime and flaky to the touch and cannot be brought to respectable condition, I do not allow them in my doll cabinet. Nor do I allow nude dolls to cavort around amongst the ladies and gentlemen in the cabinet. So, the decision is taken and the original garments are replaced. Usually the under garments being of cotton and protected

by the outer garments continue in use after proper and meticulous cleaning. The outer garments are sketched, copied and ideally, photographed on the doll -- then carefully packed away in Ziploc bags with a few moth flakes wrapped in white tissue paper. Each package is carefully tagged with the doll's name, type and accession number so that there is no danger of the doll and her original garments becoming separated should she leave my collection.

Normally the original dress is copied in a modern natural fiber fabric which is treated in any one of a variety of ways so that it appears old. I do not, generally speaking, like to use old fabrics because so often when exposed to the pollutants in our modern air they begin to crumble thus wasting my time and effort. I do use old trims and laces as they seem to hold up better than fabric. Each dress I make is very carefully labeled on the inside lower back hem with my name so that there can be no confusion in the mind of even the least experienced of doll collectors as to whether or not the dress is original.

The dress, on a 20in (50.8cm) doll, is made of yellow silk broadcloth and silk organza with white lace. It is based on designs of 1910 to 1912. The natural straw hat was purchased at the Milliner's Shop in Colonial Williamsburg and trimmed as shown with yellow ribbon and pale peach flowers and feathers.

Cut the bodice lining pieces of white batiste. Sew darts in fronts. Join front and backs at shoulder and underarm seams. Place on doll, darts and seams out. Turn neck and sleeves seam allowances out. Remove from doll and feather-stitch hems down. Make the lining sleeves of organza. Make a narrow hem in the bottoms. Sew sleeve seams and sew sleeves to lining. The seams and hems should be inside the sleeve but the sleeve should be whipped to the armscyes so that the raw edges are outside. These odd maneuvers with the darts and seams of the lining will ensure a smooth and attractive interior appearance. Trim the bottom of each sleeve and the neck with three rows of 1/2in (1.3cm) lace as shown in sketch of finished lining.

Cut organza lining pieces. Form and baste pleats in bodice pieces. Baste bodice pieces to organza lining. Gather lining pieces along double dotted lines at waist edges to control fullness. Turn bodice and lining edges under along neck edges and sleeve bottoms. Feather-stitch hems in place. Sew underarm seams, being careful not to disarrange pleats. Place lining on doll. Put bodice pieces on over lining, arranging as shown in sketch. Pin in place. Remove from doll and tack in place. Baste together along waist edge. Turn under back edges and face.

There are three skirts, each assembled separately, and finally joined at the waist edge. Make the bottom skirt of silk broadcloth lined with batiste. Sew side seams and center back seam. Turn under edges of opening and feather-stitch in place. Gather top of skirt slightly to fit doll just above natural waistline. Hem bottom of skirt to ground level. Make the second skirt of unlined organza. Use the skirt pattern but cut the organza 1in (2.5cm) wider on the side seams and 1in (2.5cm) longer around the bottom. Assemble exactly the same as the other, but do not hem yet. Finally make an overskirt from a piece of lace 8in (20.3cm) wide and 22in (55.9cm) long. Sew a center back seam, leaving open for placket to coincide with the plackets in

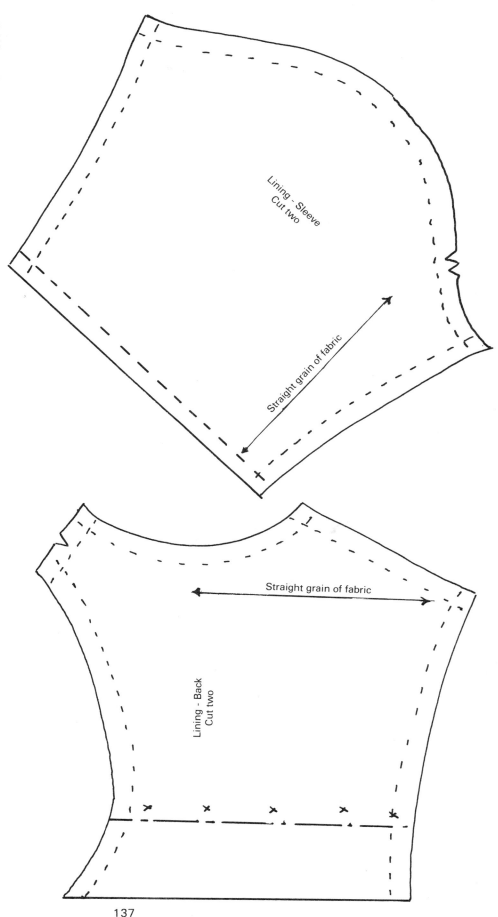

137

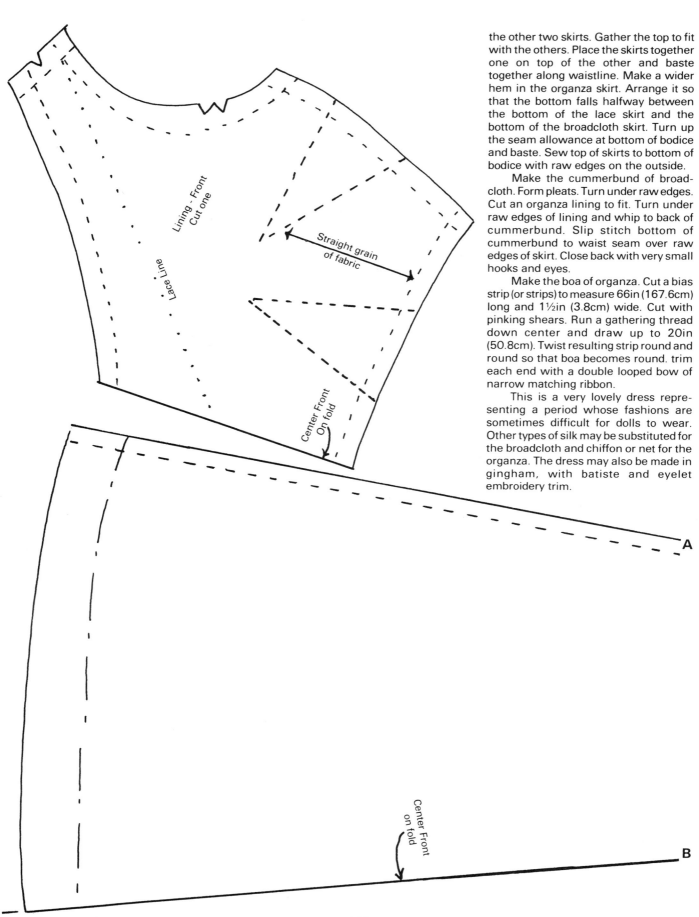

the other two skirts. Gather the top to fit with the others. Place the skirts together one on top of the other and baste together along waistline. Make a wider hem in the organza skirt. Arrange it so that the bottom falls halfway between the bottom of the lace skirt and the bottom of the broadcloth skirt. Turn up the seam allowance at bottom of bodice and baste. Sew top of skirts to bottom of bodice with raw edges on the outside.

Make the cummerbund of broadcloth. Form pleats. Turn under raw edges. Cut an organza lining to fit. Turn under raw edges of lining and whip to back of cummerbund. Slip stitch bottom of cummerbund to waist seam over raw edges of skirt. Close back with very small hooks and eyes.

Make the boa of organza. Cut a bias strip (or strips) to measure 66in (167.6cm) long and 1½in (3.8cm) wide. Cut with pinking shears. Run a gathering thread down center and draw up to 20in (50.8cm). Twist resulting strip round and round so that boa becomes round. trim each end with a double looped bow of narrow matching ribbon.

This is a very lovely dress representing a period whose fashions are sometimes difficult for dolls to wear. Other types of silk may be substituted for the broadcloth and chiffon or net for the organza. The dress may also be made in gingham, with batiste and eyelet embroidery trim.

Lining - Front
Cut one

Lace Line

Straight grain of fabric

Center Front
On fold

A

Center Front
on fold

B

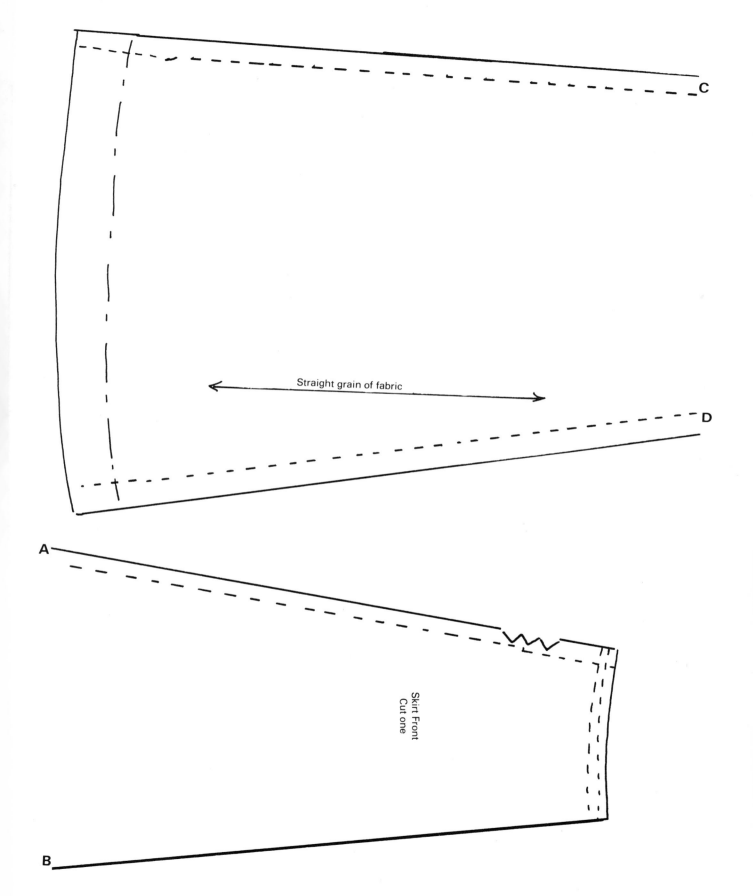

Straight grain of fabric

C

D

A

B

Skirt Front
Cut one

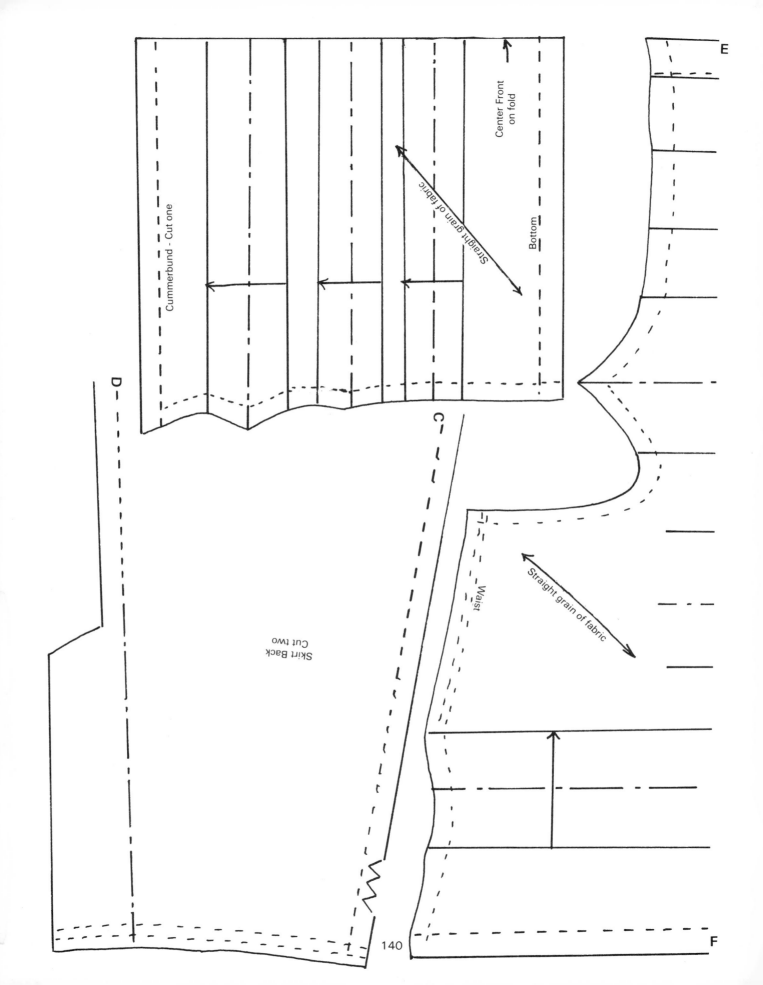

Cummerbund - Cut one

Center Front
on fold

Bottom

Straight grain of fabric

E

D

C

Waist

Straight grain of fabric

Skirt Back
Cut two

140

F

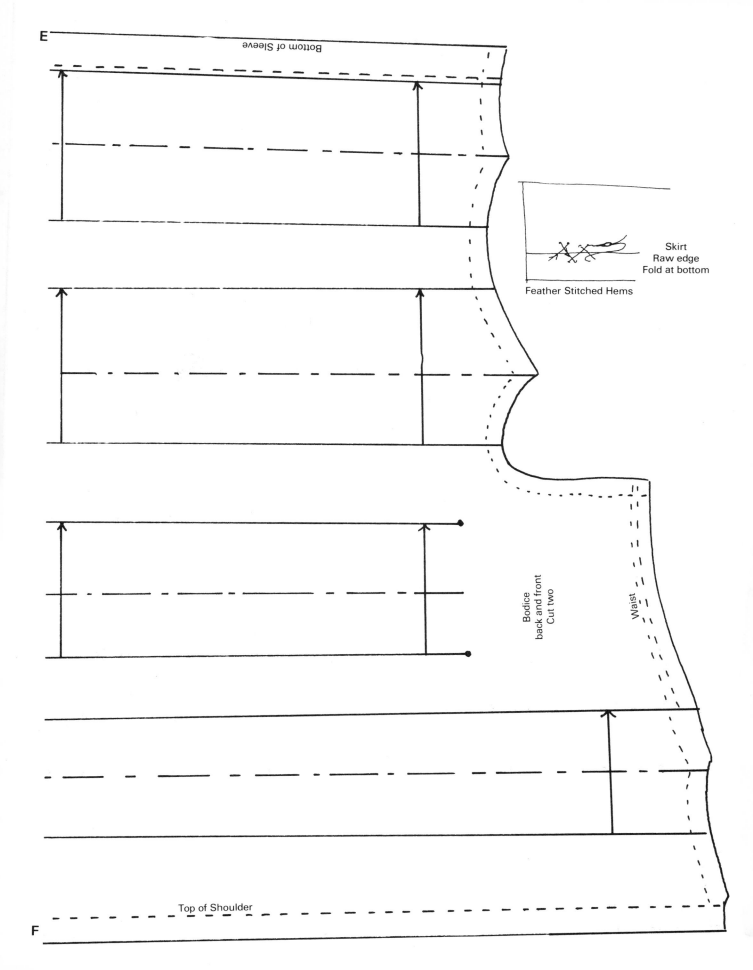

E

Bottom of Sleeve

Skirt
Raw edge
Fold at bottom

Feather Stitched Hems

Bodice
back and front
Cut two

Waist

Top of Shoulder

F

THE DOLL'S WARDROBE

from *The Delineator*, November 1911

Design 347.

How many little girls know what treasures are rolled up and tucked away in the chest of drawers in the sewing room? How many have rummaged in the trunk in the attic to see if they can find some pieces of silk or muslin there? How many know what they can make if mother lets them have the extra yard or so of material which was left from her last pretty dress? Design 347 for a girl doll's Empire dress answers that last question. It is just like those real people wear now. It has a large collar, and a plaited peplum at the high waistline, and a ruching around the bottom of the skirt, all the fashionable features of the dresses for grown-ups. It is easy to make, too, because the skirt is just gathered and the sleeves are cut in one with the body.

For a doll 22in (55.9cm) long, 7/8yd (.77m) of material 36in (91.4cm) wide, with 3/8yd (.33m) of contrasting material 27in (68.6cm) wide for the collar will be required for the dress with the collar and plaitings; and for the dress without these, 3/4yd (.69m) of material 36in (91.4cm) wide.

Design 347 comes in nine sizes, from a 14in (35.6cm) to 30in (76.2cm) doll.

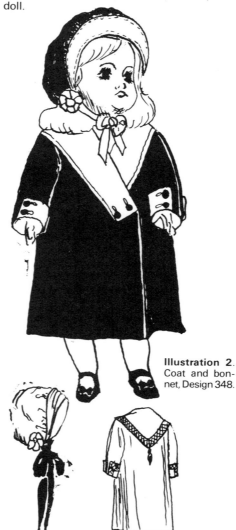

Illustration 1. Empire dress, Design 347.

Design 348.

Design 348 will appeal to many little mothers who think that it is not any fun to take out their doll children in the same coats and hats they wore last year, for it gives a coat with the fashionable kimono sleeves and broad collar and a cunning little bonnet.

For a doll 22in (55.9cm) long, 3/8yd (.33m) of material 20in (50.8cm) or more wide, with 1/4yd (.23m) of silk 20in (50.8cm) wide for the brim, and 3/8yd (.33m) wide for the lining will be required for the bonnet. For the coat 5/8yd (.55m) of material 36in (91.4cm) wide, with 1/2yd (.46m) contrasting material 20in (50.8cm) wide for the collar and cuffs will be required.

Design 348 comes in nine sizes, from a 14in (35.6cm) to 30in (76.2cm) doll.

Illustration 2. Coat and bonnet, Design 348.

Design 345.

A Lady doll has a certain fascination, for one can make her do and say things just like mother or like the beautiful aunty who has such pretty clothes and goes to parties; a boy doll is nice for a change, and a baby to wheel and rock; but nothing equals the pleasure of having a little girl doll who will do the most dreadful forbidden things and have to be scolded good and hard. Her clothes are more interesting too.

It is usually great fun for a little girl to dress her doll in the same kind of clothes that she wears herself. Now most little girls when they are having a splendid time, playing just as hard as they can, wear rompers, and so dolly, of course, must have a pair of rompers too. Design 345 shows how to make them and also a sun hat, for she must have that when she plays outdoors or in the sandpile with her mother, who pretends that they are by the seashore again. The rompers can have high neck with a turnover collar, or a square neck trimmed with bands, a belt and a pocket if you want them, and full-length or shorter sleeves. Having the sleeves cut in one with the body, they are both up-to-date and easily made. The sun hat is simple but too cunning for words with its puff crown, wide brim, and ruffle edge, and a doll rarely looks sweeter than when her soft curls are pulled out in front of it and crisp bows are tied under her chin.

For a doll 22in (55.9cm) long, 1yd (.91m) of material 27in (68.6cm) or more wide, with 1/4yd (.23m) of contrasting material 27in (68.6cm) wide for belt and bands will be required for the rompers, and 5/8yd (.55m) of material 20in (50.8cm) wide for the sun hat with 3/8yd (.33m) of ribbon for ties.

Design 345 come in nine sizes, from a 14in (35.6cm) to 30in (76.2cm) doll.

Design 346.

Part of the pleasure of playing with dolls is dressing and undressing them, and the more things a dolly has to put on and take off the more fun it is. How cunning she looks, too, in a little nightgown, especially when it slips on over the head and has kimono sleeves just like her mother's. As she must have drawers and a petticoat as well which should be fine and dainty so that they may be shown with pride, this set, design 346, has been made for her wardrobe.

For a doll 22in (55.9cm) long, 1yd (.91m) of material 27in (68.6cm) or more wide will be required for the nightgown, 1/2yd (.46m) of material 36in (91.4cm) wide for the drawers.

Design 346 comes in nine sizes, from a 14in (35.6cm) to 30in (76.2cm) doll.

Back.

Illustration 4. Nightgown, drawers and petticoat, Design 346.

Illustration 3. Rompers and a sun hat, Design 345.

The two pretty garments shown in the illustration would make a very stylish outfit for little Miss Dolly. The cape is made of red cashmere trimmed with black velvet ribbon, and the dress of green China silk, with dark green velvet bretelle and neckband, trimmed with gold braid.

The cape consists of a circular piece, fitted on each shoulder by a dart. To its lower edge the graduated four-piece flounce is attached. The neck edge is completed by a flaring collar.

The dress has a yoke fitted by shoulder seams and fastening in the back. To the lower edge of the yoke the straight one-piece skirt is gathered, the joining being concealed by the bretelle. The neck is finished with a binding. The sleeves are one seamed and gathered along the seam edges. They are surmounted by shaped epaulets.

This pattern is cut in seven sizes, for dolls measuring 12in (30.5cm) to 24in (61cm) from crown of head to sole of foot. The 18in (45.7cm) size requires, for dress, 1¼yd (1.14m) of silk 22in (55.9cm) wide, with 1/4yd (.23m) yard of velvet 22in (55.9cm) wide for bretelle. Cape requires 1/4yd (.23m) of 44in (111.7cm) goods and 2yd (1.82m) of braid.

Girl Doll's Set

The Designer - November, 1898

Illustration 1. Girl doll's set.

Getting Miss Dolly Ready for Easter

from *The Delineator*, March 1910

Illustration 5. Facing the neck edge.

Illustration 6. Making the bretelles.

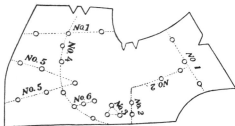

Illustration 1. An Easter bride.

If you are going to have an Easter bride now is the time to make the wedding dress. *Illustration 2* shows you how to lay the pattern on your material. It is made with short sleeves so piece 4 is cut off at the crossline of single perforations near the top. Pieces 1, 5 and 7 are cut with the triple perforations on a lengthwise fold, the others with the double perforations lengthwise.

Turn under the hems on the backs at the notches, baste and hem them. The waist is put together with outlet seams. Baste through the single perforations near the seam edges. Take up the darts in the fronts bringing the dart perforations together and basting through them. There are so many perforations in the front that *Illustration 4* explains them.

Try the waist on the doll. If it is too small, let out the deep seams. When it fits nicely, sew the seams and darts. Cut the neck away at the square line of single perforations on the front and back. Turn under the neck edge 1/4in (.65cm), clip it at the corners so that it will lie flat, baste and face it.

Put the sleeve together with the notches in its side edges matching, sewing the seam 1/4in (.65cm) from the edge. Turn up the lower edge of the sleeve 1/4in (.65cm) and face it like the neck of the waist. Gather the top of the sleeve between the notches and sew it into the waist with its notches matching those in the armhole.

Turn the hems under on the side edges of the bretelles and hem them down. There are two plaits in each bretelle. The first plait is made by bringing the fold of the hem on the notched side of the bretelle over to the nearest row of triple perforations and basting it. The second plait is made by creasing through the single perforations and bringing the crease over to the next row of triple perforations and basting. The plaits turn toward the armhole. Tack the underfolds of the plaits to a narrow tape to hold them in place. Gather the ends of the bretelles and place them on the waist with the ends marked with double notches at the front. The double notches of the bretelles should be placed on the triple perforations on the waist. The bretelles should be sewed flat to the waist with invisible stitches. The ends are covered by the girdle of the skirt.

Put the skirt together with the notches matching, basting the seams 1/4in (.65cm) from the edges. Leave a placket opening on the left side of piece 7. To make the box plait in the back, crease through the lines of single perforations in piece 7 and bring the crease over to the triple perforations. Baste and press. Tack the underfolds of the plaits to a piece of tape just below the hips to hold them in place.

Join the skirt to the waist with the double perforation in pieces 5 and 6 at the lower edge of the waist. The underarm seams of the skirt and waist should come together, and the upper edge of pieces 5 and 6 should fall on the line of single perforations in the waist. Turn under the upper edge of the belt and girdle 1/4in (.65cm) and tack it to the waist. Turn under the right end of the girdle 5/8in (1.6cm) and shirr it 1/8in (.31cm) from the fold. Try the dress on and turn under the left end of the girdle as much as is necessary, gather it and tack it to the waist. Turn under the lower edge of the girdle on piece 6 1/4in (.65cm) and tack it to the back of the skirt. Turn up the lower edge of the skirt 1/4in (.65cm) and face it.

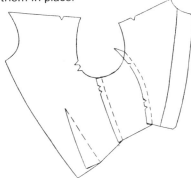

Illustration 3. Putting the waist together.

Illustration 4. No. 1, Outlet seam perforation. No. 2, Square neck. No. 3, Triple perforations for cutting. No. 4, Where the skirt joins the waist. No 5, The dart perforations. No. 6, Line for the bretelle.

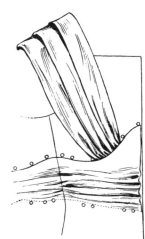

Illustration 7. Sewing the skirt to waist.

Illustration 2. Pattern laid on material.

The Latest Fashions for Toyland

Illustration 1. Party dress and cape, Design 386.

Since yours is a gay, flighty doll who likes to go to parties, she should have a party dress (Design 386). This pretty frock if made of flowered material, will surely cause all the other dolls to look up. The Empire style is charming, and the little bretelles add to the dainty effect. These may be finished off at the waistline with rosettes. The circular cape is not only appropriate but unusually distinctive, and both make an attractive combination.

This girl dolls' dress in 24in (61cm) size requires 1½yd (1.36m) material 36in (91.4cm) wide.

Design 386 in nine sizes, 14in (35.6cm) to 30in (76.2cm).

Illustration 2. Dress, cap, coat, petticoat and envelope chemise, Design 385.

Mother will not mind making this set for her little girl's doll because it is so easy to make; and both her little girl and dolly will like it because it is in excellent taste. This frock is fresh and youthful in appearance, and the lace and insertion make it dainty. The cap and coat with its round collar and belt — the latter may be omitted — help carry out the idea of simplicity. The petticoat and envelope chemise should be in the wardrobe of every well-dressed doll.

This girl dolls' dress in 24in (61cm) size requires 7/8yd (.77m) material 36in (91.4cm) wide, 5½yd (5m) insertion, and 1½yd (1.36m) edging.

Design 385 in nine sizes, 14in (35.6cm) to 30in (76.2cm).

Illustration 3. Coat, skirt, blouse and tam-o'-shanter, Design 388.

You must take dolly out to get the air; and if it be only for a walk she will need an outdoor costume (Design 388). This set of sport clothes will be just the thing. If dolly has golden curls she will look beautiful in a black velvet tam-o'-shanter. The skirt has real pockets, and the blouse a pretty sailor collar. On cold days dolly will be comfortable if only she buttons her coat collar high.

Coat and skirt in the 24in (61cm) size require 1yd (.91m) 44in (111.7cm) material, 1½yd (1.36m) fur band, and 3/8yd (.33m) material 18in (45.7cm) or more for hat.

Design 388 in nine sizes, 14in (35.6cm) to 30in (76.2cm).

from *The Delineator* November 1916

Illustration 4. Russian blouse dress, coat and hat, Design 387.

If you have a Russian blouse dress, dolly will surely want one (Design 387). And if you do not, she will want it just the same; for Russian blouses are now the best of style for grown-ups, little girls, and dolls. This dress has a pretty soft gathering from the yoke. If the coat and hat are made of the same materials, for instance, velveteen or corduroy, dolly's mother will have reason to be proud of her.

This girl dolls' dress in 24in (61cm) material requires 1⅛yd (1.02m) 36in (91.4cm) material, with 1/4yd (.23m) contrasting material 27in (68.6cm).

Design 387 in nine sizes, 14in (35.6cm) to 30in (76.2cm).

DOLLS' FASHIONS FOR THE COMING SEASON

from The Delineator, **November 1913**

It will delight any wee miss to possess a set made from Design 362, for it consists of a regular bath robe and pajamas. Madras, mercerized cottons and silks may be used for the pajamas.

For a doll 24in (61cm) tall, 1⅛yd (1.02m) of material 27in (68.6cm) wide and 2yds (1.82m) of ribbon to bind are required for the bath robe. The pajamas require ⅞yd (.77m) of material 36in (91.4cm) wide.

Design 362 comes in nine sizes, from 14in (35.6cm) to 30in (76.2cm).

If you decide to dress a little girl doll, Design 361 will be found a most complete set. There is the cap and the coat, a yoke dress, a petticoat and drawers.

For a doll 24in (61cm) tall, the coat requires ⅞yd (.77m) 36in (91.4cm) wide, the dress requires 1yd (.91m) of material 27in (68.6cm) wide, the petticoat requires ¼yd (.23m) of material 36in (91.4cm) wide for body and ⅜yd (.33m) 32in (81.3cm) wide for skirt, and the drawers require ½yd (.46m) 27in (68.6cm) wide.

Design 361, in nine sizes, from 14in (35.6cm) to 30in (76.2cm).

Design 364 consists of a coat, hat and Russian blouse dress.

For a doll 24in (61cm) tall, the coat requires 1yd (.91m) of material 36in (91.4cm) wide; the dress 7/8yd (.77m) 36in (91.4cm) wide and 3/8yd (.33m) 27in (68.6cm) wide; the hat requires 3/8yd (.33m) 27in (68.6cm) wide, 1/4yd (.23m) of contrasting material 27in (68.6cm) wide, 1/2yd (.46m) of ribbon and 3/8yd (.33m) of crinoline 27in (68.6cm) wide.

Design 364, in nine sizes 14in (35.6cm) to 30in (76.2cm).

361

362

Illustration 1. Cap and coat, yoke dress, petticoat and drawers, Design 361.

To include in the girl doll's trousseau when her young mother takes her to play on the sandpile is set 363, consisting of a dress, bloomers and hat.

For a doll 24in (61cm) tall, the dress requires 1yd (.91m) of material 27in (68.6cm) wide, with 3/8yd (.33m) of contrasting material the same width. The bloomers require 3/4yd (.69m) of material 27in (68.6cm) wide, and for the hat 1/2yd (.46m) of material 27in (68.6cm) wide, 1/4yd (.23m) of canvas or butcher's linen 27in (68.6cm) wide and 1/8yd (.11m) of crinoline 27in (68.6cm) wide.

Design 363 comes in nine sizes, from 14in (35.6cm) to 30in (76.2cm).

Illustration 3. Dress, bloomers and hat, Design 363.

363

362

Illustration 2. Bath robe and pajamas, Design 362.

Illustration 4. Coat, hat and Russian blouse dress, Design 364.

364

Styles for Dolls

December 1916, <u>The Delineator</u>.

Illustration 1. Empire dress with jumper and underblouse, hat, coat, petticoat and envelope drawers, Design 392.

Susan Simplicity Simpson has a modern mother with a great many newfangled notions about bringing up children. She favors the set of Design 392 because it is plain and easy to make, and we agree that Susan looks charming in it. It has an Empire dress with a jumper and underblouse that can be changed to freshen up the costume. There is a hat, and a coat that has a stylish Russian closing and loose belt. The petticoat and envelope drawers are necessary, for Susan will not look right outside unless dressed right underneath.

Design 392 in nine sizes, 14in (35.6cm) to 30in (76.2cm).

Illustration 2. Wedding gown, Design 390.

"To love and to cherish," Design 390 was surely created. There are always weddings in the best doll families, and one satisfactory thing about them is that a bridegroom is not really necessary, unless you happen to have one handy, but a gown is. If your dolly tells you that she is falling in love with the idea that she must be a bride this month, you set right to work and see about the gown. Period costumes are very much in vogue for the bride of today. Nothing would suit your doll's classic type of beauty better than the simple lines of this Grecian gown. It falls from the shoulder in soft folds. The long braided sash comes over the shoulder in surplice effect, gathers in the waist loosely and ties in a graceful knot at the knee. The angel sleeves may be omitted, but they are more discreet and very becoming for the bridal gown. You will like this design for it is so simple to make.

Design 390 in nine sizes, 14in (35.6cm) to 30in (76.2cm).

Illustration 3. Dress, coat and bonnet, Design 391.

Do not be so rushed that you will overlook Design 391. We know that you are pretty busy with the Christmas entertainment at school and going down to see Santa Claus, and trying to tell him what you want, and seeing all the things in the toy department, and saving up your pennies to buy mother a Christmas present, and wondering if you will really get the doll with the blue eyes and the golden curls. But take care of the old love before you bring on the new. See that Mary Edith's wardrobe is replenished. This set offers a dainty frock with cunning puff sleeves and a smart panel down the front that drops from a yoke. There is a coat that will protect the frock in stormy weather, with a popular cape collar and a belt if you like. The bonnet has the sweetest puffed crown and frames her face charmingly. Drawers and a dainty petticoat complete the outfit.

Design 391 in ten sizes, 12in (30.5cm) to 30in (76.2cm).

Illustration 4. French dress, Empire coat and hat, Design 389.

A come-hither look in those brown eyes makes you want to snatch her up and hug her in spite of her lovely frock (Design 389). You always want to have your child well-dressed. It keeps up her self-respect, and she is more apt to have a restraining influence on her cousin, Jemima Rag, who is continually falling down stairs and spilling her sawdust in a most untidy fashion. A tea party is the dearest social duty of dolly, and there frocks are discussed and worn that would startle the ideas of French designers. The dress in this set is French and quite charming for that fluffy type of doll. The skirt has two ruffles that are edged with lace or made of embroidery flouncing. A bit of ribbon around the waist does wonders. Dolly will look charming if she wears the round neck and short sleeves, but of course, if she is subject to colds, have a high neck and long sleeves. A simple Empire coat comes with the design, and to top off the costume there is an adorable bonnet with Dutch points and real streamers down the back, so your child will be well prepared to go out on nice winter days.

Design 389 in nine sizes, 14in (35.6cm) to 30in (76.2cm).

WHAT THE DOLLS WILL BE WEARING FOR CHRISTMAS

from *The Delineator* December 1912

Illustration **1**. French dress and bonnet, Design 357.

Illustration **2**. Empire dress and bonnet, Design 358.

Illustration **3**. Coat and dress, Design 359.

Illustration **4**. Kimono, Design 360.

A very little girl will adore the dolly who wears a dress like that in design 357. I know she will, because I know that little mothers like to dress their children just like mother's children, and love best the dolly with a frock like their own. Little girls wear French dresses, with long waists and gathered skirts, made, in many cases of white lawn or batiste trimmed with lace, or of embroidered flouncing and edging. By means of design 357 dolly can have one too, and not only that, but a quaint and cunning bonnet for wearing with it.

For a doll 22in (55.9cm) long, 1⅝yd (1.46m) of flouncing 5in (12.7cm) deep for the sleeves and skirt, 3/8yd (.33m) of material 36in (91.4cm) wide for the body and yokes, and 1⅛yd (1.02m) of edging 3½in (8.9cm) deep for bretelles, will be required for the dress as shown on the figure, and 1/4yd (.23m) of material 30in (76.2cm) or more wide for the bonnet.

Design 357 comes in nine sizes from 14in (35.6cm) to 30in (76.2cm) doll.

S ince Empire dresses are becoming more and more fashionable for you little girls, it seems that no time should be lost in providing your girl doll with one. You want her to look well dressed when she calls on her cousins, and you can be sure she will be if she has an Empire dress like your new holiday frock. You have one, haven't you, with a plain skirt, and a peplum, and lace or different-colored collar and cuffs? Lots of little girls are having them very much like that shown in design 358, and I am sure the dolls will be wearing them for Christmas, too. Included in the design is a bonnet which came from Paris. It is really smart with its point on top and frill about the face and will be wonderfully becoming.

For a doll 22in (55.9cm) long, 3/4yd (.69m) of material 36in (91.4cm) wide, 1/4yd (.23m) 20in (50.8cm) wide for the collar, cuffs and belt, and 1/8yd (.11m) 18in (45.7cm) or more wide for the frill, will be required for the dress, and 1/4yd (.23m) 20in (50.8cm) wide with 5/8yd (.55m) of edging 2in (5.1cm) wide for the frill, and 3/4yd (.69m) of ribbon for ties and bows for the bonnet.

Design 358 comes in nine sizes, from a 14in (35.6cm) to 30in (76.2cm) doll.

T here is a lull in the middle of Christmas morning, after the stockings have been emptied or the Christmas tree stripped of its fruit, when there is only one thing for a little girl to do — and that is to take the new dolly out for an airing. You will want to draw her up and down on your sled, or take her over next door for a visit, and what on earth will you do if she does not have a coat? I should speak to mother about that at once and ask her to make you one like the one in design 359. It is a copy of a real little girl's coat, a really fashionable little coat. There is also a pretty dress in the design with a smart and up-to-date cut and cunning collar and cuffs.

For a doll 22in (55.9cm) long, 7/8yd (.77m) of material 36in (91.4cm) wide, and 1/4yd (.23m) of contrasting material 36in (91.4cm) wide for the collar and cuffs, will be required for the coat, and 3/4yd (.69m) 36in (91.4cm) wide and 1/8yd (.11m) 18in (45.7cm) or more wide for collar and cuffs for the dress.

Design 359 comes in nine sizes, from 14in (35.6cm) to 30in (76.2cm) doll.

D o you mean to say that your doll does not have a kimono? Nothing to put on when you take off her dress to comb her hair, and none to take with her when she goes away to spend the night? You surely are going to make her one, then, and are only waiting to wonder how. In design 360 is a darling kimono for a doll and one that you can make her yourself, too, for it is very simple. There is also a dress, quite like those you children are wearing, and bloomers to make it seem complete and real. They are easy to make too.

For a doll 22in (55.9cm) long, 1⅛yd (1.02m) of material 27in (68.6cm) wide for bands to trim will be required for the kimono, 3/4yd (.69m) 36in (91.4cm) wide and 1/4yd (.23m) of contrasting material 27in (68.6cm) wide to trim, for the dress, and 3/8yd (.33m) 36in (91.4cm) wide for bloomers.

Design 360 comes in nine sizes, from 14in (35.6cm) to 30in (76.2cm) of doll.

THE LATEST FASHIONS
FOR XMAS DOLLS

from *The Delineator,* December 1913

SET 365, for a doll 24in (61cm) tall, will require 7/8yd (.77m) of material 36in (91.4cm) wide for the coat; for the dress 7/8yd (.77m) 36in (91.4cm) wide, with 3⅛yd (2.84m) of insertion, 2⅝yd (2.37m) of edging, and 3/4yd (.69m) of ribbon for the sash, for the hat 3/8yd (.33m) 20in (50.8cm) or more wide.

Set 365 was available in nine sizes, from 14in (35.6cm) to 30in (76.2cm).

SET 366, for a doll 24in (61cm) tall, will require for the coat 1yd (.91m) of material 36in (91.4cm) wide; for the dress 1yd (.91m) of material 27in (68.6cm) wide with 3/8yd (.33m) of material 27in (68.6cm) wide for the collar, cuffs, belt and tie; for the hat 1/8yd (.11m) 27in (68.6cm) wide, with 1/8yd (.11m) 20in (50.8cm) wide for the brim.

Set 366 was available in nine sizes, from 14in (35.6cm) to 30in (76.2cm).

SET 367, consisting of a hat, draped coat and dress for a doll 24in (61cm) tall, will require 1yd (.91m) of flouncing 10in (25.4cm) deep for skirt, with 7/8yd (.77m) of edging 5in (12.7cm) deep, 3/8yd (.33m) 36in (91.4cm) wide, 1/2yd (.46m) of edging, 1/8yd (.11m) of allover embroidery 22in (55.9cm) wide and 1/2yd (.46m) of beading.

Set 367 was available in nine sizes, from 14in (35.6cm) to 30in (76.2cm).

SET 368 consists of a coat, dress and gored hat; and for a doll 24in (61cm) tall 1yd (.91m) of material 36in (91.4cm) wide will be required for the coat, 5/8yd (.55m) 36in (91.4cm) wide for the dress, with 1/4yd (.23m) of contrasting material 36in (91.4cm) wide for the collar, cuffs and belt. The coat and hat are equally attractive.

Set 368 was available in nine sizes from 14in (35.6cm), to 30in (76.2cm).

ABOVE LEFT: Illustration 1. Coat, dress and hat, Design 365.

ABOVE RIGHT: Illustration 2. Coat, dress and hat , Design 366.

BELOW LEFT: Illustration 3. Hat, draped coat and dress, Design 367.

BELOW RIGHT: Illustration 4. Coat, dress and gored hat, Design 368.

Sailor Suit from Captain January

to fit 12in (30.5cm) Shirley Temple   by **Joan Chiara**

Editor's Note: This is an adaption of the sailor suit worn by Shirley Temple in the 1936 movie "Captain January."

Pattern to fit 12in (30.5cm) *Shirley Temple* dolls and some 12in (30.5cm) boy dolls.

Blouse and Pants fabric: Navy blue cotton.
Blouse buttons: white.
Pants buttons: red.
Tie: red 1in (2.5cm) soft ribbon.
All edging: 1/8in (3.2mm) soutache braid.
Arm emblem: 1 red anchor applique about 7/8in (22.2mm)

1. SAILOR PANTS—Cut Pants Front, Back, and Front Flap, of Navy blue cotton -- not heavier than percale weight. Sew center back seam around crotch up to waist. Sew center front seam around crotch. Sew side seams from waist to bottom of leg. Match inseams front and back, and sew together starting at bottom of one leg, up to crotch, then down to bottom of opposite leg. Using narrow bias cut strips of same fabric (or matching bias tape), face hem each leg bottom. Face hem entire waist, sewing to inside forming a casing just over 1/4in (6.4mm) wide. Insert 1/4in (6.4mm) wide elastic from the ⊗ on one side, and pull for a snug fit around back waist of pants, fastening at same mark on opposite side.

2. Face hem the front opening of the pants along side and bottom edges, stitching flat to inside.

3. With right sides together on the front flap, stitch bottom edges (curve) together. Clip curve, turn right side out and press flat. Turn in side edges, press, and blindstitch together. Match big dot at center front bottom of flap, to the same dot at center front crotch seam of pants. Stitch flap to front of pants along broken line shown. Using 1/4in (6.4mm) red buttons, sew three on each side of flap, tacking to the pants edge to close up to the waist.

4. SAILOR BLOUSE—Cut Front, Back, Collar, and Insert, and Sleeves of Navy blue cotton. Sew shoulder seams together on front and back.

5. With bias, face hem bottom edge of each sleeve. Sew 1/8in (3.2mm) white braid along broken lines on each sleeve. On *left sleeve only,* sew a tiny red anchor applique (embroider on, if this is not available to you).

6. Slightly gather top of each sleeve between the X's. Fit into armholes and sew in place. Sew down underarm of sleeves, then down side seams of blouse. BE SURE TO CLIP ALL CORNERS AND CURVES, AND PRESS WELL, ON EACH PIECE.

7. Sew both collar pieces together along sides and bottom edge. Turn right side out and press. Sew 1/8in (3.2mm) white braid along broken line. Fit center back of collar neck edge to center back neck edge of blouse, and match the dots on the collar to the shoulder seam and center front dot on the blouse front; then baste all around this edge. Fold facings back over the outside front, tack neckline edge in place, and fit a strip of bias tape along back neck edge to bind. Sew all together with collar between. Trim off excess seam edges, turn right side out with facings on inside, and press. Press collar down in front and back.

8. Turn in lower edges of blouse, and face hem with bias tape. Close front with two white 1/4in (6.4mm) buttons on front, and tiny snaps inside.

9. On the insert, sew two rows of 1/8in (3.2mm) white braide on broken lines. Turn in side and bottom edges, and blindstitch together all around, then press flat. Sew a tiny snap at the O on each corner, and sew remaining half of snap at same mark on inside of blouse front (under collar). Tuck insert inside blouse.

10. Use a softened 1in (2.5cm) wide red rayon ribbon about 13in (33cm) to 14in (35.6cm) long, for the tie. Miter the ends of the ribbon inward and tack together to form a point; then lay under collar, and tie in a loose flat knot at center front.

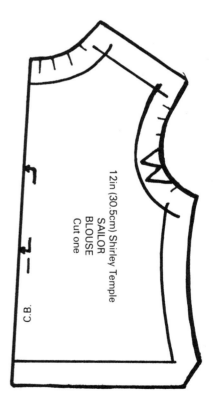

12in (30.5cm) Shirley Temple
SAILOR
BLOUSE
Cut one

C.B.

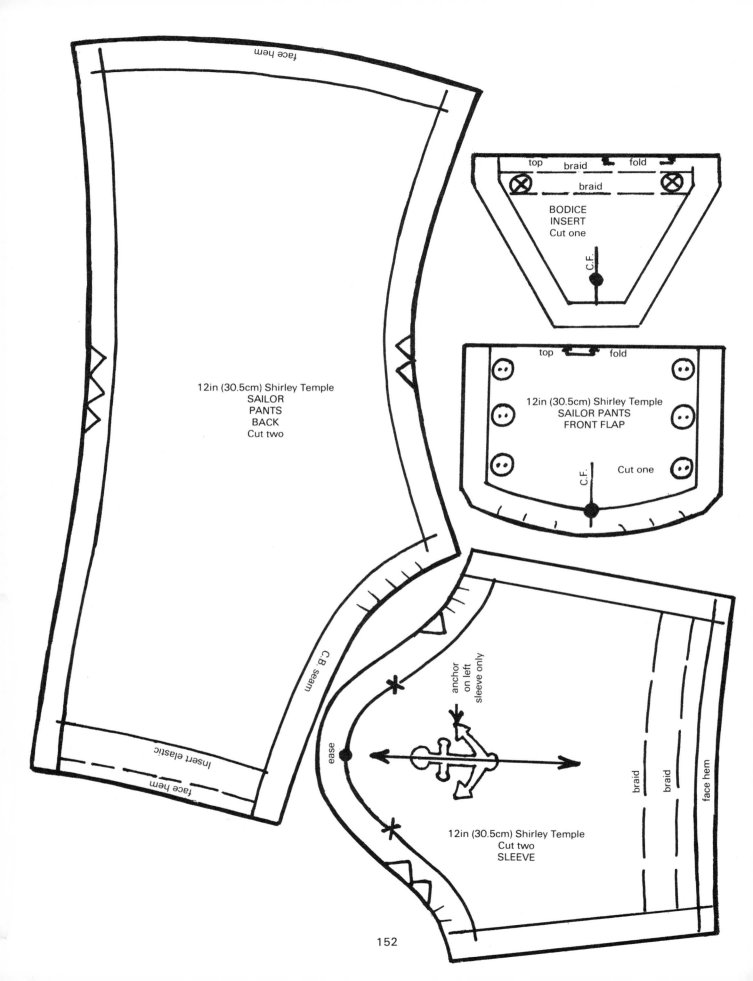

face hem

12in (30.5cm) Shirley Temple
SAILOR
PANTS
BACK
Cut two

top braid fold
braid

BODICE
INSERT
Cut one

C.F.

top fold

12in (30.5cm) Shirley Temple
SAILOR PANTS
FRONT FLAP

C.F.

Cut one

C.B. seam

Insert elastic

face hem

ease

anchor
on left
sleeve only

braid braid

face hem

12in (30.5cm) Shirley Temple
Cut two
SLEEVE

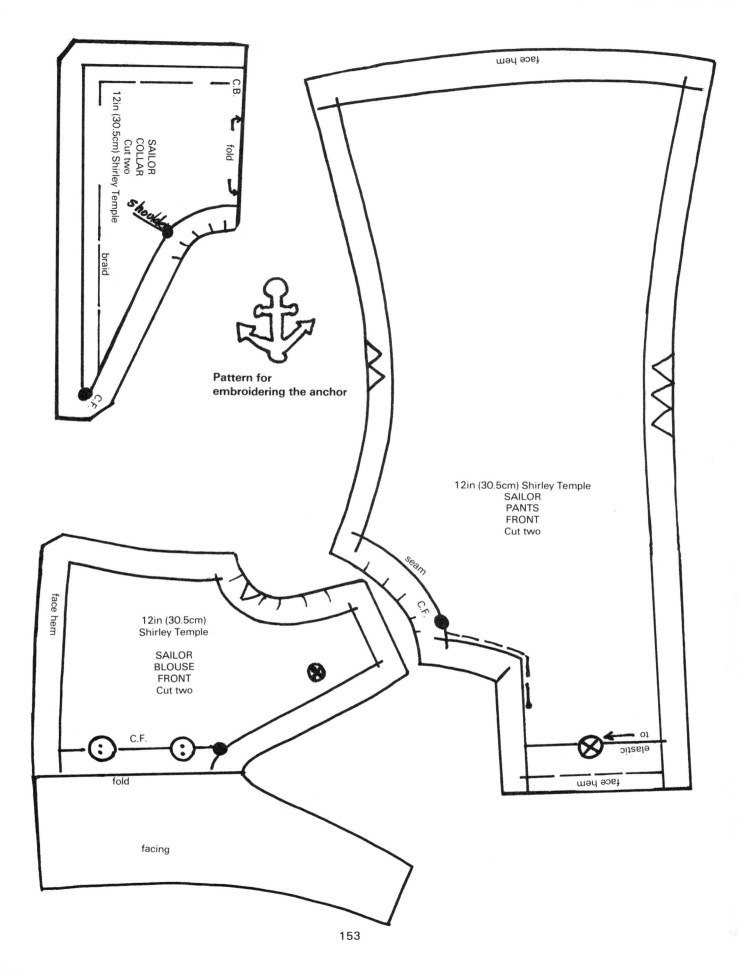

C.B.

fold

SAILOR
COLLAR
Cut two
12in (30.5cm) Shirley Temple

shoulder

braid

C.F.

**Pattern for
embroidering the anchor**

face hem

12in (30.5cm) Shirley Temple
SAILOR
PANTS
FRONT
Cut two

seam

C.F.

face hem

face hem

12in (30.5cm)
Shirley Temple

SAILOR
BLOUSE
FRONT
Cut two

face hem

C.F.

fold

facing

to

elastic

face hem

153

RUFFLED DRESS AND BONNET

1920s GERMAN BISQUE   by **Susan Sirkis**

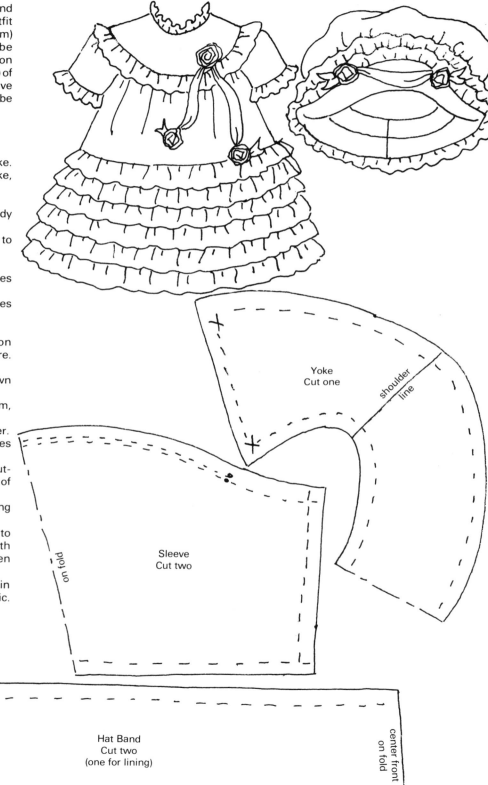

The original version of this dress and bonnet was a commercially made outfit of pink organdy. It fits an 18in (45.7cm) to 20in (50.8cm) doll, but can be lengthened or shortened at the notch on the dress. You will need 6⅞yd (6.23m) of ruffling 3/4in (2cm) wide. It should have a picoted edge. Lace ruffles may be substituted.

DRESS:
1. Sew side seams.
2. Sew shoulder seams.
3. Gather top on dotted lines to fit yoke.
4. Baste ruffle around outside of yoke, right sides together.
5. Sew yoke to neckline.
6. Trim sleeve bottoms with organdy ruffles.
7. Sew sleeve seams. Sew sleeves to dress.
8. Trim neckline with lace ruffle.
9. Face placket. Close with buttonholes and buttons on X's.
10. Sew organdy ruffles to dotted lines on skirt.
11. Hem skirt.
12. Trim front with narrow ribbon rosettes and streamers. See picture.

BONNET:
1. Sew back seams of brim and crown and their linings.
2. Baste ruffle around outside of brim, right sides together.
3. Sew brim and brim lining together.
4. Sew hat band to brim, right sides together.
5. Run a gathering thread around outside of crown. Draw up to fit top of band. Sew together.
6. Whip band lining in place, concealing raw edges of crown and brim.
7. Fold up front of brim. At X's tack to band. Trim with rosettes on X's with a loop of ribbon twisted between them.

Note: Always try any pattern in muslin or tissue before cutting into good fabric.

Yoke
Cut one

shoulder line

Sleeve
Cut two

on fold

Hat Band
Cut two
(one for lining)

center front
on fold

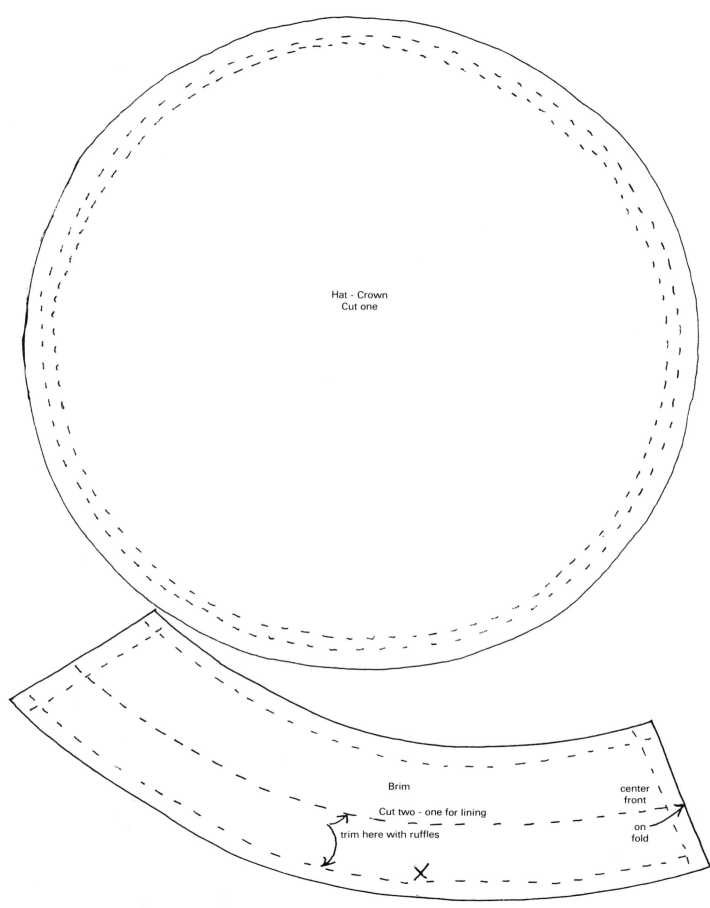

Hat - Crown
Cut one

Brim

Cut two - one for lining

trim here with ruffles

center
front

on
fold

155

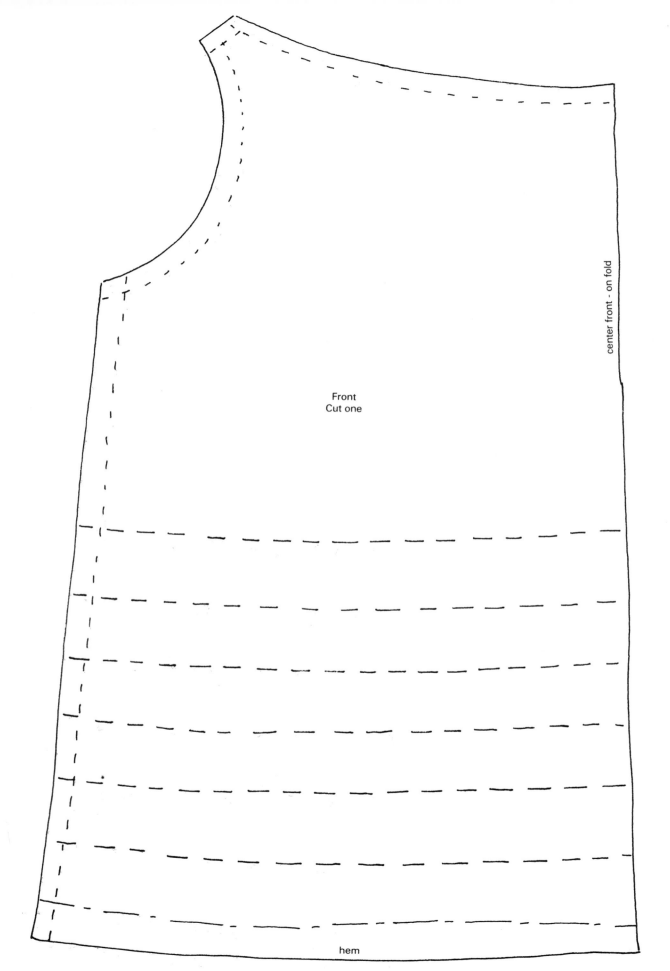

Front
Cut one

center front - on fold

hem

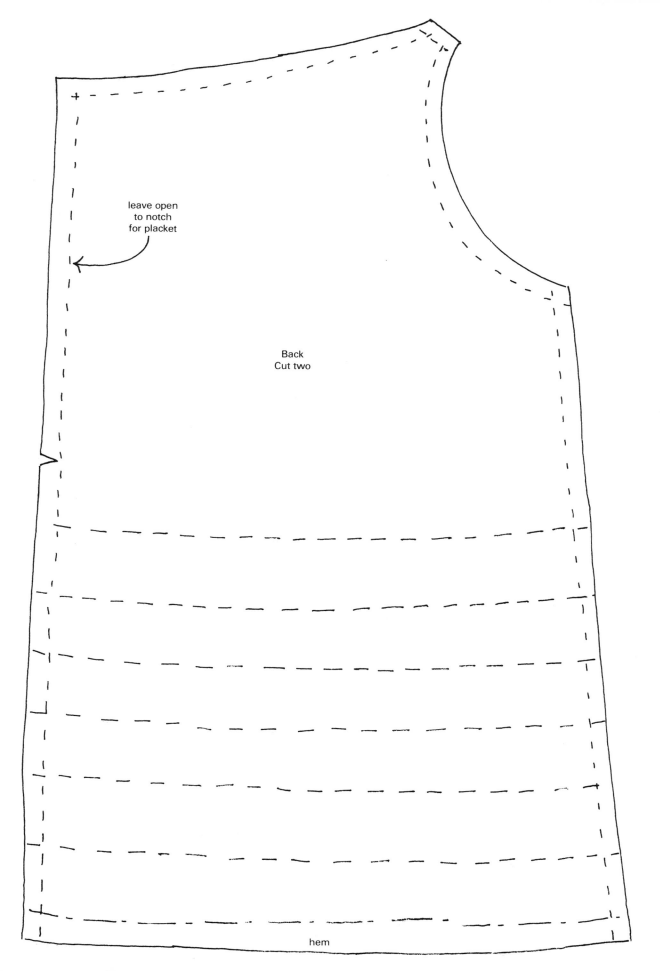

leave open
to notch
for placket

Back
Cut two

hem

10in (25.4cm) Dionne Quint Baby

Dionne Quint Baby Doll Pattern

by **Sandy Williams**

This chubby 10in (25.4cm) *Dionne Quint* baby doll was produced by Madame Alexander in 1935. Each composition doll had a chubby baby body, bent limbs movable at shoulders and hips, rotating head, molded straight, brown hair, brown sleep eyes and closed mouth. The dolls were marked "DIONNE" on the nape of their necks and MADAME/ALEXANDER on their backs. Their dresses had a white cloth label with red printing sewn on the back of the dress which read: Madame/Alexander NEW YORK. The dolls' white organdy outfits consisted of teddy, slip, dress and bonnet. All laces and neckline braid are white. The closing of each garment is a tiny brass safety pin. The only color in the outfit was the identifying Quint-color on the bonnet ribbons and a double row of stitching on the bonnet ruffle. According to *The Collectible Dionne Quintuplets* book by John Axe, Madame Alexander assigned these identifying colors to the Quint dolls: Emilie—lavender; Marie—blue; Cecile—green; Yvonne—pink and Annette—yellow. In real life each Quint was identified with an entirely different color. Most seams on the Quint baby's clothes were just turned in and left raw or had the raw edges covered by braid or lace. All stitching was done by machine. Set your machine at ten stitches per inch. White

thread was used throughout except for the bonnet ruffle. Press after you complete each seam.

Materials needed for each doll:
White organdy
Four tiny brass safety pins
1/4in (6.4mm) wide white lace
1/2in (12.7mm) wide white lace
1/4in (6.3mm) white braid (or substitute 1/2in [12.7mm] wide white lace folded lengthwise)
18in (45.7cm) of 3/8in (9.5mm) wide satin ribbon in desired Quint-color
Fine white and Quint-color threads

Teddy: The original teddy is a one-piece combination underpants/undershirt with a pleated petticoat sewn onto the teddy just under the arms. The original petticoat had pleats spaced approximately 1/2in (12.7mm) apart though quite a few were irregularly spaced. The back bodice is closed with two tiny brass safety pins. Cut out the three teddy pattern pieces from white organdy. Mark petticoat sewing line on teddy with a faint pencil. Sew CB (Center Back) seam from crotch to dot on teddy backs together. Turn rest of CB seam in to wrong side of teddy and topstitch seam down about 1/8in (3.2mm) in from edge. Sew shoulder seams in front and back teddy together; press these seams to the back of teddy. Finger-press neck and armhole seams

to wrong side and topstitch close to edge. Sew side seams together. Finger-press leg seams to *right* side of teddy; topstitch 1/4in (6.4mm) wide lace over leg seam so no raw edge can be seen (*Illustration 1*). Mark pleats on petticoat. Turn petticoat hem up on *right* side of petticoat; topstitch 1/4in (6.4mm) wide lace over raw edge. Pin pleats in place following direction of arrows on pattern; baste. With right sides of petticoat and teddy together (*Illustration 2*), sew petticoat waist to teddy on pencil line. Sew petticoat CB seam to dot. Press.

Slip: The original slip (as well as the dress) had its raw neckline edge covered with a 1/4in (6.4mm) wide white scalloped edged braid. If you cannot find the braid, substitute 1/2in (12.7mm) wide white lace and fold lace in half lengthwise and place half of lace on wrong side of neckline and other half on right side of neckline; topstitch down.

Dress: The original white organdy dress had its neck edge covered by a 1/4in (6.4mm) wide white braid (you may substitute 1/2in [12.7mm] wide lace; see slip neckline edging) and the armholes had 1/2in (12.7mm) wide white lace tucked around the armhole about every 3/8in (9.5mm). Cut out the dress pattern piece and mark tucks. Press hem up; turn raw edge in and press; topstitch hem down. Pin and baste armhole tucks in place. Topstitch 1/2in (12.7mm) wide lace on armhole seam line—making a small tuck every 3/8in (9.5mm) around entire armhole seam. Sew shoulder seams together; press seam to back of dress. Pin and baste CF (Center Front) tucks and back tucks in place; sew braid or 1/2in (12.7mm) wide lace over raw edge (see slip neckline edging directions). Sew CB seam together to dot; press each side of back opening in and topstitch each edge down. Close dress with one tiny safety pin.

Bonnet: Cut out the three bonnet pattern pieces. Turn seam allowance of longest edge of bonnet to *right* side of bonnet; press. Gather 18in (45.7cm) of 1/2in (12.7mm) wide white lace and sew over this raw edge (*Illustration 3*). Turn seam

158

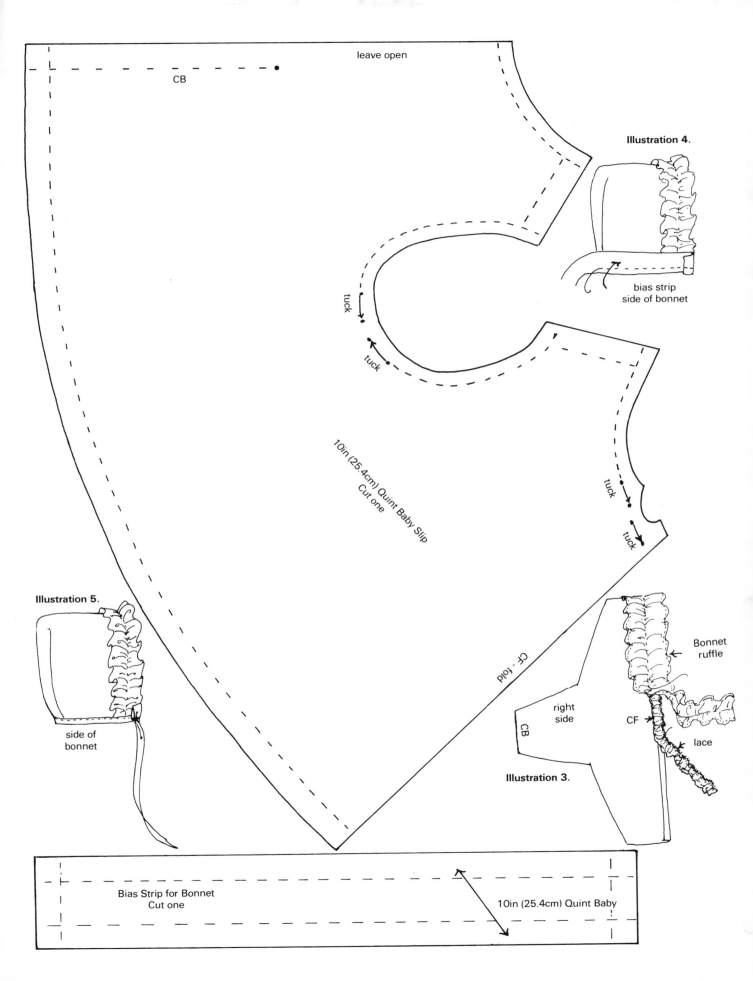

leave open

CB

Illustration 4.

bias strip
side of bonnet

tuck

tuck

10in (25.4cm) Quint Baby Slip
Cut one

tuck

tuck

Illustration 5.

CF - fold

Bonnet
ruffle

right
side

CF

CB

lace

side of
bonnet

Illustration 3.

Bias Strip for Bonnet
Cut one

10in (25.4cm) Quint Baby

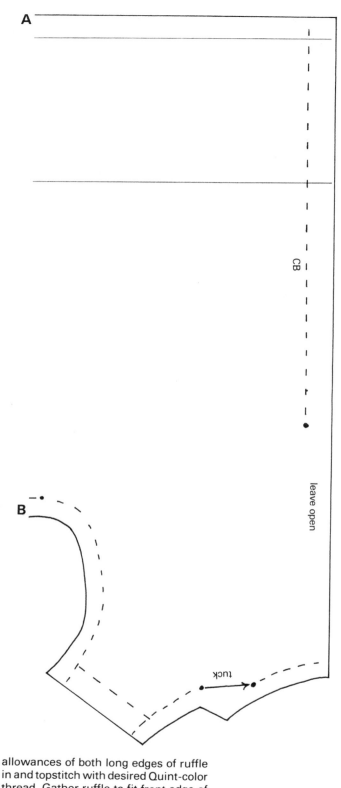

A

B

tuck

CB

leave open

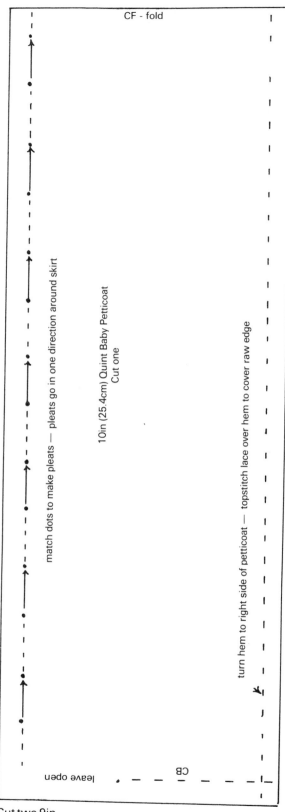

CF - fold

match dots to make pleats — pleats go in one direction around skirt

10in (25.4cm) Quint Baby Petticoat
Cut one

turn hem to right side of petticoat — topstitch lace over hem to cover raw edge

leave open

CB

allowances of both long edges of ruffle in and topstitch with desired Quint-color thread. Gather ruffle to fit front edge of bonnet. Sew gathering line of ruffle over sewing line of lace. Remove gathering thread. Sew up the two back sides of bonnet. With right side of bias strip and bottom edge of bonnet together (*Illustration 4*), sew together with a 1/4in (6.4mm) seam. Turn strip in to inside of bonnet; turn raw edge in and topstitch

close to edge (*Illustration 5*). Cut two 9in (22.9cm) strips of ribbon; make a 5/8in (15.9mm) loop at one end of ribbon; sew ribbon loop to bias strip (*Illustration 5*). Repeat with other strip of ribbon. Pinch the two edges of ruffle so they stand up. The lace ruffle frames the doll's face.

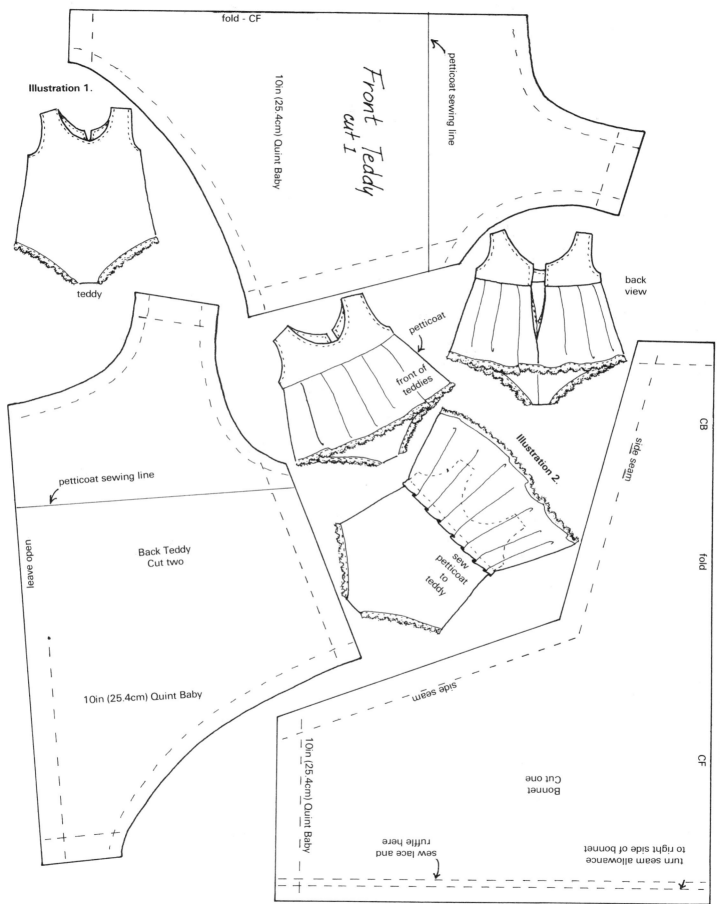

Illustration 1.

teddy

fold - CF

Front Teddy
cut 1

10in (25.4cm) Quint Baby

petticoat sewing line

back view

petticoat sewing line

Back Teddy
Cut two

leave open

10in (25.4cm) Quint Baby

petticoat

front of teddies

Illustration 2.

sew petticoat to teddy

CB

side seam

fold

side seam

CF

10in (25.4cm) Quint Baby

Bonnet
Cut one

sew lace and ruffle here

turn seam allowance to right side of bonnet

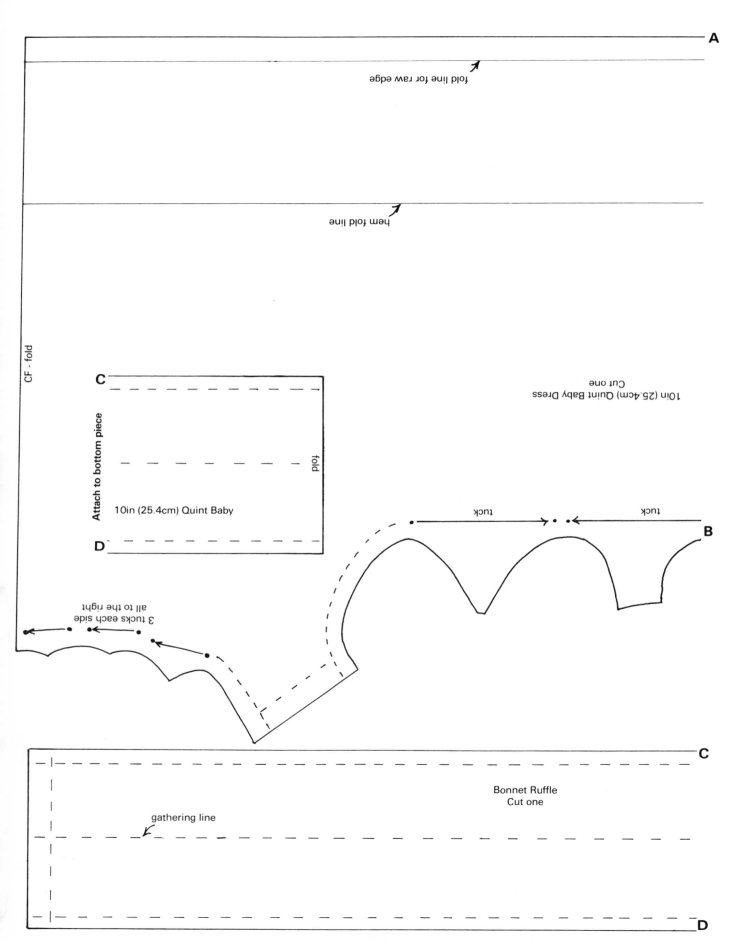

A

fold line for raw edge

hem fold line

CF - fold

C

10in (25.4cm) Quint Baby Dress
Cut one

Attach to bottom piece

fold

10in (25.4cm) Quint Baby

D

tuck   tuck

B

3 tucks each side
all to the right

C

Bonnet Ruffle
Cut one

gathering line

D

11-1/2″(29.1cm)
Dionne Quint Toddler Clothes

BY SANDY WILLIAMS

Photographs by Paul Emmett Hamilton.

Madame Alexander produced an 11½in (29.1cm) toddler doll in 1936. The all-composition doll had a chubby toddler body, bent arms, straight legs, molded curly brown hair and brown sleep eyes. She is marked "ALEXANDER" across her back and at the nape of her neck.

Her outfit, reproduced here in pattern form, consists of a teddy, dress, bonnet, shoes and socks. A gold-colored name medallion was pinned to the center front dress bodice on the original doll. The teddy is made of white organdy while her dress and bonnet are of a colored organdy. Lace and cording loop trim are white as are her shoes and socks. The closing of the teddy and dress are tiny brass safety pins. Most seams on the clothes are just turned in and left raw or had the raw edges covered by lace. All stitching is done by machine except for the dress hem which is done by hand. Set your machine at ten stitches per inch and use very fine thread.

Madame Alexander chose the following colors for this group of dolls: Emilie—deep pink; Marie—pale blue; Cécile—mint green; Yvonne—pale pink; and Annette—pale yellow. These colors were not the ones used to identify the Quints in private life. Also, Madame Alexander chose to spell Emilie as "Emelie" on her name medallion.

Materials needed for each doll's clothing: White organdy; colored organdy for desired Quint dress and bonnet; 4

tiny brass safety pins; very fine thread to match organdy; 1 yard of 3/8in (9.5mm) wide white lace; 20in (50.8cm) of 1/2in (12.7mm) wide white lace; 18in (45.7cm) of 3/8in (9.5mm) wide satin ribbon to match dress color; ball of white KNIT-CRO-SHEEN put out by J.&P. Coats (available in dime stores); white vinyl or felt; thin (cereal box) cardboard; tan leather or felt; iron-on interfacing, 2 silver snaps or buttons; pair of white baby socks size 0-3-1/2 and 7in (17.7cm) of *soft stretch* 1/4in (6.3mm) wide white elastic.

Teddy: The original white organdy teddy is a one-piece undergarment. It consists of a one-piece combination underpants/undershirt with a pleated petticoat sewn onto the teddy just under the arms. The back bodice is closed with two tiny brass safety pins.

Cut out teddy pattern pieces from white organdy. Mark petticoat sewing line on teddy with faint pencil line. Sew CB seam from crotch to dot on one-piece teddy. Turn rest of CB seam in to wrong side of teddy and topstitch seam down about 1/8in (3.2mm) in from edge. Sew shoulder seams together. Turn neck and armhole seams to wrong side and top-stitch down 1/8in (3.2mm) in from edge.

Sew side seams together. Turn leg seams to *right* side of teddy; topstitch lace over leg seam so no raw edge can be seen (*Illustration 1*).

Mark pleats on petticoat. Turn petticoat hem up on *right* side of petticoat; topstitch lace over raw edge. Pin pleats in place following direction of arrows on pattern; baste. With right sides of petticoat and teddy together (*Illustration 2*) sew petticoat waist to teddy on pencil line. Sew petticoat CB seam to dot; sew crotch seam together. Close teddy with safety pins.

Dress: The dress is lined only on the bodice with matching organdy and closed with two tiny brass safety pins. On the original dress a white cloth label was sewn onto the dress. In blue writing it reads: "GENUINE//Dionne Quintuplet Dolls/ALL RIGHTS RESERVED// Madame Alexander-N.Y."

Bodice: Cut out dress pattern pieces from desired color of organdy. Sew shoulder seams of front and back bodice together. Do same with bodice lining. Press shoulder seams toward back bodice. With right sides of bodice and bodice lining together, sew one CB seam, back neck, front neck and back down other CB seam (*Illustration 3*). Trim seam allowance and notch corners. Slash square front neck seam. Turn right-side-out and press.

Skirt: Mark tuck fold lines on skirt with faint pencil lines. Press top fold line; sew tuck 1/8in (3.2mm) from fold line catching cording every 1/2in (12.7mm) or do cording by hand after the two tucks have been machine sewn (*Illustration 4*). Repeat for bottom tuck. Blindstitch resulting hem behind the top tuck; press. Gather skirt between dots to fit bodice. Pin front skirt to front bodice and sew together. Pin CB seam allowance of skirt to wrong side of skirt. Pin one back skirt to corresponding back bodice, sew together. Repeat with other back skirt. Press.

Sleeve: Turn bottom hem to wrong side of sleeve; press. Sew tuck 1/8in (3.2mm) from bottom edge catching cording every 1/2in (12.7mm) (*Illustration 4*). Gather armhole between dots to fit bodice. Pin sleeve and bodice together matching arrow on sleeve to shoulder seam of bodice. Evenly adjust gathers; sew together. Press waist seam of bodice and skirt up facing neckline. Cut elastic into two 3½in (8.9mm) pieces. Mark center of elastic and pin on wrong side at center of sleeve hem; pin elastic at each end of sleeve. Stretch elastic as you sew. Sew underarm seam of sleeve, bodice and dart together. Repeat with other sleeve. Sew CB seam of skirt together from dot to hem. Topstitch skirt opening 1/8in (3.2mm) from edge. Press dress.

Bonnet: Cut out bonnet pattern pieces from organdy to match dress. Sew CB seams of A piece together. Match dots of B (bonnet circle) to A. Make evenly spaced tucks around A to fit B. Sew A and B together. Trim seam. Turn right-side-out; press. Turn neck seam of A to wrong side of bonnet and topstitch 1/16in (1.6mm) in from edge.

Turn outer edge of organdy ruffle to wrong side of ruffle, topstitch 1/8in (3.2mm) in from edge and sew cording loops on (Illustration 4, except sew loops on *wrong* side of ruffle). Gather ruffle to fit outer bonnet brim; evenly adjust gathers; sew together (Illustration 5). When bonnet is finished the exposed raw edge of ruffle will face the back of bonnet. Press or baste interfacing on wrong side of other bonnet brim. Pin right sides of brims together along outside edge as shown. sew together, trim seam; turn right-side-out and press.

Sew brim to bonnet (Illustration 6); press. Gather 20in (50.8cm) of 1/2in (12.7mm) wide lace to fit over this edge; evenly adjust gathers and sew lace ruffle over inner bonnet brim seam (Illustration 6).

Cut two 9in (22.9cm) lengths of ribbon. Make a 5/8in (15.9cm) loop of one end of ribbon, make a tiny pleat in ribbon (Illustration 7) and tack to front side of bonnet. Repeat with other side of bonnet.

Socks: The original white short-ribbed rayon socks had scalloped borders. Make new socks out of pair of white ribbed nylon baby socks, size 0-3-1/2. Turn baby sock wrong-side-out. Pat sock so it lays flat. Pin CF fold edge of pattern on fold of sock so top of pattern just covers scalloped edge of sock. With machine set at ten stitches per inch, sew close to pattern. Sew again close to first stitching. Remove pattern and trim seam close to stitching. Turn sock right-side-out. Repeat for other sock.

Shoes: The shoe uppers were originally made from a white simulated leather; the soles from tan leather and the bow from shoe upper material passed through a silver-colored buckle. A silver snap closed the shoe strap. You may make the shoes out of white vinyl (leather simulated) or white felt stiffened on one side with iron-on interfacing. Cut innersoles out of lightweight cardboard (from a cereal box) and cut the soles from thin stiff tan leather (from old wallets, purses, and so forth) or tan felt.

Trace shoe pattern on white vinyl with sharp pencil. Using ten-stitches-per-inch setting on your machine, top-stitch 1/16in (1.6mm) around entire upper edge of shoe (you may need to place tissue paper over shoe pattern so machine will not skip; tear tissue off after topstitching). Cut shoe out. Sew CB seams together. Turn right-side-out and finger press seam open. Finger press bottom shoe seam allowance in. Apply glue to *bottom* edge of innersole; *let glue get tacky*; place upper shoe seam allowance onto bottom of innersole; place shoe innersole on plastic wrap or wax paper and with your thumb inside shoe press innersole edges down onto wax paper to give a firm bond; let dry. Glue shoe sole onto bottom of innersole and repeat process of pressing thumb down inside shoe to get a good firm bond; let dry.

Shoes may be closed with tiny silver snaps; tiny button or bead with a button-hole cut on strap. Glue or sew bow and buckle (or bow knot) to center front of shoe.

teddy illus.#1

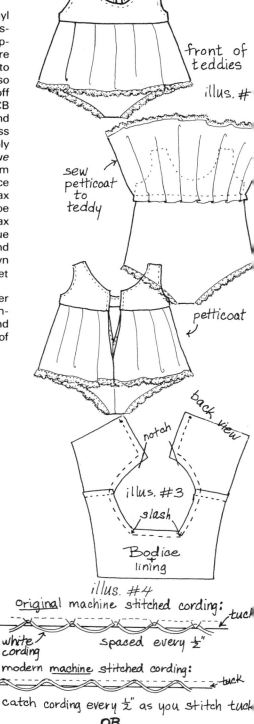

front of teddies

illus. #

sew petticoat to teddy

petticoat

back view

notch

illus. #3

slash

Bodice + lining

illus. #4
Original machine stitched cording:
white cording
spaced every 1/2"
tuck

modern machine stitched cording:
catch cording every 1/2" as you stitch tuck
tuck

OR

hand stitched cording:
knots
tuck

First stitch tuck. Sew 2 knots to hold loop so it will not slip out; slide needle thru tuck 1/2" away to make next loop.

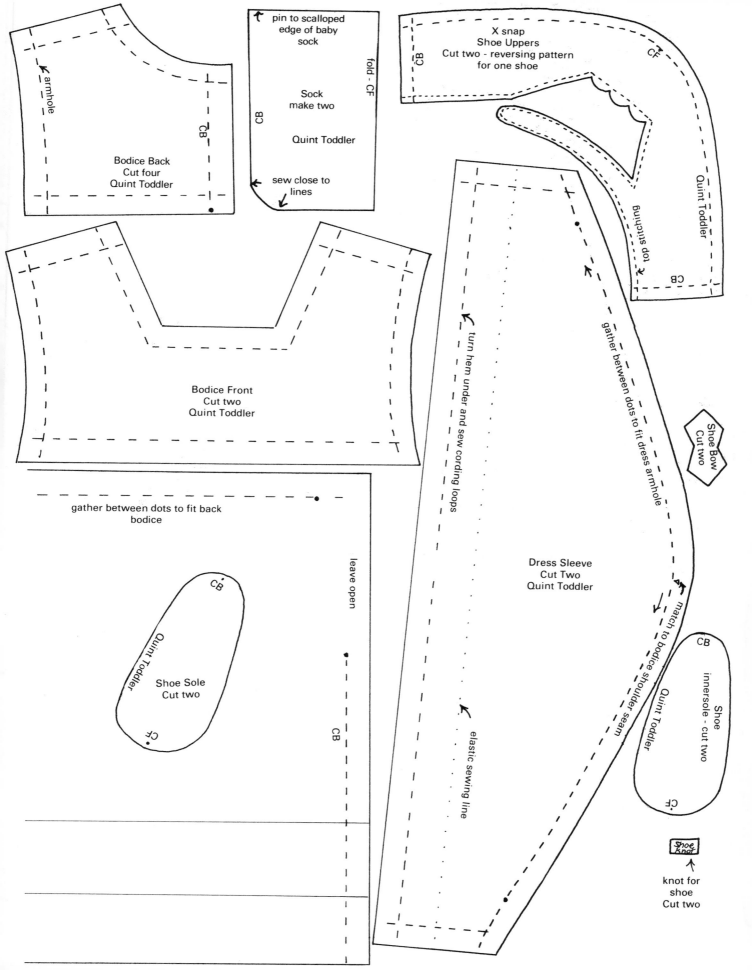

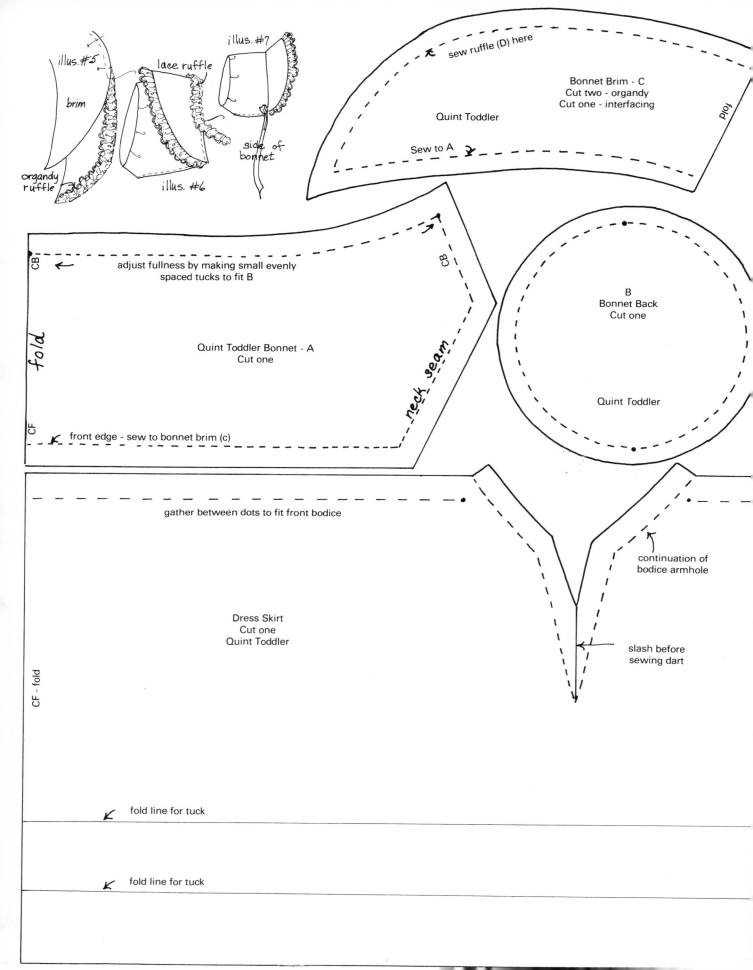

illus. #5

illus. #7

lace ruffle

brim

side of bonnet

organdy ruffle

illus. #6

sew ruffle (D) here

Bonnet Brim - C
Cut two - organdy
Cut one - interfacing

Quint Toddler

fold

Sew to A

CB

adjust fullness by making small evenly
spaced tucks to fit B

CB

fold

Quint Toddler Bonnet - A
Cut one

neck seam

B
Bonnet Back
Cut one

Quint Toddler

CF

front edge - sew to bonnet brim (c)

gather between dots to fit front bodice

continuation of
bodice armhole

Dress Skirt
Cut one
Quint Toddler

slash before
sewing dart

CF - fold

fold line for tuck

fold line for tuck

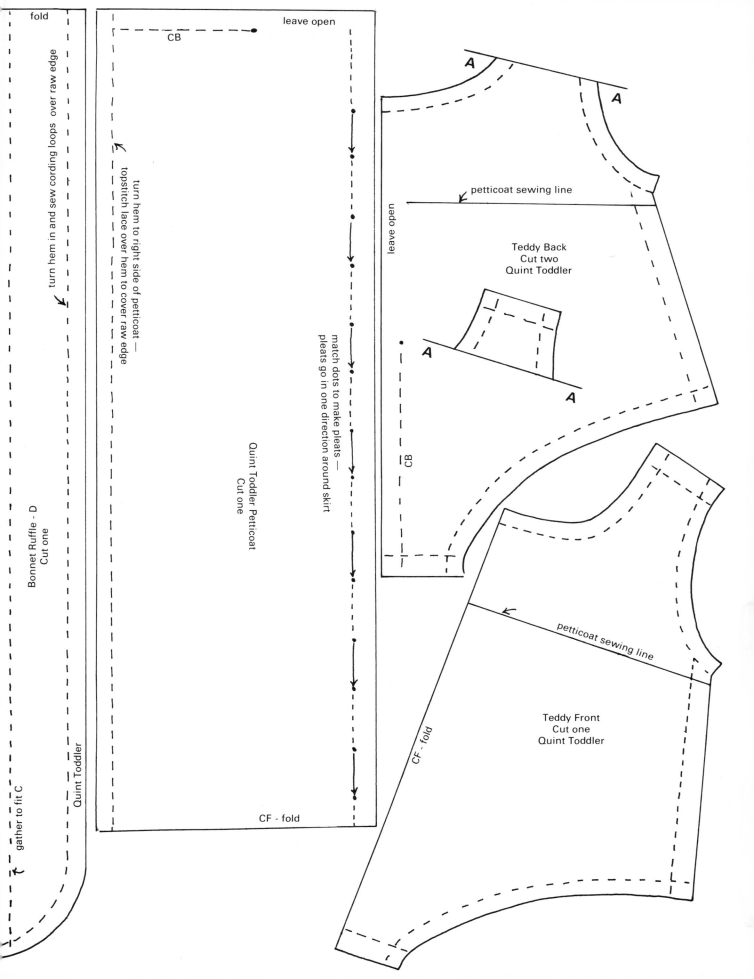

fold

turn hem in and sew cording loops over raw edge

Quint Toddler

Bonnet Ruffle - D
Cut one

gather to fit C

leave open

CB

turn hem to right side of petticoat —
topstitch lace over hem to cover raw edge

Quint Toddler Petticoat
Cut one

match dots to make pleats —
pleats go in one direction around skirt

CF - fold

leave open

A

A

petticoat sewing line

Teddy Back
Cut two
Quint Toddler

A

A

CB

petticoat sewing line

CF - fold

Teddy Front
Cut one
Quint Toddler

Dressing The Modern Collectible Doll

by Patricia Gardner

The aristocratic bisque-headed doll, though rarely found in her original garments, has a wealth of currently available patterns from which to select an entire wardrobe. Many excellent books have been written concerning her accurate costuming and there is no longer any need for the doll made prior to 1930 to sit around in dowdy, cut-down baby dresses or absurd-looking modern doll clothes.

The more recent dolls, long step-children to the doll collecting world, have had relatively few means of restoring the lost clothing. Worse, it seems that the dolls who need clothing the least, by dint of their monumental commercial wardrobes, are the very ones for whom most modern patterns are published. *Barbie, Crissy* and their near relatives can hardly decide what to wear on Saturday night, while their less abundant friends are lucky to have an old sock to call a dress. Johana Gast Anderton's excellent book, *Sewing for Twentieth Century Dolls,* has done much to dress the modern doll properly. Reprints of old commercial patterns are sometimes available, but it is still difficult for the newer doll with an established identity to find exactly the right replacement garments.

Now that the older bisque dolls are both scarce and expensive, more recent dolls are becoming welcome additions to most collections, and with this trend comes a need to properly costume them. Even the collector of modern dolls who intends to "adopt" only perfect or near-perfect dolls will someday find that one special doll, too nice to be passed by, but missing some or all of the original clothing. Let us then try to sift out some of the confusion that can overtake the owner of a less-than-perfect modern doll.

The first step with *any* new addition to your collection is thorough research. Check all marks on the doll and try to establish the maker, the era in which the doll was produced and any special identities the doll may have had. This is not always easy, for many dolls have no identifying marks on them, and even when the manufacturer is positively known, the individual identity of the doll can remain well-hidden. Most doll makers used heads, bodies and part of

bodies in a variety of combinations, and many used exactly the same basic doll for a number of personalities. As if *this* were not enough confusion, differing heads and/or bodies were often used for the *same* personality. The collector must find most of the clues to his or her doll's identity alone, for the opinion of the dealer or even the original owner cannot always be taken as a correct assessment. This is particulary true if the doll comes from a shop which specializes in a field of collecting other than dolls. (When I first began collecting, I purchased a lovely Alexander composition doll from a shop which dealt mainly in glass and furniture. The dealer told me the doll was *Princess Elizabeth,* the doll was *marked Princess Elizabeth* and I was convinced she *was Princess Elizabeth.* She *was McGuffey-Ana.*)

Illustration 1. Front and back view of *McGuffey-Ana* from Patricia Gardner's GA 1300 Madame Alexander's McGuffey-Ana and Flora McFlimsey patterns.

This brings me somewhat prematurely into an area I call "denying the inevitable." The advanced collector already knows that the "rare" vinyl *Mae West* she bought may turn out to be a common *Barbie,* still available in toy shops. The beginner does *not* know this, and tends to deny it hotly and publicly. I have technicolor, total-recall pictures of all the denying I have done in my own collecting, all of it totally embarrassing, and I am sure that the collector without any such denial story had led a particularly dull life. This gets even worse when fancy is allowed to enter the otherwise rational mind: "My doll looks like Marilyn Monroe, therefore she *is* Marilyn Monroe, and you are only telling me that she is a common Alexander *Cissy* to ruin my morning." Trust me; no one wants to rain on your parade, but you had better be careful in identifying your doll(s)...no fantasies allowed at this point.

Once your doll has been firmly identified, find as many pictures as possible showing the outfit(s) that the doll originally wore. Some dolls, such as Alexander's *Cissy* or American Character's *Sweet Sue,* wore many different outfits while others, like Alexander's *Grandma Jane,* wore only one costume, and in such a case that one outfit will be the *only* one to duplicate for your doll.

This brings us to another sticky wicket: The Case For Authenticity. Drawing the line for authenticity is an individual thing, and I am not going to come over to your house and confiscate your doll just because you chose not to dress her the way I would have if she were mine. I am, however, inclined to think that if a doll is one which came with many costumes, and for whom contemporary commercial patterns were designed, it is perfectly acceptable to use such an old pattern (or a reprint of it) in dressing your doll. Included in this category would be such dolls as Effanbee's *Patsy* family, Ideal's *Shirley Temple,* Mattel's *Barbie,* Alexander's hard-plastic *Maggi* and *Wendy,* any of the 20in (50.8cm) high-heeled dolls and all of the 8in (20.3cm) dolls such as *Ginny, Muffie* and the *Alexanderkins*. The reasoning here is that while a costume may not be a copy of any factory-produced garment, it will be representative of the time in which the doll was produced and will replicate the clothes in which little girls have dressed dolls of this sort in. The one-costume doll, such as Alexander's 14in (35.6cm) hard plastic *Cinderella,* or those with an identity so specific that they will look a bit silly in the "street clothes" generally presented in contemporary commercial patterns like *Alice in Wonderland, Scarlett O'Hara* or *Tinkerbell* should be dressed in a style which underlines the special identity of the doll. From here we progress into a number of "gray" areas, among them being *artistic license*.

Artistic License

You must realize that you are creating a replica costume. No amount of care will ever make it more than a replica. What you are trying to capture is the "feeling" of the original costume; a matter of essence rather than substance. If the doll is not a very recent one, it may be difficult or impossible to find the exact trim or fabric used for the original garment. You may not be happy with the precise finishing details used on the original, for example, safety pins in place of snap or raw sash ends and unfinished seams. You may prefer a color or fabric print other than that used on the original. How far you can deviate from the original costume is a matter of individual judgement -- *Cinderella,* for example, will still be recognizable in almost any pastel color, while *Peter Pan* will look peculiar in anything but green.

Fantasy Figures and Blank Walls

Often, after the most exhaustive research, you will still have a doll who defies positive identification. You must make an educated guess concerning her probable date of manufacture and proceed from there, dressing her in a style suitable to both her actual age and the age group she was intended to represent (such as infant, toddler, pre-teen, adult, and so on).

A non-descript doll of uncertain parentage can take on a special meaning

Illustration 2. Front and back view of *Little Genius* from Patricia Gardner's GA 0802 Madame Alexander's 7½in (19.1cm) to 8in (20.3cm) *Little Genius* and *Fischer Quintuplets* pattern.

if she is dressed in a costume of personal significance to her owner. A slim-bodied composition doll can wear a copy of a family wedding gown or formal from the 1940s; a hard plastic child will be super in a replica of the dress you (or your daughter!) wore in 1956. If you have an unidentifiable doll, try to find a suitable fantasy in which to clothe it.

If you already have a fantasy in mind, look for an appropriate doll to fill it. Please remember that if an existing original wig or garment must be discarded to make the doll fit your fantasy, the doll is *not* suitable. *Never* sacrifice an existing identity to create a new one you like better. Trade or sell the unwanted doll to get the one you really want rather than try to perform an identity change on the doll.

Once you have established an identity for your doll and have carefully researched the costumes she may have worn when new, made your selection and purchased your fabric, you can begin to intelligently dress the doll.

You will find making clothing for more recent dolls easier than dressing your bisques for many reasons. First, recent dolls have standard bodies, and a pattern made specifically for your doll may be trusted to fit without alterations, thus bypassing the need for a muslin mock-up of the dress. Second, fabrics and trims are more readily available, for synthetic fabrics need not be avoided in many cases, though you do have to be a bit careful in using polyesters...these are

no more suitable for a composition or early hard plastic doll than they are for a bisque. Third, because these clothes were mass-produced, many of the "fine" sewing techniques needed for an antique doll's clothing are eliminated. Snaps and even safety pins were commonly used as fasteners, so there is no need for tiny handworked buttonholes unless you really enjoy making them. Hems were frequently sewn with machine-done topstitching and garments were rarely lined. Modern dolls need less clothing than an old doll...often simply a dress and panties, while for an older bisque to look and feel right, she needs many layers of underthings. Elastic, which should never be used in dressing an old doll, makes gathered cuffs and waistbands far easier for your modern dolls.

I find that, in general, an old bisque-headed doll takes two or three times as long to dress as a more recent doll, and costs at least twice as much in materials alone. (I am very fussy about my dolls' clothing, and use only natural fabrics for my old dolls, lining them in silk organza and using French seams whenever possible.)

In dressing any doll, old or new, an attention to age, detail and accessories is most important and in the case of a newer doll, this is perhaps even more important. Many examples of the same doll in original clothing are apt to be in books and the collections of friends, so your re-dressed doll's differences will be more glaringly apparent. We are more

Illustration 3. *Fischer Quintuplet* from Patricia Gardner's GA 0802 Madame Alexander's 7½in (19.1cm) to 8in (20.3cm) *Little Genius* and *Fischer Quintuplets* pattern.

aware of style trends and short-term "fads" as they approach our own time. Most of us can immediately associate a pink felt circular skirt sporting an appliqéd poodle with the mid-1950s and know that skirt would have been laughably out-of-date by 1960. How many of us can tell the difference between an 1874 bustle and an 1883 bustle?

The habitual collector of less-than-perfect dolls should be aware of trims and small accessories now available that may be hard to find later, and keep a small supply of these things on hand. The search for a "just-right" trim or fabric can be exhausting and frustrating if you wait until you *must* have it to look for it. Party favor shops are a good source of doll supplies too. The doll's dressmaker should have perhaps a dozen Japanese paper parasols on hand, as well as tiny plastic fans, cocktail picks shaped like swords, arrows and the like. Tiny woven straw baskets are also good to keep in stock.

Thrift store clothing and jewelry can also provide needed older trims and fabrics at low cost. Old straw hats and placemats can be cut down and re-blocked to provide hats, and fake pearls, mellowed to an ivory color with age, are a necessity for composition dolls, who look silly in a too-white new string of pearls.

Look for the unlikely source too -- regular girls or ladies helanca knee socks will make wonderful doll tights and socks, often without the need to make a special waistband finish. (Be sure to cut them with the top of the sock to the top of the doll item, for helanca will run down-to-up, never up-to-down, and cutting a doll sock the wrong way will fill your doll items with unsightly runs.) Dime store earrings can make fine necklace pendants for your dolls. Fuzzy children's socks make nice sweaters and winter caps. A single white fake fur hat, salvaged from a thrift store, has been soaked in strong tea to tint it tan and cut into strips to trim several Eskimo parkas. Miniature liquor bottles found

on airplanes have given my *Cissy* the best-stocked bar in town, with the addition of tinted water. Sample-sized perfume bottles fill her dressing table.

Make-it-yourself jewelry shops specialize in jewelry findings which can be broken up into crowns, bracelets, necklaces, earrings and even shoe buckles for your dolls. Be on the alert for tiny pendants, fine chains, small jewelry clasps, artificial fabric flowers, tiny beads and the like. (Your dolls will love them!)

Narrow elastic is important too -- I try to keep several packets in varying widths at hand. This is easiest to apply if you do not cut all the way through the elastic at first...just fit it from start to finish around whatever part of the doll (waist, upper arm, thigh, and so forth) you will need it to encircle, notch it at the end point and do not cut it through until after it has been entirely sewn to the garment...this will give you something to hold onto as you near the end of your stitching, for elastic must be stretched as it is sewn to be effective. If you cut the

elastic to size before it is sewn in place, you will reach a point where you must let go of it to avoid sewing your fingers into the seam. This will probably ruin the garment.

Set-in sleeves are best handled exactly the way they are on most full-size factory-made garments -- gather the sleeves into the bodice before the side seams are sewn, and then sew the side seams of the bodice in one with the underarm sleeve seams.

A male efficiency expert once made a study of sewing techniques and claimed that an efficient seamstress should be able to make a full-sized dress in two hours. While I think this figure probably was based on the worst possible sewing methods, he *did* make some constructive observations which may especially help the doll's dressmaker. The most helpful of these was the fact that the fastest way to sew is to make several seams at once, without cutting the thread. Your garment sections will look rather like wash hung out on a clothesline while it is under construction, but it really *is* much faster. An error he made was the skipping of the very important pressing after every seam -- to make an attractive garment in any size, you *must* press as you sew.

If you habitually acquire undressed dolls -- and there are some great bargains here -- you had better learn to sew for yourself. You are not really saving anything if you buy a naked doll for $25 and then spend another $25 having her dressed, if she only sells for $50 in original clothing. Of course, there is always the truly amazing bargain; an undressed but otherwise perfect one-

Illustration 4. Patricia Garner's GA 0801 Madame Alexander's 8in (20.3cm) *Indian Boy* and *Girl* pattern.

owner doll for a very low price can sometimes have a full wardrobe costom-made by a professional dressmaker and still cost less than "market price," but this is rare indeed.

My own "pet peeve" is the person who says, "Oh, I just do not have the *patience* to sew for a doll." Dressing a doll requires no patience at all, though it does call for a certain level of skill and dexterity. A child who will not hold still for a fitting or an adult who will abruptly gain or lose ten pounds needs patience to dress...a doll does not do any of these annoying things. A doll will never lie to you about her size or weight, and she will be as available at 2:00a.m. for a fitting as she is at noon. Unless she has a cloth body she will not suck in her breath for a fitting and then complain that the finished garment is too tight. She will not even complain if you accidentally stick her with a pin. A doll dress takes less than a quarter of the time its full-size counterpart would take. If you start on a doll's underwear by, say, ten in the morning, after the family is out of the house and you have your eyes open and are on your last cup of coffee, you should have a shiny doll in complete undies watching you eat lunch at noon, and if that is not an immediate reward requiring no patience whatsoever, I do not know what is. By bedtime, including time-out to fix dinner and do a load of wash, your doll should be nearly or entirely finished, needing only a few final touches the following day. Your first dress, even for a very small modern doll, may take a week or more, but you will speed up with practice.

In my own series of patterns, I am trying to reach a wide range of collectors with patterns for dolls frequently found undressed...the dolls once used as play dolls, now turned collectible. For this reason, the incredibly rare and/or initially expensive dolls, such as Alexander's *Portrait* series, as well as dolls already supplied with a plethora of patterns and ready-made garments, such as *Barbie* and *Crissy,* will be avoided. Most of my patterns are taken directly from existing original garments, while a few have been done from photographs. Those done from photographs are bound to be less accurate, and in my current series, one pattern was actually pulled from production and revised prior to release when I found the all-original doll to differ substantially from the one I had dressed from photographs alone. (See the 8in [20.3cm] Alexander *Indian Girl's Illustration 4*).

Once you have made your copied outfit, I hope you will have enough pride in your work to label it with your name (and the date, if possible). I use name tapes (like the ones you sew into a child's camp gear) on very small garments and larger embroidered tags for non-sheer dresses sized for dolls 12in (30.5cm) and taller. These are available by special order from most yardage stores at low cost, and unless you are unusually prolific, a single order should last for years. The purist would have you write your name and the date of completion into a seam allowance with indelible ink, and this is a fine idea, but India ink is difficult to manage on fabric and will ruin the appearance of a sheer garment even if the inking is skillfully done. For the dressmaker who sews only for her own collection, this is a matter of record. Years from now, your granddaughter may mistake your copy of a dress for an original, so you should tell her now, by means of a clear label. For the person who dresses dolls for others as a livelihood, it is a question of morality and conscience -- not just your own, but the customer's as well. If you do not want your things passed off as the work of another, you *must* mark them. It is difficult or impossible to produce a replica garment so exact that it will fool the really discerning buyer into believing it is "all original," but you can sometimes come pretty close with a lot of effort. While this sort of effort is immensely satisfying for your own collection, it is commercially unprofitable, for the price of a good collectible doll undressed verses her price in all-original clothing will seldom compensate you for the time and effort invested. You should also remember that some excellent doll's dressmakers become so renowned that a dress with their label will bring more than the factory original would. An artist's work should always be signed...please sign yours.

Now that your doll is all cleaned, dressed properly and correctly identified, isn't she pretty? Now all she needs is a little hug from you. You worked hard to make her the beauty she is...enjoy her.

Dress Pattern for 18 in. (45.7cm)
~Victoria~

by Sandy Williams

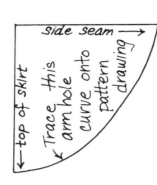

Who can resist cradling a newborn baby in their arms--especially one named Victoria? Victoria is marked at the nape of her neck: c ALEXANDER 1966. She has all the characteristics of a tiny baby: chubby cheeks, bent limbs and a plump body. She has blue sleep eyes; molded honey-blond hair; a vinyl head, forearms, hands and legs; and a pink stuffed cloth body. Her original white batiste dress almost covers her curling toes. Wide pink satin ribbon peeps through the scalloped-edged eyelet trim (which hides the center front closing of the dress). Fine white gathered lace edges the neck and sleeves. A white cloth label is sewn on the back dress neck; printed in blue ink it states: " 'Victoria'// by MADAME ALEXANDER//NEW YORK, U.S.A."

Materials Needed: ½ yd. (45.7cm) of white 1¼ in. (3.2cm) wide white scalloped-edged eyelet trim; ½ yd. (45.7cm) of 5/8 in. (1.6cm) wide pale pink satin ribbon; 1 yd. (91.4cm) of 3/8 in. (.93cm) wide pale pink satin ribbon; 1½ yd. (137.1cm) of ½ in. (1.3cm) wide fine white lace; 6 in. (15.2cm) of 1/8 in. (.31cm) wide white soft-stretch elastic; four white 3/8 in. (.93cm) buttons; a tiny silver snap; 7/8 yd. (80cm) yard of white batiste; extra fine white thread.

Sewing hints: Press after each sewing step. Use ¼ in. (.65cm) seams throughout. Use 12 stitches per inch (per 2.5cm) setting on sewing machine. Use a number 11 sewing machine needle and extra fine thread when making doll clothes as regular thread looks too bulky on doll garments. The following sewing directions follow as close to the original dress as possible--so, most seams are left raw.

Sewing directions: Cut two each of front and back bodice: machine stitch each two-layer bodice piece together ¼ in. (.65cm) from all edges; from now on treat each two-layer bodice as one piece. Enlarge back skirt drawing onto paper (these measurements include seam allowance). Place armhole curve pattern in upper right corner of enlarged back skirt

pattern and trace the armhole curve onto skirt pattern. Cut a back skirt pattern from batiste placing center back (CB) seam on fold of fabric. To make front skirt pattern, use back skirt pattern except: add 1 in. (2.5cm) to CB fold line so that the new hem width will be 12 3/4 in. (32.5cm) and the new "gather to fit bodice" width will be 11¼ in. (28.6cm) wide (see drawing). Cut 2 front skirts from batiste.

Sew shoulder seams of front and back bodices together; press shoulder seams toward back bodice. Sew two rows of gathers (¼ in. (.65cm) and 1/8 in. (.31cm) in from raw edge) across top of back skirt: pull the two gathering threads until same width as back bodice seam; adjust gathers evenly; sew bodice and skirt together; sew again 1/8 in. (.31cm) from raw edge; trim seam close to second stitching; press seam toward bodice. To gather the two front skirts: start the two rows of gather 1 3/4 in. (4.5cm) in from center front seam to within ½ in. (1.3cm) of armhole. Follow back skirt directions to gather and sew the front skirt to the front bodice.

Gather top of sleeve between dots to fit bodice/skirt armhole; match shoulder of sleeve to bodice shoulder seam; sew sleeve and dress armhole together; press seam toward sleeve. Press sleeve hem up ¼ in. (.65cm) to *wrong* side of fabric; lay

lace on *right* side of sleeve hem (about half of lace will extend beyond sleeve edge); stitch lace to hem; on wrong side of sleeve stretch and stitch 3 in. (7.6cm) of soft-stretch elastic close to edge of hem. Repeat with other sleeve.

Machine gather rest of the lace. Turn neck edge of dress bodice to wrong side of bodice along ¼ in. (.65cm) basting line; hand baste this seam down, pressing and clipping curve so it lies flat. Using a small machine zig-zag stitch, sew lace to outside edge of neck. Trim excess seam close to zig-zag stitching.

On *right* front dress press CF raw edge in ¼ in. (.65cm): press in again 3/4 in. (2.0cm); top stitch down (about 5/8 in. (1.6cm) in from CF edge). Make a machine buttonhole on right bodice following bodice pattern markings. Two inches (5.1cm) below this bodice buttonhole, mark and make another buttonhole; 2½ in. (6.4cm) below this finished buttonhole make another buttonhole; then 2½ in. (6.4cm) below this buttonhole make another for a total of four buttonholes.

Center the wide pink satin ribbon under eyelet; top stitch both edges of pink ribbon to eyelet. Using the completed drawing as a guide, place eyelet (with pink ribbon peeping out through eyelet holes) over right

---

side seam →

top of skirt

Trace this armhole curve onto pattern drawing

bodice center front edge just so the one scalloped edge juts out over the center front dress edge. Tuck top raw edge of eyelet under ¼ in. (.65cm) and pin to neck lace edge; top stitch neck edge of eyelet down; then continue the top stitching down the eyelet edge nearest to the sleeve right on top of the previous ribbon top stitching--this forms a "flap" that covers up the buttonholes. Cut off excess eyelet at hem edge.

Pin and sew the underarm sleeve seam and the skirt side seams together in one seam; press.

Press *left* center front raw edge of dress in ¼ in. (.65cm); press in again 3/4 in. (2.0cm); top stitch down about 5/8 in. (1.6cm) in from dress CF edge. Sew the four buttons on left CF edge of dress to correspond with the buttonholes. Sew the tiny snap as marked on pattern.

Press dress hem up ¼ in. (.65cm); then press up again 1 in. (2.5cm); blind stitch hem.

Make a tiny bow with the narrow ribbon and tack to right dress CF neck edge as illustrated. Remove all visible basting threads.

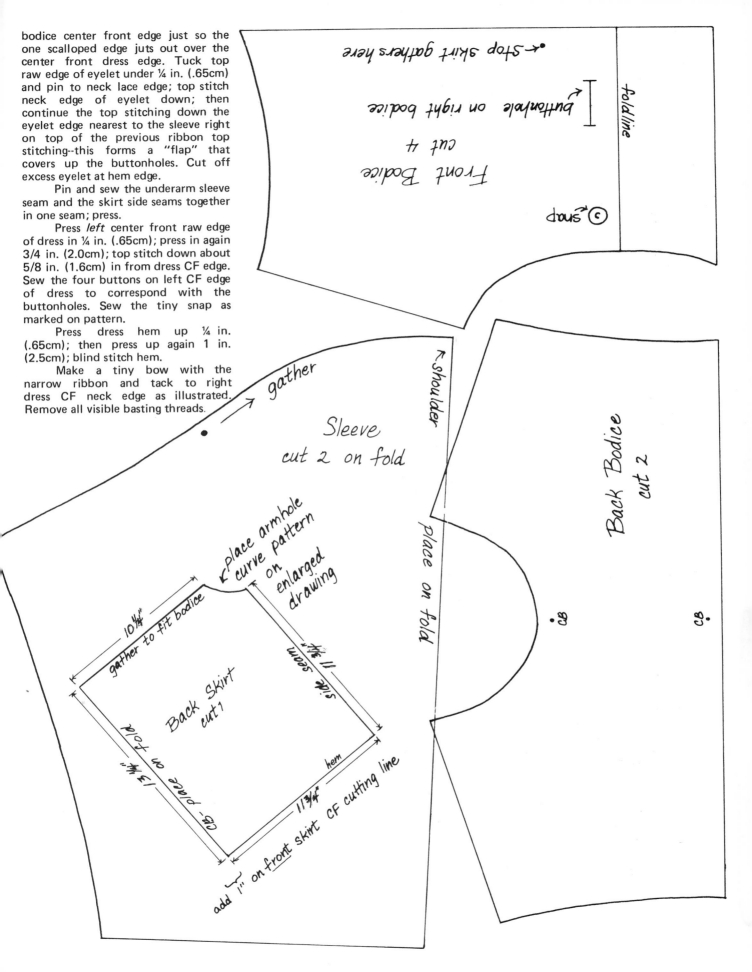

A Sweater For Mary Marie

fits 16in (40.6cm) doll

Editor's Note: Our thanks to Kathryn Gresham of Gladewater, Texas, for sharing her book on doll knitting and crochet with us. In the book crochet is spelled "Crow Shaw".

Doll's Sweater (taken from *Mary Frances Knit and Crochet Book*)

Material: old blue or peacock blue knitting worsted. Bone crochet hook No. 5.

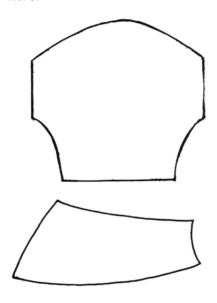

Directions for sweater. This work is begun in front.

1. Make a chain of 26 stitches.
2. Make 25 single crochet stitches.
3. Chain 1 to turn.
4. Make 12 rows (in all) of 25 sc stitches, taking up both loops of the stitches below.
5. On the 13th, make only
   15 sc for 6 rows (in all). These rows come under the doll's arms. You will then have made 18 rows.
6. On the 19th row, make 15 sc and 11 chain stitches.
7. On the 20th row, make 25 sc.
8. Make 21 rows of 25 sc for the back of the sweater. This makes 39 rows from the beginning.
9. On the 40th row make 15 sc for 6 rows under arm.
10. On the 47th row add 11 chains and crochet 12 rows of 25 sc stitches.

To make armholes:

Thread a needle with the worsted and sew 6 rows of the front to 6 rows of the back (A to A, B to B). Do the same to the other side.

To make border on the edge around the sweater:

1. Hold the outside of the sweater toward you. Starting at the left side of the neck, take up both loops of each stitch with sc all around sweater to right side of neck. (Note: In turning corners at bottom use 3 sc in each stitch.)
2. Make 1 chain stitch to use in turning, make another row of sc in the same way all around the sweater. This will bring you back to the starting stitch of border.
3. Make 1 chain to use in turning, and make third row, only putting 2 sc in the corners at the bottom.

To make collar band:

1. Hold right side of sweater toward you, and take up each stitch across the neck with sc.
2. Make 5 rows of sc, using 1 ch stitch to turn. Make slip stitches all around sweater taking up back thread only of the stitches.

To fasten sweater:

The sweater is fastened with loops and buttons.

To make loops:

1. On the right hand side of the sweater, commencing at the bottom make 4 slip stitches.
2. Make 2 chain stitches.
3. Skip 2 stitches in the row below, and make 4 more slip stitches. The chain stitches form the loops.
4. Continue doing this until the neck is reached.
5. Make 1 loop on the end of the collar. Sew buttons on the left side opposite the loops.

To make the sleeves:

1. Make 9 chain stitches.
2. Make 8 sc stitches.
3. Always make 1 chain stitch to use in turning sc.
4. Second row: Taking up both threads of the row of sc just made, make 2 sc in the first stitch, and 1 in each

stitch to the end of the row. This will make 9 stitches
5. Make three chains, and turn work.
6. Third row: Make 1 sc in each of the two chain stitches, and sc to the end of the row making 11 stitches in all. Make 1 chain to turn.
7. Fourth row. Make 2 single crochet in the first stitch and sc to the end of row making 12 stitches in all.
8. Fifth row. Make 5 chain stitches. Make 4 sc in the chain stitches and sc to the end of the row, making 16 stitches.
9. Sixth row: Make 2 sc stitches in the first stitch and sc to the end, make 17 stitches.
10. Seventh row: Make 17 sc.
11. Eighth row: Make 2 sc in first stitch and sc to the end of the row, making 18 sc.
12. Make 6 rows of 18 sc.
13. 15th row: Make sc, but skip next to the last stitch, making 17 sc (decreasing).
14. 16th row: Make 17 sc.
15. 17th row: Make sc across row, but skip next to the last stitch, making 16 sc.
16. 18th row: Make 16 sc.
17. 19th row: Make slip stitches in the first four stitches. Sc to the end, skipping next to the last stitch making 11 stitches.
18. 20th row: Make 11 sc.
19. 21st row: Make 2 slip stitches, and sc to the end of row, skipping next to the last stitch making 8 stitches.
20. 22nd row: Make 8 sc. Cut thread and fasten yarn. Make another sleeve like this one.
21. Sew up sleeves.
22. Pin seam to the front corner of the armhole and sew into place.
23. Put 2 rows of sc around the end of sleeve at wrist. Add one row of slip stitches below these. Do not make this row of slip stitches very tight.

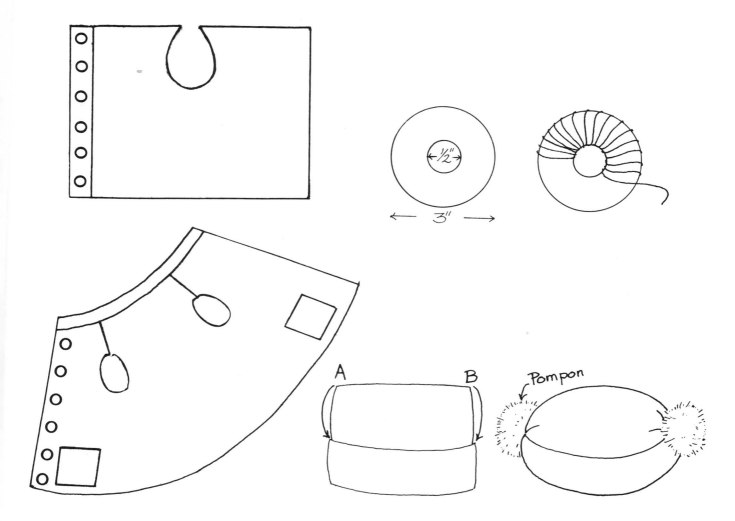

Pockets:
1. Chain 7.
2. Sc in chain 7. Make 7 rows of 6 sc.
3. Put 1 row of sc across the top of pocket.
4. Put 1 row of slip stitches across the top of the pocket. Make another pocket this same way. Sew pockets on the sweater, about 1in (2.5cm) from the bottom and 1in (2.5cm) from the sides.

Doll's Crocheted Toque or Cap (taken from *Mary Frances Knit and Crochet Book*)
   Material: Old rose (double) wool floss. Gray floss to be used in making pompons. Bone crochet hook number 2.
   Directions for Hat:
   Make 50 chain stitches. Join the last chain stitch to the first chain stitch with a slip stitch.
   Make 50 single crochet stitches and work around for 20 rows.
   Make two slip stitches; turn and work on wrong side.

Make 50 single crochets for 25 rows. Fasten the end of the floss.
   Thread a zephyr needle or a darning needle with the floss. Lay the chain-stitched edge together like the top of a stocking laid flat, and sew it overhand together from A to B to form top of cap.
   Fold up on the outside of cap, 12 rows of the single crochet stitches last made. Fold up about 13 rows. This roll forms the part around the doll's head.
   Bring points A and B down to meet the roll; pin in place. Fasten points in place by sewing on pompons for trimming.

Directions for Pompons:
   Cut two cardboard circles 3in (7.6cm) across.
   Cut out a circular hole in the center of each making it ½in (1.3cm) across.
   Cut off one piece of old rose and one piece of gray floss, making each about 3yd (2.73m) long. Put the ends together side by side.
   Holding the two cardboard circles together, thread the gray and rose floss into the center hole, over the edges, into the center, over the edges, doing this over and over again until the entire length of floss is used.
   Put one leg of a pair of scissors between the two cardboard's edges of the circle and cut the floss apart.
   Put a short double thread of floss between the two cardboard circles and tie the ends of the double thread firmly together.
   Tear out cardboard, carefully clip the surface of the pompon evenly.

Miniature Projects For Dolls

From *The Mary Francis Sewing Book* by Jane Eayre Fryer.

a project in miniature sewing by **Susan Sirkis**

These patterns and ideas were developed for a doll house doll in the 1in (2.5cm) to 1ft (30.5cm) scale. My original idea was to make the doll and her costumes and accessories and display them in a breakaway box. The box should measure about 8in (20.3cm) high by 18in (45.7cm) wide by 6in (15.2cm) deep and be lined in red velvet. She could be standing in front of an elegant Victorian dressing table with a mirror. On the dressing table would be dressing table accessories of the usual sort. The rest of the box should have the clothes arranged on dummies; the under things and accessories pinned to the walls, with some on the flap of the box. I never quite got the box finished but the dresses and accessories turned out well.

Make the lingerie of very light batiste trimmed with very narrow lace. Embroidery floss can be used for draw strings and laces for the corset.

1 - CHEMISE: Make V-shaped tucks over shoulders. Hem neck edge and trim with lace. Hem sleeves and trim with lace. Sew underarm seams. Hem bottom. Close front with small white bead.

2 - PANTALETS: Make tucks in bottoms. Hem bottoms and edge with narrow lace ruffle. Sew leg seams and hem crotch edges. Make narrow casing in top and run embroidery floss through for tie.

3 - SHORT PETTICOAT: Cut a piece of material 8in (20.3cm) by 3in (7.6cm). Hem bottom and edge with narrow lace. Make pin tucks above hem to match pantalets. Sew center back seam and make a narrow casing in top. Run embroidery floss through.

4 - CORSET: Make darts in corset as shown. Hem top and bind bottom. Face front edges. Trim bottom with lace ruffle. Lace up front with embroidery floss.

5 - LONG PETTICOAT: Cut fabric 5in (12.7cm) by 10in (25.4cm). Make as described under 3, short petticoat.

6 - HOOPS: The hoops may be made of thin wire covered with ribbon or pipe cleaners. Cut lengths of wire 7in (17.8cm), 6in (15.2cm) and 5in (12.7cm) long. Shape into circles. Fasten together with embroidery floss tapes as shown in sketch. Anchor tapes to ribbon waistband.

7 - NIGHTGOWN: Make V-shaped tucks over shoulder. Hem neck and front edge and trim with narrow lace. Hem bottom of sleeves and trim with lace. Gather to fit wrist. Sew underarm seams. Hem bottom. Close front with bead "buttons."

8 - DRESSING GOWN: Cut fabric 10in (25.4cm) by 5½in (14cm). Hem short edges and bottom. Gather top to fit around doll's chest. Sew lengths of ribbon over shoulders as shown in sketch. Trim with doubled lace ruffle and close with ribbon ties.

9 - AFTERNOON DRESS: Line bodice. Make darts as shown. Use embroidery floss as shoulder straps. Trim with doubled lace ruffle and flower. Cut a piece of batiste or other soft fabric 11in (27.9cm) by 4½in (11.5cm). Make a ½in (1.3cm) hem in bottom. Make two 2in (5.1cm) slightly gathered ruffles and sew to batiste skirt. Sew back seams. Gather top to fit bottom of bodice and slip stitch in place. Close back with hooks and eyes and tie sash around waist as shown.

#1 - CHEMISE

#2 - PANTALETS

#3 - SHORT PETTICOAT

#4 - CORSET

#5 - LONG PETTICOAT

#6 - HOOPS

#7 - NIGHTGOWN

#8 - DRESSING GOWN

#9 - AFTERNOON DRESS WORN WITH LACE SCARF & MITTS. HAT, TOO!

10 - EVENING DRESS: Make bodice as described in 9. Trim with lace ruffles as shown. Cut batiste skirt 11in (27.9cm) by 4½in (11.5cm). Hem. Sew back seam leaving open 1in (2.5cm) for placket. Trim with ruffles of ½in (1.3cm) lace. Trim front with swags of material and bead clusters or flowers. Close back with hooks and eyes.

11 - WEDDING DRESS: Make bodice of white satin, as previously described. Trim with ½in (1.3cm) lace; sew a piece of lace around shoulders with scalloped edge pointing toward neck and un-gathered. Then add lace ruffles. Trim with ribbon swag and flowers as shown. Make skirt as previously described and trim with two 2in (5.1cm) ruffles of lace. Make train 7in (17.8cm) by 6in (15.2cm). Line with net. Gather one 6in (15.2cm) to fit back of waist. Cut placket in center back. Sew to bottom of bodice with skirt.

12 - BURNOOSE: Make the burnoose of very lightweight wool. Trim with lace appliques and tassels made of embroidery floss. Sew tassels to x's. Sew hood seam. Buttonhole stitch all raw edges.

13 - COMB AND BRUSH: Cut pattern shapes of index card; paint gold. Glue a bit of cotton to the brush to simulate bristles.

14 - GLOVE BOX (With Gloves): Make the glove box of index card covered with velvet and lined with silk. Cut the glove shapes of kid and place in box.

15 - PERFUME ATOMIZER: Glue beads, bell cap and wire together to make the atomizer.

16 - LACE HANKIES: Cut 1in (2.5cm) squares out of lace or batiste. Buttonhole stitch all edges. Make a silk pocket to hold them.

17 - BOUQUET OF FLOWERS: Make the bouquet holder of jewelry findings as shown in sketch. Glue artificial flowers into holder.

18 - MITTS: Cut pieces of double-edged lace long enough to go around doll's wrist and hand. Whip ends together.

19 - FUR MUFF AND TOQUE (Make toque and muff of white velvet): Sew ends of toque together. Cut circle to fit top and sew in place. Embroider ermine with lazy daisy stitch and one strand of black embroidery floss. Line with silk.

20 - HAT: The hat is a circle, 2in (5.1cm) in diameter. It can be made of straw or cloth-covered index card. Trim with tiny flowers, feathers or ribbons.

21 - FAN: Cut the "sticks" of index card. The paper is a scrap of lace. Hold the sticks together with a loop of thread.

22 - LACE SCARF: Cut a piece of lace 2in (5.1cm) wide by 12in (30.5cm) long. Drape around doll's arms.

23 - WEDDING VEIL: Cut a square of very fine net or lace measuring 12in (30.5cm). Arrange over doll's head. Hold in place with some small flowers and sequin pins.

#10 - EVENING DRESS

PLUMES OR FLOWERS IN HAIR - FAN - BURNOOSE FOR WRAP

#11 - WEDDING DRESS

#13 COMB & BRUSH FULL SIZE

#12 BURNOOSE

ACCESSORIES
#13 - COMB & BRUSH
#14 - GLOVE BOX (WITH GLOVES)
#15 - PERFUME ATOMIZER
#16 - LACE HANKIES (IN CASE)
#17 - BOUQUET OF FLOWERS
#18 - MITTS
#19 - FUR MUFF & TOQUE
#20 HAT
#21 - FAN
#22 - LACE SCARF
#23 - WEDDING VEIL

WIRE — BEAD — BELL CAP — BEAD — PEARL
#15 - PERFUME ATOMIZER

#16 HANDKER-CHIEF CASE MADE OF SILK, LINED WITH SILK.

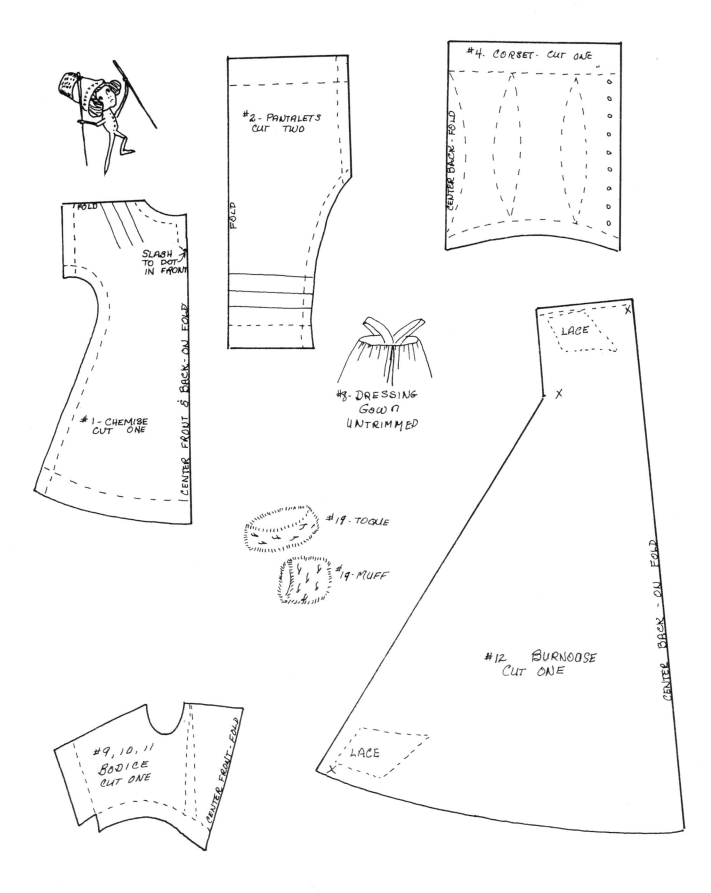

#2 - PANTALETS
CUT TWO

FOLD

#4. CORSET. CUT ONE

CENTER BACK · FOLD

FOLD

SLASH
TO DOT
IN FRONT

#1 - CHEMISE
CUT ONE

CENTER FRONT & BACK · ON FOLD

#8 - DRESSING
GOWN
UNTRIMMED

#19 - TOQUE

#19 · MUFF

LACE

X

X

LACE

X

#12 BURNOOSE
CUT ONE

CENTER BACK - ON FOLD

#9, 10, 11
BODICE
CUT ONE

CENTER FRONT - FOLD

180

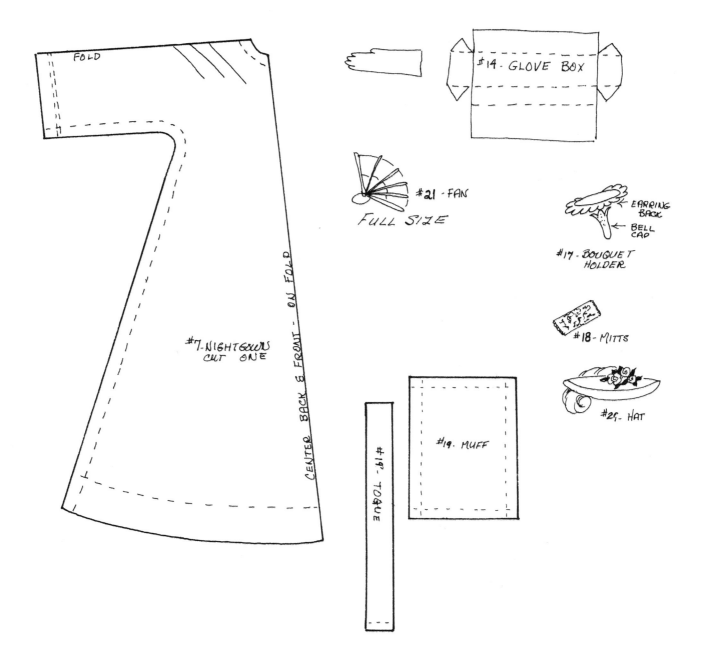

FOLD

CENTER BACK & FRONT - ON FOLD

#7 - NIGHTGOWN
CUT ONE

#14 - GLOVE BOX

#21 - FAN
FULL SIZE

EARRING
BACK

BELL
CAP

#17 - BOUQUET
HOLDER

#18 - MITTS

#29 - HAT

#19 - MUFF

#19 - TOQUE

Tulip Quilt

by **Sandy Williams**

1in (2.5cm) to 1ft (30.5cm) Scale

A

B

Need a quilt for your miniature bedroom and you do not want to spend hours stitching it? Here is your answer. This 7½in (19.1cm) square Tulip Quilt is in 1in (2.5cm) to 1ft (30.5cm) scale and is "painted" with liquid embroidery or fabric paints onto unbleached muslin.

The original quilt was about 87½in (247.6cm) square of Pennsylvania origin (circa 1865). The Pennsylvania Germans made quilts in bold colors and this is certainly bold. Personally, I prefer to make up this quilt in blues. Simply substitute light blue for the orange and navy blue for the red; keep the avocado green. Choose what colors you wish to complement your miniature room setting. The quilt size may be adjusted by adding or subtracting the tulip blocks and borders.

Materials Needed: Iron-on transfer pencil (available at needlecraft and craft stores), tracing paper, liquid embroidery or fabric acrylic paints in desired shades, ruler, unbleached muslin.

Place tracing paper over quilt. Trace quilt with transfer pencil (keep point sharp). It is helpful to use a ruler on all straight lines. Place traced quilt face down on muslin; leave at least a 2in (5.1cm) margin around quilt. Press with hot iron until quilt design is entirely transferred onto the muslin. Do not cut quilt out yet. Color the quilt with either the liquid embroidery or fabric acrylic paints—be sure and follow the manufacturer's instructions. Dry thoroughly. Cut another piece of muslin out using quilt as pattern. This is the quilt backing. With right sides of two quilt pieces together, sew around quilt from dot to dot. Trim seams and corners. Turn right side out. Blindstitch opening closed. Press.

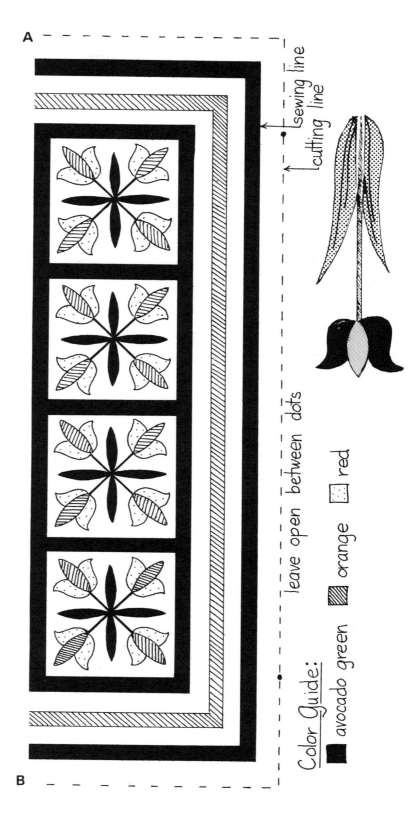

Some of the most charming displays of dolls I have seen have involved quilts. A quilt tucked around a doll sitting in an antique child's sled, in a cradle or in a bed produces a charming effect. I know that to a small child nothing is more pleasing than to wrap their dolls in quilts and to rock them in a cradle. Sometimes, but not often, old doll's quilts were in scale with the doll. Most often the quilts were made up from several blocks from a regular sized quilt pattern. The Windmill pattern given here is reduced to a 4in (10.2cm) completed block to be more in scale with a doll setting.

A quilt consists of three layers: a pieced or appliqued top, a middle layer of quilt batting and a backing. The three layers are held together by quilting or tufting (knots with small ends left on) through all three layers. Quilting is simply to sew a running stitch. Quilts may be pieced into patchwork blocks or appliqued onto one piece of fabric. Sometimes a quilt is made up of the two processes. A patchwork block (*Illustration 4*) may be made up of triangles, squares, rectangles and curved pieces of fabric. There are some tricks to patchwork: press each seam after it is sewn to the side of the darker fabric; do not press seams open unless many seams meet at one point; keep pencils sharp when tracing your pattern onto fabric, follow the grain line on the pattern. This pattern and most patchwork uses a ¼in (.65cm) seam. To make sure you sew a ¼in (.65cm) seam, tape a piece of masking tape exactly ¼in (.65cm) from the needle on your machine. On some machines the right edge of the presser foot is exactly ¼in (.65cm) from the needle making it a handy guide.

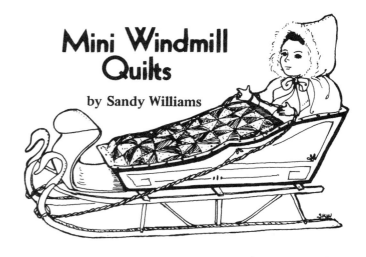

Mini Windmill Quilts

by Sandy Williams

The Windmill pattern is a four-patch block pattern and one of the simplest to sew on a sewing machine. Another name for the Windmill pattern is Pinwheel. You may make the quilt up in two colors or use up your scraps (a variety of colors). I made it up in a blue print on white (substituted for muslin) and a white print on blue with the dark print used for the borders. If you use fabric scraps, remember to use two colors for each Windmill block. If you use more than two colors for each block you will lose the windmill effect. By adding or deleting blocks and borders you can easily change the size of the quilt. If you decide to omit the borders, sew bias tape around the quilt's edges. If you add blocks you will need to increase the size of the borders; be sure to add a ¼in (.65cm) seam allowance where needed.

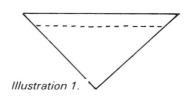

Illustration 1.

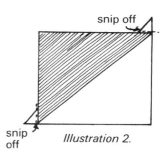

snip off

snip off

Illustration 2.

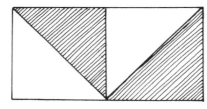

Illustration 3.

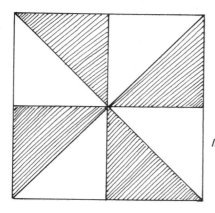

*Illustration 4.*Completed block.

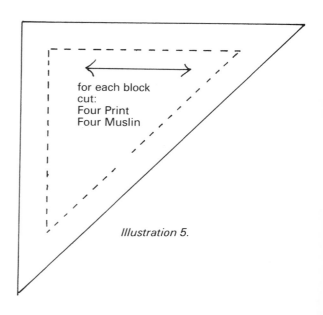

for each block cut:
Four Print
Four Muslin

Illustration 5.

184

2½in (5.1cm) by 12½in (31.8cm) border

2½in (5.1cm) by 20½in (51.1cm) border.

ᏇWindmill QuiltᏇ

Illustration 6. Windmill Quilt, 16in (40.6cm) by 20in (50.8cm).

Materials needed: print fabric, un-bleached muslin, thread, quilt batting, sharp pencils, ruler, embroidery thread (if you tuft the quilt).

Trace the windmill diamond onto lightweight cardboard or on fine sandpaper (make two patterns so that when the edges of one pattern wear down, you will have another pattern). Wash and press fabrics to be used (to shrink fabric and remove sizing). With a sharp pencil, mark triangle on wrong side of fabric. For this size of quilt you will need to cut 48 print triangles and 48 muslin triangles. From the print fabric cut *two* borders of *each* size: 2½in (5.1cm) by 12½in (31.8cm) and 2½in (5.1cm) by 20½in (51.1cm).

For each block:

1. With right sides of print and muslin triangles together, sew together on their longest side (*Illustration 1*). Press seam toward print triangle and snip off two extra points of material (*Illustration 2*). Repeat with rest of triangles from your block. You now have four squares.

2. With right sides of two squares together, sew along one side so when squares are opened the resulting rectangle will look like *Illustration 3*. Press seam toward print triangle. Repeat with other two squares.

3. Sew the two rectangles together so you have a new square (*Illustration 4*). This is your completed Windmill "block".

4. Repeat steps 1 through 3 until you have completed 12 blocks. Using completed quilt illustration as a guide: sew three blocks together. Press seams toward one side. Repeat until you have four strips of blocks. Sew these four strips of blocks together; press. Sew the smaller borders to the top and bottom edges of the quilt; press. Sew the longer borders to the sides of the quilt; press. You have now completed the pieced top of your quilt.

Using the pieced top as a pattern, lay it on backing fabric (muslin or print fabric). Cut out backing fabric the same size as pieced top. Cut out quilt batting the same size, too.

Place right sides of Windmill top and backing fabric together; lay quilt batting on top of this. Pin the three layers together and sew along three sides using a ¼in (.65cm) seam. Notch corners of quilt. Turn quilt right side out. Blind stitch fourth side closed. Press edges of quilt. Pin quilt together through all three layers.

The easiest way to finish off the quilt so that all three layers are held together is to sew a small knot (tufting) at each corner of blocks leaving ends of knot about 1/4in (.65cm) long. Use a three-strand length of embroidery thread in a coordinating color.

The traditional way to finish a quilt is to "quilt" it. Take a single length of thread and make a small knot at one end of it; place needle through backing of quilt and up through top of quilt; pull knot through to middle of quilt; sew small running stitches through the three layers of fabric; try to keep stitches even and neat. Quilt just inside each triangle and just outside of border seams.

A New Method For Miniature Needlepoint

by **Joan Meshirer**

Have you ever spent countless hours working on a piece of miniature needlepoint? After every stitch is correct and you have done a perfect job of blocking, then comes the realization that the edges have to be bound.

I find the binding always seems to show. It sometimes even curls slightly around the edges. After spending countless hours in getting it just right, I am still never completely satisfied.

Thinking I was the only one with this problem, I went through my miniature how-to books and found pictures of handworked rugs. Many of them had the same unsightly edges.

After several days I came upon what was for me, the perfect answer. Not only did this new method of finishing do away with added bulk but it also kept the smaller rugs from distorting in shape. A few tugs and my rugs were blocked.

Practice Piece:

Cut a 3in (7.6cm) by 3in (7.6cm) piece of canvas, 18 gauge. Pull out six to eight threads on each side of your canvas piece. See *Illustration 1*.

Bend under the loose threads, firmly pinching the edges to get an even line. For this practice piece use a brightly

CONTINENTAL STITCH   ILLUSTRATION #2

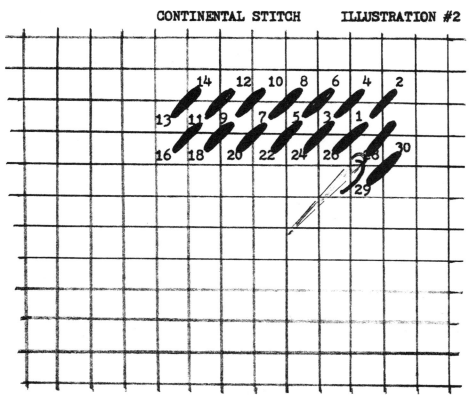

Illustration 2. "Continental Stitch." This stitch fully covers the back of your needlepoint. Work rows right to left, bringing the needle up at 1; crossing the intersection thread diagonally, insert the needle at 2. Bring the needle up at 3, to the left of 1. Work horizontal rows, turn the canvas upside down for each new row.

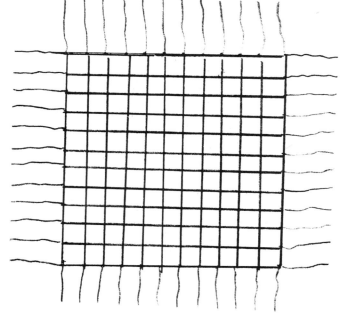

Illustration 1. Canvas with six to eight end threads pulled out on each side.

colored four-strand piece of embroidery thread. Using the continental stitch, see *Illustration 2,* work three rows around entire piece of canvas. Be careful to hold loose threads under the canvas firmly with your fingertips as you work the stitches. If you happen to miss securing a loose thread on your first round, be sure to catch it on the second. The third row will fully secure the threads. Do not cut off the excessive length from the loose threads; your background stitches will completely cover them.

You will master this technique in a very short period, and more than likely, you will never return to the bulky finishing method again.

NOTE: If your rug has a border you will want to use the border colored

Hen On Nest Design for small rug to be placed in front of kitchen sink.

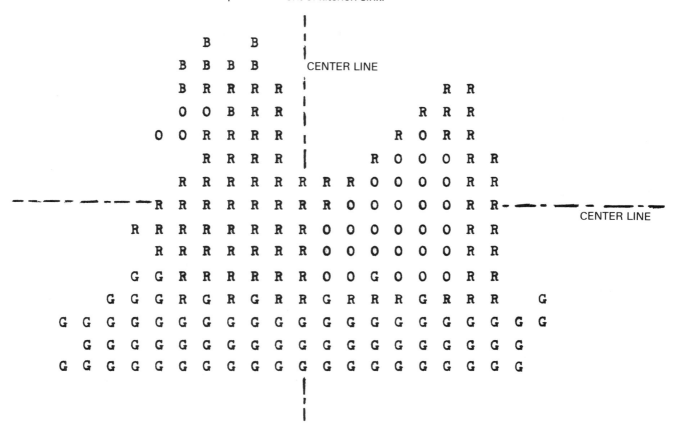

CENTER LINE

CENTER LINE

thread for the three rows of securing. For larger rugs, especially those with lots of center designs, you may want to do the detail work while piece is attached to a frame. Remove the rug from its frame when you get to within 1 in (2.5cm) of outside edge.

Put away your practice pieces. It is time for the "real thing!"

Work both design and background in three-strand embroidery thread.

"B"—Black
"R"—Red
"O"—Orange
"G"—Green

Background—Yellow
Fringe—Red, yellow; green sewing thread is used for a decorative fringe

Directions:

Using a 2¼ in (5.8cm) by 3 in (7.6cm) piece of canvas (No. 18), fringe six to eight rows as shown in *Illustration 1*. Fold under your fringe threads and work three rows of yellow around entire piece in a continental stitch, as shown in *Illustration 2*. Find your center thread and chart your design on the canvas. Work entire design, then fill in yellow background. Make a fringed edge of the two short ends using sewing thread or one strand of embroidery thread.

187

Doll Repair

From *The Mary Francis Sewing Book* by Jane Eayre Fryer.

Notes On Doll Restoration

by Robert and Karin
MacDowell

*A summary of mutually accepted
concepts subscribed to by professional
conservators, curators and collectors*

Illustration 1. French Schmitt. Head had
been broken into 15 pieces. Careful recon-
struction yielded excellent museum speci-
men.

Introduction

Soon after founding a laboratory
specializing in repair, restoration and
conservation of historic ceramic art
objects, it became evident that the current approach to preservation of antique dolls was far from being very
ethical, or even vaguely practical.

We offer this article to illustrate
the present state of the art, and to en-
courage those who become involved in
any way with the care of antique dolls
to adopt a professional approach to
the task at hand.

Responsibility for proper care is
divided between all parties involved;
improved communications must logi-
cally benefit both parties and objects.

Collectors should note that any
restoration work done on their behalf
should follow the general concepts
outlined here; these principles are subscribed to by the professional conservators who deal with priceless institutional material, and there is no justi-
fication for supporting non-conform-
ing practices where fine dolls are concerned.

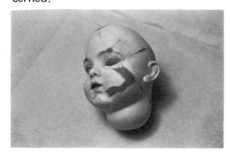

Illustration 2. Broken bisque head after
pieces assembled, missing ones made and
contoured. Note previous sanding damage.

Ethics

The widely-recognized, major
points to consider when doing any
type of conservation work are given
below. In the planning stages of a pro-

ject, the principles will aid in developing a logical approach, and the finished
work will reflect the consideration
given.

Reversibility. All materials used
should be removable; it should be possible to completely dismantle and
clean the restored object, should this
become necessary or desirable at some
future time.

Strength of materials. Avoid
using materials stronger or harder than
the object being treated. For example,
don't use epoxy putty to repair a
papier-mâché body, nor epoxy adhesive to set eyes. Find a material of
proper strength—use the same material
used originally, if possible.

Illustration 3. A head shown after removal
of eyes, dismantling of previous badly-
aligned cement joint and the cleaning off of
excess adhesive.

Preserve the original. Such practices as grinding pieces to make them
fit, grinding anchor grooves, drilling
holes and sanding any part of the object—especially the colored or decorated surfaces—should be avoided.
These practices produce irreversible
damage; they complicate and raise the
cost of future treatment.

Stability of materials. Within the
confines of reversibility and compati-
ble strength, materials should retain
their characteristic strength, color and
general appearance. There is little
value in accomplishing artwork to render a repair unobtrusive, only to have
the colors change soon after the work
is finished, or to have the paint peel or
chip off.

Restorations to deceive. The primary reason for cosmetic work to render a restoration unobtrusive or vir-
tually invisible, is to prevent the damage from interfering with a viewer's
study and appreciation of the object.
To achieve this, it is customary to cos-
metically treat only the surfaces which
will be normally seen. For example, a
doll head can be made to look virtual-
ly "mint" on the outside, while cracks
and replaced pieces show clearly on
the inside. Wigs should not be cemented on. In this way, the extent of restoration is easily determined when
necessary, and at the same time, the

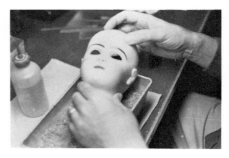

Illustration 4. Same head as in *Illustration 3*
being assembled with low-viscosity adhesive.
Head is left in sandbox to maintain position
while adhesive sets.

head may be thoroughly enjoyed as
part of a display.

To carry a restoration project so
far as to render the work very difficult to detect (such as painting the inside of a doll head with opaque white
or smearing over the cracks with plaster of Paris) is *most* unethical, as it increases the risk of that head being sold
as undamaged. Restored parts must be
handled more carefully than undamaged parts, as the paints and coatings
used to effect the restoration are more
easily scratched than fired-on materials. (Incidently, re-firing of ceramic
articles is not technically feasible).

Buyers of restored articles should
always be told the extent of restoration, and advised to take care to keep
these items clean and safe from unnecessary or uninformed handling.
Given proper care, a restored object
has prospects for a long and satisfactory exhibition.

Illustration 5. Applying clear protective
coating with artist's airbrush.

A Typical Bisque Restoration

The following are the steps we
subscribe to in the average doll-head
restoration project: unpack, check for
mail damage, log in; plan approach to
project; provide estimate to client—
wait for instructions; dismantle recent
restoration, clean and reconstruct in
the following manner:

1). Wet eye-securing plaster, wait,
gently remove eyes.

2). Soak head in industrial epoxy
stripper to dismantle poor bonds and
loosen previous over-paint.

3). Remove remaining epoxy
with commercial paint stripper.

4). Assemble pieces with medium-speed proprietary adhesive.

5). Make up foundations for filling missing pieces with commercial, white, room-temperature-curing (RTC) epoxy system.

6). Finish filling missing pieces with polyester resin putty and shape correctly.

7). Airbrush isolation sealer over cracks and filled pieces.

8). Smooth with soft sandpaper, only over protective film. Avoid sanding original surfaces.

9). Airbrush appropriate colors to blend restored areas and cracks with original.

10). Airbrush protective clear coating.

11). Airbrush matte coating to reduce gloss to match bisque finish.

Recommended Materials and Tools

Items used generally in the course of doll restoration are presented in the following table. Selection of tools and materials is based on compliance with the ethical considerations previously described, and reasonable efficiency in carrying out actual conservation work.

MATERIAL	PURPOSE	SOURCE
Elmer's School Glue	Similar to regular Elmer's, but easily removed with soap and water; good for setting eye pieces, repairing composition bodies	Variety stores; craft shops
Devcon 5-Minute Epoxy	Forms strong bonds, reversible	Hardware stores
Epoxy Putty	Hand-forming missing pieces	Hardware stores
White Industrial Epoxy (RTC)	Filling missing pieces where great strength is required	Industrial plastics supplier
Polyester Body Filler	Filling chips and making pieces where moderate strength is required	Automotive paint supplier
Masking Tape	Holding parts together while adhesive sets, general use (ie making labels)	Automotive paint supplier
Plaster of Paris	Setting eyes	Doll parts supplier
Elastic Cord	Stringing dolls	Doll parts supplier
Galvanized steel, wire, various gauges	Making clamps to secure elastic, making other hooks, fixtures, etc.	Hardware store
Paint Remover (non-flammable)	Removing paint, adhesives	Hardware; paint store
Epoxy Stripper (non-flammable)	Dismantling bonds, removing epoxy	Plastics supplier
Modeling Clay	Simple molds, making models from which to make molds in which missing pieces are cast	Hobby or craft shop
Acetone	Solvent for general cleaning	Automotive paint shop
Xylol	Solvent for cleaning; removes wax, modeling clay; used for thinning paints	Automotive or general paint shop
Acrylic Lacquer Thinner	Solvent for lacquer	Automotive paint shop
White Acrylic Lacquer	Airbrushing over repairs	Automotive paint shop
Clear Acrylic Lacquer	Top coat	Automotive paint shop
Artist's Pigment Powders	Tinting white or clear acrylic lacquer	Artist's supply shop
Matting agent	Reducing gloss in above paint products	Automotive paint shop
Clear Seal	Aerosol, non-glossy, use as above (clear)	G & H Products, P.O. Box 571, Greenfield, Indiana 46140
Matte Seal	Aerosol, matte finish, clear	G & H Products (above)
Brown Sandpaper; various grits	Smoothing—do not use black wet-or-dry paper—it is much too harsh	Hardware store
Files, good selection	Shaping replaced parts. Files much better than sandpaper, does not as readily damage ceramic surfaces	Hardware store
File Card	Cleaning files	Hardware store
Miscellaneous Hand Tools	General use	Hardware store
Artist's Airbrush	Applying colors, sealers, glazes	Artist's supply shop
Air Compressor, piston and tank type	Air supply for airbrush	Artist's supply shop
Adjustable Air Gauge and Regulator	Controlling air supply to airbrush	Artist's supply shop; Automotive paint shop

WARNING: Paints and solvents are generally flammable; explosive if sprayed in unventilated areas. Vapors are harmful to health. Read all labels and observe instructions.

Materials and Methods to Avoid

The following table highlights items we note most frequently as sources of damage, inconvenience and causes for much unnecessary additional work.

ITEM	REASON NOT RECOMMENDED
Silicon Rubber Adhesive	Poor adhesive, almost impossible to remove. Contaminant; other adhesives and paints will not bond to areas affected.
Epoxies used as coatings or exposed fills	Epoxy changes color, generally turns yellow or orange with time
'Instant' Adhesives	Bonds too quickly to allow proper alignment of pieces. Dangerous, inconvenient to clean up. Moisture-sensitive.
Heat-Cure Epoxy	Almost irreversible, damage to object very likely during dis-assembly.
Sanding (especially wet-or-dry paper)	Easily damages original artwork, especially features which protrude above general surface, such as eyebrows. Almost impossible to fully recover from such irresponsible damage.
Excessive tightness in Doll Stringing	Causes structural failure of body parts, excessive wear at joints, wear to ceramic parts. Breaks ceramic attaching points, necks of heads.
Excess Adhesive	Generally tight, carefully aligned bonds with very little adhesive are strongest. Adhesive to outside joints does not improve strength. Excess cement on wigs damages wigs, pulls chips of ceramic material from heads. Best not to cement wigs at all—never when head is restored.
Excess Over-paint	Destroys character of original. Many paints almost impossible to remove from bodies and other non-ceramic, perishable parts. Most of this type of abuse unnecessary. Paints which discolor most are generally hardest to remove (oil based, containing lead, epoxy, alkyd).

Antique Doll Restoration

by **Robert & Karin MacDowell**

In response to many requests for specific details on the procedures used in the course of conservation treatment of fine antique dolls, we are pleased to offer the following illustrated material. We should emphasize that all procedures used in our laboratory and described here meet the strict institutional standards for stability, reversibility and minimal obscuration of the original visual intent of the maker, and that all of these objects could be returned to their pre-treatment status should the need ever arise.

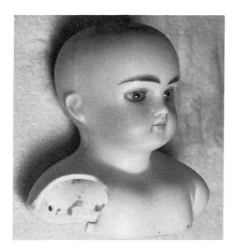

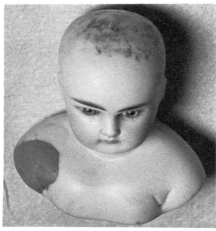

Illustration 2. Modeling clay was pressed into void left by missing piece and modeled to duplicate missing piece exactly. Modeling clay and surrounding bisque were sprayed with two light coats of wax-based mold release.

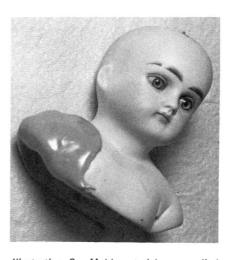

Illustration 1. German bisque shoulder head in perfect condition, except for piece broken out of shoulder and missing.

Illustration 3. Mold material was applied over modeling clay and surrounding bisque to form shell mold. After mold hardened, modeling clay was removed and the mold was gently removed. Then, shoulder and mold were thoroughly cleaned with xylol (toluol or mineral spirit could be used) to remove all traces of modeling clay and release. Two coats of wax-based mold release were sprayed inside shell mold and allowed to dry.

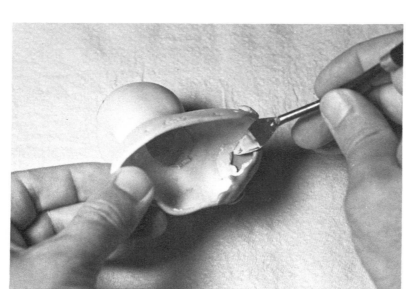

Illustration 4. Shell mold was held in place with adhesive clay (Mortite or similar product sold for use as household weather stripping). Void was filled with two-part room-temperature-curing (RTC) white industrial epoxy and then epoxy was removed from all areas outside the filled void with acetone and cotton swab before epoxy hardened. This leaves original bisque free of extraneous epoxy and clearly delineates extent of repair.

Illustration 5. After epoxy was fully cured, shell mold was gently removed and all traces of mold release were removed with xylol. Minor surface pits were filled with automotive lacquer putty and shaping was done with a fine, round needle file.

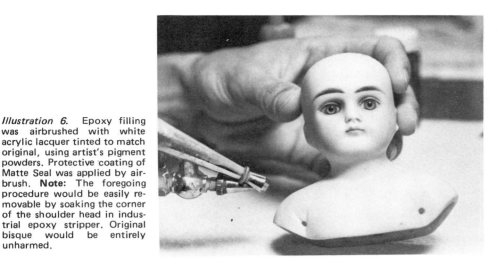

Illustration 6. Epoxy filling was airbrushed with white acrylic lacquer tinted to match original, using artist's pigment powders. Protective coating of Matte Seal was applied by airbrush. **Note:** The foregoing procedure would be easily removable by soaking the corner of the shoulder head in industrial epoxy stripper. Original bisque would be entirely unharmed.

Illustration 7. Modeling clay was pressed into the hand of the half-figure and modeled to form the shape of the inside of the finger (in reverse). Finger stub was cleaned with xylol and acetone to ensure a good bond, epoxy was applied to make general form of finger.

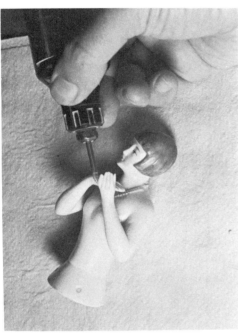

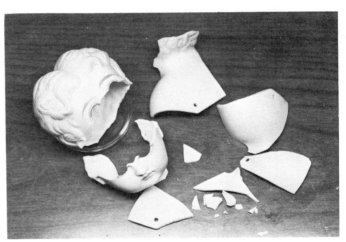

Illustration 9. Tinted bisque with molded hair after old repair was dismantled and pieces were cleaned. **Note:** Much time and expense could be spared in such projects if it were not necessary to dismantle and scrupulously clean all such objects.

Illustration 8. Modeling clay was removed, all areas were thoroughly cleaned with xylol and the finger was given a final shape with a high-speed motor tool and conical cutter.

Illustration 10. Just prior to final assembly, note the numerous small missing pieces in the shoulder and at the corner of the right eye.

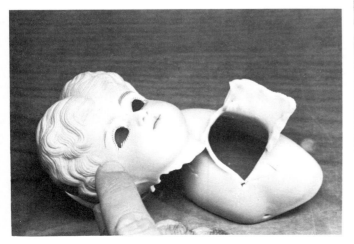

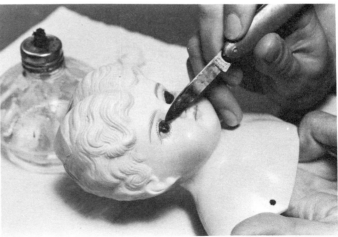

Illustration 11. Using a knife blade warmed over an alcohol lamp, wax was dripped on the front of the eyes; this temporarily holds the eyes in good alignment. Wax was then applied around the inside of the eye openings to prevent any plaster of Paris from showing through.

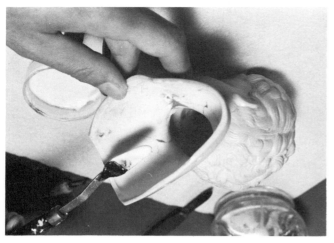

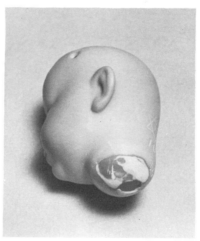

Illustration 12. A small quantity of plaster of Paris was applied to encapsulate the eyes and firmly attach them to the inside of the head.

Illustration 13. Temporary wax was carefully removed with a dull carving tool. Remaining film of wax was removed with mineral spirit and soft cotton swab.

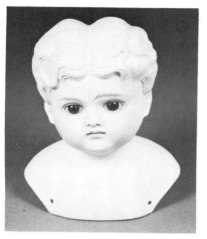

Illustration 14. The finished project.

Illustrations 15 & 16. Old repair to the neck of a K*R 101 done with plaster of Paris and unknown dark material. Note excess material inside head.

Illustration 17. Head was soaked in plain water to soften plaster and render it more easily removable.

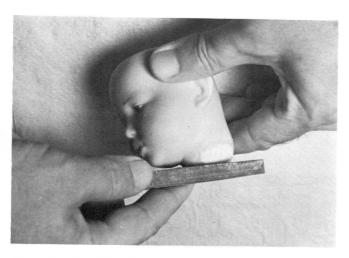

Illustration 18. White RTC epoxy applied over temporary modeling clay support placed inside of head. Epoxy was allowed to cure and then shaped with a file.

Illustration 19. Modeling clay was removed and the inside of the head was scrupulously cleaned with xylol. Because stringing hardware will cause considerable stress to the neck, this restoration is reinforced with an internal application of fiber glass cloth and clear RTC epoxy resin built up of small, overlapping pieces of cloth dipped in catalyzed resin. The resulting laminate covers the replaced piece and overlaps the original bisque, adding considerable strength. The laminate remains rather clear, so the extent of repair is not obscured by this additional material, nor is the weight of the head appreciably increased.

Illustration 20. The finished head assembled onto its original composition body.

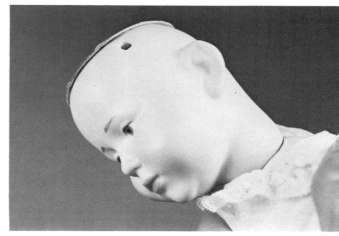

Illustration 21. China head cemented together with unknown adhesive, broken pieces badly out of alignment and inside reinforced (??? !!!) with fantastic buildup of unknown, unsightly material. Note missing corner.

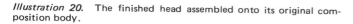

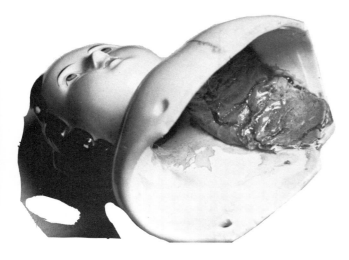

Illustration 22. China head after it has been dismantled, cleaned, recemented, missing corner made and outside airbrushed to cover crack and new piece. Repairs are not discernable outside, but are easily seen inside.

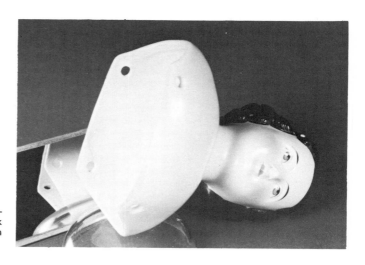

You the Doll Eye Doctor

by **Ruth Davis Glover**

For many collectors, the fun of a collection is restoring an "as-is find" to its original beauty. Most repairs, such as painting and stringing are easily accomplished, but the eye jobs are sometimes a bit more difficult.

The following should be of help in solving some of your eye-repair problems.

When New Eyes Are Needed

1. Check the cork in the bottom of the head where the weight hits. If missing, glue a small piece of cork in place.

2. Select eye large enough to cover the eye opening from inside.

3. Melt 1/2 cup white-tinted candle wax with a small amount of pale pink or orange candle wax. Add one teaspoon of powdered alum and two teaspoons talcum powder. Do Not Boil as crystals will form. It is best to heat over hot water; a double broiler will do.

4. Lay one eye in place, inside head.

5. Inside head, drop melted wax around eye with paint brush.

6. Check setting of eye by holding the head above your eye level. Move eye to the desired position while the wax is still soft.

7. Add more wax around eye to hold firmly.

8. Lay other eye in place; set the same way.

9. Check eye wire and weight. Ends of wire must fit into each open end of eye and the weight must rest on bottom cork. Adjust wire until you have correct fit.

10. Make sure weight is not too long or it will hit back of head and eyes will not open wide enough. Caution: weight must always contact cork—never ceramic head material—otherwise head may become cracked.

11. Measure two tablespoons of water into a dish, add enough patching plaster to make putty, or mix a sufficient amount of Epoxy Putty to cover top of wire.

12. Drop mixture across wire and press onto eyes. Do not extend plaster too far down on eyeballs as it will keep the eyes from opening when plaster is applied for setting.

13. Set aside until hard.

14. To remove eyes from head, melt the wax around eyes with a soldering gun, tip pressed against wax until soft or soften wax with paint thinner.

15. Push eyes gently from the front.

16. Measure one tablespoon of Plastico Rok in a jar or dish.

17. Add a drop of coral, red or henna and tiny bit of black Flo-Paque paint to color. Try to match the bisque color of bisque head. Water colors will also tint the Plastico Rok since it is soluble with water.

18. Paint tinted Plastic Rok across top of eyeballs and over the bridge. Set aside to dry.

19. Lay eyes in head, check color on lids. If not down far enough, apply second coat, paint lower. If too far down on eyes, moisten a cloth and wipe off the excess at edge. Let dry thoroughly.

20. Melt wax. Dip eyes in wax, twice if necessary.

21. Paint melted wax around inside eye opening so eyes will not be scratched when they are opened and closed.

22. Rub any cooking oil on sides of eyes so plaster will not stick. Also around inside eye opening.

23. Lay eyes in place.

24. Place three tablespoons of water in dish or rubber cup and add enough patching plaster to absorb all water. Set aside until water works its way to the top; stir. Plaster is ready to use when it stands in peaks like beaten egg whites. Do not use plaster of paris—it is too hard.

25. Drop plaster on outside of eye, but not too much on top side as eyes will not open far enough. The bridge will hit the plaster.

26. Check setting every five minutes. When plaster is firm but not hard carefully move eyes to closed position and move back and forth several times. Continue checking until plaster is firm and hard. Drying time may vary.

27. If plaster hardens too fast and eyes will not move freely, drop water on each piece of plaster.

28. Pry off pieces, mark left and right so you will replace them on the correct sides.

29. Shave off a very small amount of plaster resting against eye; trim off small amount from outside edge.

30. Glue pieces back in place, making sure you have shaved off enough so eyes move freely. Elmer's School Glue, which is water-soluble works well.

31. Mix small amount of plaster and drop over outside edge of plaster, holding eyes to make sure plaster secures them.

32. Check top cork. If missing cut a triangular piece of cork and glue or plaster in place.

NOTE: Sometimes eyes stick but do not need resetting. From inside the head, drop a little thin oil on sides of each eye.

When eyes are still mounted and need color and wax, drop water on the plaster pieces. Mark left and right. Follow above directions.

To Replace Eyelashes

1. Measure last strip. Cut long enough to touch each side of eye opening.

2. Put small amount of Duco Cement across top of eye, a thin line above eye color, from side to side.

3. Put cement sparingly on edge of eyelash strip.

4. Attach lash to eyelid.

5. Before glue hardens, position lash. Hold center of lash down and draw ends up to make curved lashes. If too straight across top of eye, the sides will be too long.

6. Dry thoroughly.

7. Paint tinted Plastico Rok on lid and top of eyelash strip.

8. Let dry; apply additional coats of color until there is no line left between lash strip and eye top. Make a smooth lid.

9. Paint melted wax above lash strip and top of eye.

10. Set same as you would eyes without lashes.

What Is Restoring A Doll?

by John Axe

Something that I feel very strongly about is preserving dolls in their original condition, whether they be antique dolls, collectible dolls or modern dolls. Most responsible collectors feel the same way.

Oftentimes, the beginning collector follows improper advice and has a doll that had minor flaws "repaired" to the point where it hardly resembles the doll that it was meant to be. Coats of new paint do not improve an old doll when the "restorer" is simply trying to erase or hide the aging process that all dolls go through. This is no more flattering to a doll than heavy make-up is to a person who is trying to create the illusion of possessing the "bloom of youth" long after it is gone. In addition, new costumes or improper costumes do not benefit a doll whose original garments are in worn condition. What a person does with their own doll is their own business, but they should be aware that unnecessary so-called "restoration" only detracts from the value of the doll, no matter how much money they invested to have this done.

Dorothy S. Coleman, whose judgment every doll person respects, told me that she considers *The Collector's Book of Doll Clothes* (Crown Publishers, Inc., 1975) the most important of the works by the Colemans because it stresses the originality of dolls. In *A Treasury of Beautiful Dolls* (Weathervane Books, 1971) John Noble cites in the Introduction that dolls are part of the "decorative arts." Even minor art is real art if it is permitted to retain is originality. It does not hurt for an old doll to be missing a finger. Fading of an original costume does not spoil it. Old dolls can not look like new dolls.

Many uninformed persons justify "restoring" a doll based on the fact that paintings and other artworks are restored. *Restore* means to return to the original state — *not* to make modern additions. In 1946 Italy's Ministry of Fine Arts began an eight-year program to restore Leonardo da Vinci's *Last Supper.* In this instance, restoring meant removing the incrustations of many previous repaintings until Leonardo's original paint base was reached and secured. After the Great Flood of Florence on November 4, 1966 desperate measures were adopted to restore damaged artwork. Almost all of the work involved was to *clean* paintings and sculpture, *not* to *hide* the damage. One casualty, Donatello's carved wooden masterpiece, *Mary Magdalene,* was soaked to the hips by oil-laden flood waters. It was the task of

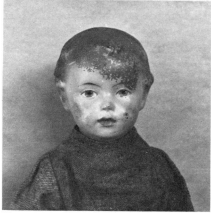

Illustration 1. Unmarked boy doll with an early composition head dating before 1920. The paint has flaked off the forehead and there are rubs on the cheeks. It would be a crime to repaint this head as the original matte patina could never be matched! The delicate coloring, which does not show in the photo, could not be duplicated.

the restorers to return this figure to how it looked when it was completed in 1455, not to repaint it to hide the problems.

There is no reason at all to repaint a composition doll whose original paint is rubbed, scratched or crazed. Many of the individuals who slap rouge over cheeks and fingernail polish over mouths do not bother to spend the same amount of time cleaning the doll. This is very inconsistent. Cracks and chips can be prevented from spreading with the application of Elmer's Glue, which does not

discolor the finish. If a doll is "beyond hope" it is all right to "touch it up" but one should realize that he is not restoring the value of the doll with new paint layers. Some people claim to be experts in repainting old dolls. Yet, no matter how cautiously they apply new paint, it will never look the same as the doll did when produced in a factory under different conditions. Part of the charm of old dolls is that they are not new, and that they do not look new.

A doll that has been unnecessarily restored is worthless as a collectible because it is no longer original. "A little bit of powder and a little bit of paint can make a gal look like what she ain't." In both instances the aim of the paint applier is to fool someone. The value of a composition doll can not be compared to the sculpture of Donatello. But both forms of art are more beautiful in their original condition, even if they do show the passing of time.

Not all collectors can afford high-priced "mint dolls." Sometimes we have to make do with new wigs, new clothing, new arms. That is because we would rather have a doll that needed some attention than not to have it at all. It is better to have a worn Schoenhut than not to have a Schoenhut. It is very foolish to pay a high price for a poorly repainted Schoenhut. It is just as foolish to re-wig a doll with a clumpy looking synthetic wig just because the original one was skimpy or to hire a seamstress to make a copy of an original dress that required repair which is obvious, but is still original.

Those who attempt to hide the faults of an old doll are not restoring it. What they are doing is permanently damaging it. This is irresponsible.

Illustration 2. A 16 in. (40.6 cm) composition Shirley Temple with a replaced wig. The wig has been "styled," but the thick synthetic fiber makes it appear too full and out of proportion. The eyebrows are repainted and look too dark. The dress, shoes and socks are too obvious in their newness. This photo is also an example of very poor doll photography due to lack of contrast, no detail, poor background and foreground and stand shows.

Illustration 3. 13 in. (33 cm) composition Shirley Temple. She has a skimpy, but original wig, which looks far more authentic than a modern replaced one would. The face is crazed but it does not spoil her looks. Her costume is a copy of the original, which suits her better than a contemporary design.

Schoenhut
RESTORATION
AN ILLUSTRATED COMMENTARY

BY ROBERT & KARIN MACDOWELL (All Photographs by the Authors)

Schoenhut dolls, animals and other toys present the collector and the art conservator with a rather unique set of problems. There is much heated debate in all quarters over this subject; we do not claim to have universally satisfactory answers. We have applied the rigid principles of art conservation in a number of cases, and have an on-going research program aimed at general improvements in the approach to this subject. The following examples illustrate the typical problems we see and the approaches used in solving them.

Our first task, when presented with a Schoenhut case, is to determine whether any restoration work is justified. Does the object really need treatment, or would any attempt at repairs actually devalue it? Bearing in mind these subjects are made of wood and paint, one would expect some minor chips, rubs, dents and other blemishes; in fact, a certain degree of age-evidence is considered desirable. It is all too easy to alter the real Schoenhut character by undisciplined restoration.

One definite requirement, if any significant artwork will be required in a restoration project, is to have a near-duplicate of the object at hand, so that one might closely duplicate the unusual features, and produce a convincing result.

The following photographs illustrate several recent treatments.

Illustration 1. Head shows rather extreme damage, flaking, cracking and the beginning of restoration done elsewhere (the white, hard filling). Note the condition of the shoulder is quite good; minor chips around neck socket and very slight crack in left breast.

Illustration 2. All previous restoration materials carefully removed. Major areas of flaking being filled with DAP® Vinyl Spackling Compound. This material appears to be comprised of polyvinylacetate adhesive and calcium carbonate, both well recognized conservation materials; it bonds well, is softer than the surrounding paint and wood substrate, and shapes easily. Excess spackling was removed with tissue dampened with water, before the spackling hardened. Note the chips left untouched in neck socket.

Illustration 3. Here we show the process of shaping and smoothing the filling material with a fine-cut needle file. Since the filler is reasonably soft, it can be

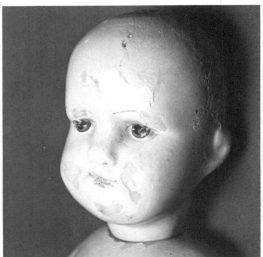

Illustration 1

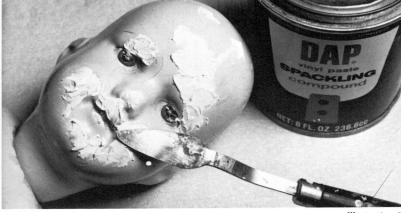

Illustration 2

Illustration 3

Illustration 4

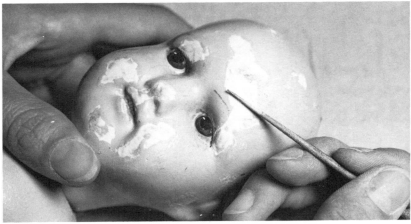

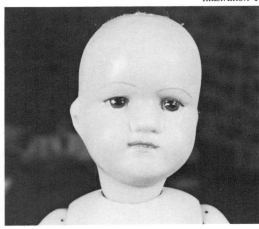

Illustration 5

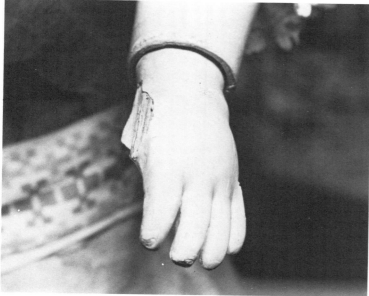

Illustration 6

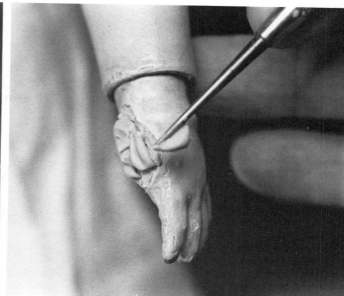

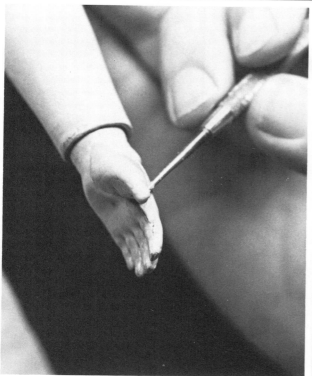

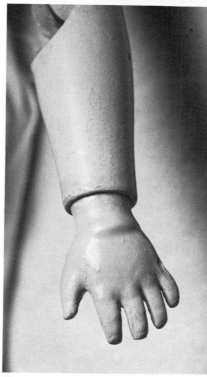

Illustration 7

Illustration 8

Illustration 9

shaped with very light pressure. Using light pressure and great care to avoid the surrounding original paint produces very little if any scratching to the original. This filling and filing continues until the surface is properly shaped and ready for airbrushing.

Illustration 4. After airbrushing, the head appears in good, but not new, condition. Prior to airbrushing, some of the cracks in the original paint film (best seen in Illustration 2) were extended into the fillings by cutting with a very sharp scalpel. If this had not been done, the large, perfectly smooth filled areas would have been very obvious. Airbrushing

does not extend over entire head; a substantial portion of the original paint is still visible. Note, again, chips around neck socket completely untouched.

Illustration 5. Typical missing thumb: it is quite easy to see how the wood splits with the grain. Note slight cracking and flaking of paint generally on hand.

Illustration 6. After cleaning wood with acetone and cotton swab, epoxy putty was mixed and worked into the general shape of missing thumb (but considerably smaller) and allowed to cure. Epoxy was applied with pointed scribe and considerable pressure to assure a good bond with the wood. No epoxy was

allowed to cure on the original surface; it was removed with cotton swab and xylol while still soft.

Illustration 7. With basic shape of thumb formed and cured, additional epoxy putty was carefully modeled over the support to render the final form.

Illustration 8. Epoxy thumb prior to airbrushing. Illustration shows clearly the original paint and its present chipped condition.

Illustration 9. Final result: airbrushed color blends new thumb with original. Finish of epoxy was left slightly rough to emulate the chipped condition of rest of hand.

Notes On Stringing Dolls

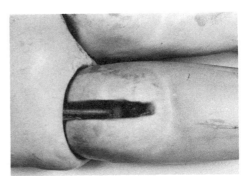

Illustration 1. Normal complement of tools and supplies used in stringing dolls includes assorted elastic (sizes from 1/16in [0.16cm] to 1/4in [0.65cm] diameter), long hooks made from coat-hanger and other steel wire, assorted neck buttons, gas pliers, diagonal wire cutters, hemostats, long-nose pliers, roll of 1/16in (0.16cm) steel wire used for making hooks and clamps for securing elastic.

by ROBERT & KARIN MacDOWELL

Photographs by the Authors

SCOPE. This article describes a number of procedures we have found useful in stringing dolls, both modern and antique. The photographs should assist in visualizing what is documented here, and in other articles on the subject.

PRECAUTIONS. As with any phase of handling dolls, especially the antique, great care is required to protect the article from damage. The finished work must be secure, as any part which unexpectedly detaches from the doll will likely fall and be broken. We find the following items deserve special attention:

Always work on a soft surface.

If possible, work out procedure so that all work can be done by one person — without assistance.

Holding doll body firmly between the knees will usually avoid the necessity for having a helper.

Make certain all hardware and attaching points are sound.

Carefully select elastic of correct strength.

Avoid over-tight stringing, as this causes much wear and damage.

Avoid temptation to over-repair minor damage to old bodies.

Touch up only areas repaired, and only if able to closely match color.

Never repaint body or major parts.

ELASTIC. We find an assortment ranging from 1/16in (0.16cm) to 1/4in (0.65cm) diameter covers all of our requirements. In most cases, a loop of elastic half the diameter of the required single strand is much more satisfactory, as the tension increases more gradually as the loop is tightened. This property is very desirable, as minor changes in elastic strength will not be evident in the finished work. Built-in tolerance yields a longer-lasting product and avoids frequent repairs, with their attendant risks.

TENSION ADJUSTMENT. Using an electrical cable tie (Ty-wrap) to terminate an elastic loop can be a very useful technique. The elastic loop is made shorter than normal; the cable tie can then be used to set the desired tension by making the cable tie loop tighter, as desired. (Most cable ties can only be tightened, but not loosened or removed, thus, if the tie is over-tightened, it will have to be replaced.) An 8in (20.3cm) cable tie makes a loop of approximately 3in (7.6cm) diameter. If the tension is

Illustration 2. Routing of elastic behind dowel in top of upper leg section; if elastic is in front of dowel, legs will not maintain their positions.

correct with the loop set in the 2in (5.1cm) to 3in (7.6cm) range, then, as the elastic ages and loses strength, the loop can be tightened to compensate.

SPECIAL NOTE ON FRENCH ATTACHING HARDWARE. We find numerous fine French dolls missing their original spring and hook head-attaching hardware, doubtless because a previous repairer failed to understand how to reassemble the doll, once it was dismantled. We feel very strongly that these original parts should be saved and used, as they help in keeping the doll more original, preserving its value, and actually are

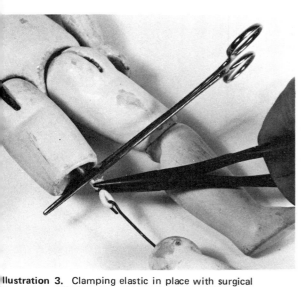

Illustration 3. Clamping elastic in place with surgical hemostat while forming and securing loop with clamp fashioned from 1/16in (0.16cm) steel wire; clamp squeezed into final form with long-nose pliers.

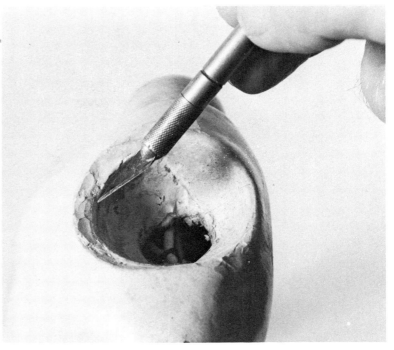

Illustration 4. Top of body showing partially collapsed neck socket (pointer shows front edge of socket cup, which should be flush with top of body). Note undamaged portion at rear of body. This type of damage is typical in cases where dolls are strung too tightly.

technically superior to the elastic system.

If, for some reason, the method we have shown photographically for dealing with the head-attaching hardware cannot be accomplished, the following procedure should work, though it does require the use of a helper:

1. Attach strong cord to eye of hook (about 12in [30.5cm] of cord).

2. Pull cord through head, lower wooden washer, spring and upper wooden washer.

3. Push hook into body, rotate and anchor to internal dowel. Pull tension on string and maintain until work is finished.

4. Thread head and hardware down cord, into final position on body.

5. Compress spring below top of hook.

6. Insert pin through eye of hook and release spring to bear on pin.

7. Check to make certain bend in pin is centered in eye of hook, and that bend is toward body.

8. Check security of hook on internal dowel by viewing through hole in arm socket.

9. Remove cord from hook eye.

SOURCES FOR TOOLS AND SUPPLIES. Most of the items commonly used for stringing dolls are available from suppliers advertising in the DOLL READER. The tools we use are available through hardware stores and electrical supply houses. Cable ties are available through electrical supply houses. Hemostats are available at medical or dental supply firms — perhaps your local doctor or hospital can supply a local name. A good, reliable source for general tools and supplies is the Brookstone Company, 127 Vose Farm Road, Peterborough, New Hampshire, 03458.

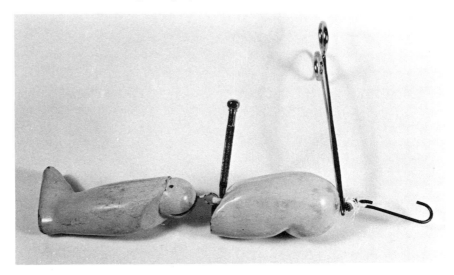

Illustration 5. Left leg of Jumeau body, showing properly sized elastic and the original upper hook which attaches to dowel in upper part of body, just below arm sockets.

Illustration 6. Long wire with hook-end pushed through body to engage leg hook. Leg hook will be pulled past internal dowel, turned 1/4-turn and secured in position.

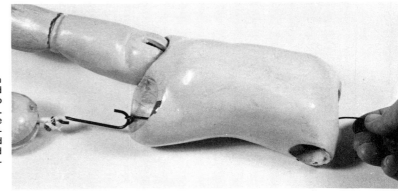

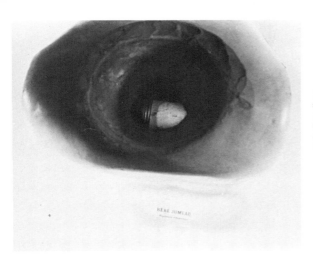

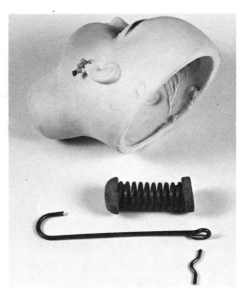

Illustration 7. Leg hook shown properly secured over internal dowel. Hook must now be slid to one side to clear area in center for attachment of head.

Illustration 8. Head and attaching hardware comprised of hook with small eye, two wooden shoulder-washers, spring and securing pin.

Illustration 9. Hardware assembled to head in preparation for final assembly to body.

Illustration 10. Holding head and compressing spring with thumb, hook is positioned parallel to dowel inside body.